D1416254

THE COMPLETE PRACTICAL ENCYCLOPEDIA OF
CYCLING
TRAINING • BIKE MAINTENANCE • RACING

THE COMPLETE PRACTICAL ENCYCLOPEDIA OF
CYCLING
TRAINING • BIKE MAINTENANCE • RACING

EVERYTHING YOU NEED TO KNOW ABOUT CYCLING FOR FITNESS AND LEISURE, TRAINING FOR BOTH SPORT AND COMPETITION, AND THE GREATEST RACES

STEP-BY-STEP INSTRUCTION, INDIVIDUAL TRAINING PLANS AND EXPERT ADVICE, ALL SHOWN IN OVER 600 FANTASTIC PHOTOGRAPHS

EDWARD PICKERING

LORENZ BOOKS

This edition is published by Lorenz Books,
an imprint of Anness Publishing Ltd
Hermes House, 88–89 Blackfriars Road,
London SE1 8HA
tel. 020 7401 2077
fax 020 7633 9499
www.lorenzbooks.com
www.annesspublishing.com

Anness Publishing has a new picture agency outlet for
images for publishing, promotions or advertising.
Please visit our website www.practicalpictures.com for
more information.

UK agent: The Manning Partnership Ltd
tel. 01225 478 444; fax 01225 478 440;
sales@manning-partnership.co.uk

UK distributor: Grantham Book Services Ltd
tel. 01476 541080; fax 01476 541061;
orders@gbs.tbs-ltd.co.uk

North American agent/distributor: National Book
Network tel. 301 459 3366; fax 301 429 5746;
www.nbnbooks.com

Australian agent/distributor: Pan Macmillan Australia:
tel. 1300 135 113; fax 1300 135 103;
customer.service@macmillan.com.au

New Zealand agent/distributor: David Bateman Ltd;
tel. (09) 415 7664; fax (09) 415 8892

Publisher: Joanna Lorenz
Project Editor: Anne Hildyard
Photographers: Phil O'Connor and Geoff Waugh
Illustrator: Peter Bull
Designer: Steve West
Copy Editor: Wendy Horobin
Indexer: Diana LeCore
Production Controller: Don Campaniello

© Anness Publishing Ltd 2009

ETHICAL TRADING POLICY
At Anness Publishing we believe that business should
be conducted in an ethical and ecologically
sustainable way, with respect for the environment and
a proper regard to the replacement of the natural
resources we employ.
Because of our ongoing ecological investment
programme, you, as our customer, can have the
pleasure and reassurance of knowing that a tree is
being cultivated on your behalf to naturally replace
the materials used to make the book you are holding.
For further information about this scheme, go to
www.annesspublishing.com/trees

Publisher's Note: Although the advice and information
in this book are believed to be accurate and true at the
time of going to press, neither the authors nor the
publisher can accept any legal responsibility or liability
for any errors or omissions that may be made nor for
any inaccuracies nor for any harm or injury that comes
about from following instructions or advice in this book.
You are advised to consult your doctor before
commencing a new exercise programme.

Page 2: Lance Armstrong during his seventh win,
descending the Col du Galibier to Briançon in the Tour
de France in 2005.
Cover illustrations
Top row L–R: **Phil O'Connor** 1–5, 7, 9, 11; **Geoff
Waugh** 6, 12; **Istock** 8; **Daniel Joubert/epa/
Corbis** 10.
Back cover bottom L–R: **Geoff Waugh** 1, 2, 3;
Phil O'Connor 4.
Front cover: Top left 1and 3: Chris Hoy and Bradley
Wiggins, gold medal winners at the 2008 Beijing
Olympics.
Main picture **Michel Krakowski/epa/Corbis**:
Australia's Robbie McEwent wins the third stage of
the Giro d'Italia in Belgium in 2006.

CONTENTS

Introduction

The bicycle symbolizes freedom, mobility, independence and self-sufficiency. It is far more than a mode of transport – it is a toy, a means to lifelong health and fitness, and the most environmentally friendly and efficient way of getting from A to B.

This book will explain everything you need to know to make the most of your cycling experience, whether you are a beginner or an expert, a road rider or a mountain biker.

The book starts with riding for pleasure and for practical purposes, taking you through the history of the development of bikes, before explaining the basic skills you need to get started. We'll describe leisure cycling, commuting, cycling for the family and how to get your children involved. For the more adventurous, the book covers the ultimate in leisure cycling – touring. We'll explain how you can make your bike part of your holiday, and advise you on

Below: Off-road biking has exploded in popularity since the first mountain bikes became available in the late 1980s.

what to take and where to go. There is a section on bike technology in which we take your bike apart and explain how the moving parts work, and how to maintain them in perfect working order.

Farther on, find out how to use your bike to get fitter, and take part in semi-competitive events. The section on sportives will guide you through the preparation, training and tactics for a middle or long-distance sportive event. These are some of the most fulfilling experiences for a bike rider, and we'll help you get the most out of them. Then the action moves off road, to take you through the different disciplines of mountain biking. We'll look at cross-country trail riding, downhilling and freeriding, as well as giving advice on the best places in the world to enjoy mountain biking. We explain how to

Above: In Amsterdam, cycling is a popular way to get around, and there are bicycles on every street.

Above: The ultimate achievement in road cycling – Tom Boonen wins a stage of the Tour de France in 2007.

Left: Many children's first experience of cycling comes through BMXing, which enables them to develop riding skills, confidence and agility.

make a training schedule for both on- and off-road cycling, with advice on how to get stronger and fitter, and how to fit a regular training schedule in your life.

The last section of the book is about fully competitive cycling – racing on- and off-road, with explanations of tactics, strategies and skills. We'll also take a look at the world's greatest bike races. Find out about off-road racing, including cross-country mountain bike racing and cyclo-cross, as well as track racing. Lastly, we look at advanced training methods, and dealing with injuries.

Why cycle?
The beauty of cycling is that you can participate at any level, be it for practical reasons such as commuting, to compete seriously, or simply just for fun. For many people, the bicycle is the first step to independence and exploration. On foot, children can explore to the end of the road and perhaps a little way beyond, but on a bike, their freedom grows exponentially. Millions, perhaps billions of children around the world have grown up with their bike as their companion. Many leave the bike behind when they enter adulthood, but increasingly, we are seeing bicycles with fresh eyes. More and more adults are riding for fun, for fitness or purely for practical reasons.

Cities around the world are following the lead of European capitals such as Amsterdam and incorporating bike lanes into their transport policy. There is no cheaper, cleaner, greener method of getting around town. Bikes are also fast. In competition with a car in a gridlocked city, the bike wins every time.

However, speed is not always of the essence. People ride bikes mainly for fun. With the invention of the BMX and its popularization in the 1980s, and the explosion of interest in mountain biking in the 1990s, cycling has been one of the fastest-growing leisure activities in the Western world.

As we become more adventurous in our choice of holiday, the bike has become a popular method of transport. It is not enough to go touring at home, people are organizing long tours all over Europe and America, and farther afield in Asia and Africa.

Cycling for fitness

One of the most effective methods of keeping fit is cycling. If you cycle, you are exercising, and by doing it you will become fitter, healthier and happier. Many leisure cyclists find that their increased fitness levels inspire them to take it more seriously. Just as joggers and fun runners enter marathons or other road-running events, leisure cyclists can find events to provide a challenge and sense of achievement.

Below: Cycling can be a sociable sport, and training in a group can be more motivating than going it alone.

Cycling events can range from 30km organized road rides up to mountainous 'sportive' events, or arduous 24-hour enduro races on mountain bikes.

Just taking a 30-minute bike ride every one or two days will have a marked effect on the fitness of a sedentary individual. For more serious cyclists, training and riding is a way of life, with races and sportive events catering for all levels of athlete.

From local children organizing BMX races, through 'weekend warriors' who are competing locally, to the winner of the Tour de France, the sport of cycling is attracting a broad audience.

When you start to ride your bike, you have deliberately chosen a fitter and healthier lifestyle. You have chosen to be practical and self-sufficient. What's more, you have chosen to have fun.

Regular cycling will result in greater levels of fitness, and by designing and following training schedules, as well as keeping a training diary, cyclists can monitor their achievements and see the improvements in their fitness. A long-term fitness plan,

Above: There is immense satisfaction to be gained by taking part, and winning, a tough cycling race.

working towards the goal of doing well in an organized event, will ensure that your cycling experience will be a positive one.

Commuting

For most people, the bike is simply a practical mode of transport, albeit one which also comes with extra fitness benefits, and one which is also enjoyable. Public transport in cities is generally crowded and expensive. In the country-side, there is often no option but to drive or cycle. These inescapable facts cause many people to come to the same con-clusion – the bicycle is a cheaper, more reliable and healthier alternative. Getting started with commuting is easy – you need a bike, motivation, and basic but effective planning. The savings are three-fold: the one-off cost of the bike is offset after a few weeks or months by the saving on public transport costs. You'll be fitter and you'll have more time – unless you have a very long trip to work. In cities the bike is a faster option than cars, trains or buses.

Group activity

The bicycle is more than a practical tool. There are few more sociable activities for families and friends than a cycling expedition into the countryside, or to a favourite café. More communities, both urban and rural, are designing and building scenic cycle paths and routes which avoid dangerous main roads. During summer weekends, there are few more enjoyable activities, and these are ideal for the entire family so the kids can get involved too, not that most children need persuading to get on their bikes and go for a ride.

Children can develop independence by exploring on their bikes, and also be encouraged to follow a healthy lifestyle from an early age. And if you do take children on family outings by bike, the journey becomes part of the adventure.

Above: Competing in international cycle events is an extremely healthy way to travel and to see different countries around the world.

Bike racing

Beyond sportive and challenge events is the world of racing. Bike racing is enjoying a real renaissance in Europe and the United States, owing to the success and popularity of Lance Armstrong, who won the Tour de France seven times, and UK success in the Olympics in 2008. To succeed at racing, you need to set even tougher targets, and have the discipline to train effectively and regularly. But you will be taking part in the most rewarding sport of all.

Whatever level you decide is suitable for you to attempt, there is a whole world out there for you to discover on two wheels.

RIDING FOR PLEASURE

There are two things you need to start cycling: a bicycle, and a lot of enthusiasm. Then you are ready to take advantage of all the opportunities cycling can offer. Getting started, you may just want to ride around town, but you will need to consider which bike to buy, what to wear and how to ride in an urban environment. Or you may want to strike out farther afield, and embark on a cycling tour. Good planning and preparation are essential to ensure that cycling is a positive experience for you.

*Left: A sociable group of cyclists take
to the road.*

HISTORY AND DEVELOPMENT

It is remarkable how little the basic design of the bicycle has changed since its invention in the 19th century. Although the overall look – two wheels, a frame, handlebars and saddle – has been constant, there has still been significant evolution. Once pneumatic tyres and efficient drivetrains had been invented, the bicycle revolutionized personal transport. From the earliest 'running machines', to the lightweight, aerodynamic carbon-fibre racing bike, bicycles have come a long way.

Above: A hobby horse from the early 19th century.
Left: An 'ordinary' bicycle, commonly known as a 'penny farthing'.

In the Beginning

In the past, most people had little choice but to walk everywhere. The invention of the bicycle provided the means for individuals to travel farther than ever before, making it the first real widespread mode of transport among the public.

Claims have been made that Leonardo da Vinci, among others, invented the bicycle, but the first reliable evidence for self-propelled two-wheeled transport comes from 1817.

Baron Karl Drais von Sauerbronn, a civil servant from Baden, Germany, invented a steerable two-wheeled device initially named the 'Draisine', after its maker. More popularly known as a running machine, or hobby horse, the Draisine was made of a wooden frame attached to two wheels. Propulsion was basic – without pedals or a drivetrain, the rider had to push the Draisine along using his feet on the ground. Following an exhibition in Paris in April 1818, Draisines enjoyed a flurry of popularity among the wealthy, but they were impractical on all but the smoothest of road surfaces.

Treadle power
Scottish blacksmith Kirkpatrick Macmillan invented a treadle-driven bicycle in 1839, the first attempt at a modern propulsion system. Pedals were attached to two rods, which connected to the back wheel and transmitted movement in a way similar to a steam train. The energy transmission was very

inefficient, but Macmillan's bicycle was reportedly capable of sustaining low speeds, as fast as 8 miles per hour, for long distances. Bicycle design took a great leap forward in 1861, when Frenchman Pierre Michaux took Drais's

Above: Baron Karl Drais von Sauerbronn and his 'Draisine' bicycle, which was propelled by the feet.

design and added pedals and cranks directly to the front wheel. Michaux's bicycle, or velocipede (which means 'fast foot' in French), was developed into what we now know as penny farthings, or 'ordinary' bikes.

The invention of gearing was a long way off, therefore the only way to increase speed was to make the driving wheel, usually the front one, larger in diameter. As one pedal revolution was equal to one rotation of the wheel, the larger the circumference, the faster the bike would travel through one revolution of the pedal.

Left: In the mid-1800s, treadle-driven bicycles made it possible to ride for long distances at low speed.

Timeline

1817 Baron Karl Drais von Sauerbronn invents the running machine, a wooden frame on two wheels, with steering ability. Propulsion came from the rider pushing himself along using his feet on the ground.
1839 Kirkpatrick Macmillan builds a bicycle with the rear wheel powered by treadles.
1861 Pierre Michaux makes the first bicycle with pedals and cranks.
1869 Solid rubber tyres mounted on steel rims are introduced in a new machine, which is the first to be patented under the modern name 'bicycle'.
1870s Penny farthings are popularized.

1885 The safety bicycle, with a chain-driven back wheel, is invented by James Starley.
1888 John Boyd Dunlop develops the pneumatic tyre.
1899 Production of bicycles in America reaches one million units per year.
1903 The first Tour de France takes place.
1927 Quick-release wheels are invented by Tullio Campagnolo.
1933 Derailleur gears are developed.
1960s BMXs originate in California. Through the 1970s they increase in popularity.
1970s Mountain biking starts, also in California, with modified cruiser bikes

ridden downhill and off-road. They become extremely popular in the 1980s and 1990s.
1985 Clipless racing pedals invented by French company Look.
1990 Off-road clipless pedals are developed.
1990 Suspension forks introduced to mass-marketed mountain bikes.
1992 Full suspension bikes are developed.
1996 Mountain biking appears in the Olympic Games.
1999 American Lance Armstrong wins his first Tour de France; this event leads to widespread popularity of bike racing outside Europe.

Painful progress

The concept of the pedal-driven bicycle was revolutionary, but bikes at this time were not built for comfort. Frames were made of heavy steel, unlike modern frames, which use lightweight tubing, and wheels were made of wood. Tyres were simply a thin strip of metal wrapped around the wheel – combined with the cobbled streets of the era, the invariably bumpy ride led to the new machines being called 'boneshakers'. It was not until 1869 that solid rubber tyres were developed, although these were scarcely less harsh than the metal strips.

The high centre of gravity and uneven weight distribution meant that accidents were common. If the huge front wheel of a penny farthing hit an obstacle, the rider, with legs trapped beneath the handlebars, was catapulted forward at the same speed as he had previously been travelling – with the direst of consequences. This way of falling became known as 'coming a cropper'. Nevertheless, during the 1870s, penny farthings were a popular means of getting around.

Right: 'Ordinary' bicycles first became popular during the 1870s. The larger the front wheel, the faster it became possible to ride.

Development of the Modern Bicycle

Following the early and bumpy start of bicycle riding, developments in engineering and technology during the late 19th century led to radical improvements in bike design. Similar-sized wheels made the bicycle much easier to ride.

Ordinary bikes were popular for leisure riding through the 1870s, mainly among young middle- and upper-class men who performed feats of reckless derring-do. The danger inherent in riding ordinaries meant that bicycles were still some way from becoming a universal transport device. However, the bicycle was on the cusp of several significant developments, which would see a radical evolution in efficiency over the next 120 years.

The invention of the 'safety bicycle' by James Starley in 1885 revolutionized bicycle design. Technological developments meant that by 1885 metals had become stronger, and it was possible to make a chain that was light enough to be incorporated into a bicycle drivetrain. Starley's Rover bicycle was the first to look like a modern model, with more similar-sized wheels, a diamond-shaped frame, and a chain connecting the pedals with the back wheel. Its weight distribution was better than that of the ordinary, and braking was improved. With the chain and sprocket drivetrain, gearing could be adjusted to make propulsion vastly more efficient.

Rubber tyres

The Rover was still hard work to ride until James Dunlop invented the pneumatic rubber tyre in 1888. The new design used hollow tyres filled with air to cushion the bumps on the roads and offered a more comfortable, faster and safer ride. At the same time, a seat tube was added to the standard frame design, to strengthen it, and this classic 'double triangle diamond' frame shape has survived to the 21st century.

The invention of freewheels, where the wheel can continue to turn while the sprocket stays still, made it possible for riders to coast down hills. Now that bikes were comfortable and fast, the 1890s saw the beginning of a

golden age for two-wheeled transport, which was interrupted by two World Wars, but which would last until the 1950s. Mass production reduced the cost of bicycles to a low level, making them accessible to the working classes.

Above: The advent of the bicycle was an important step on the road to independence for women in the early 20th century, as it was accessible to many who had previously been restricted to walking.

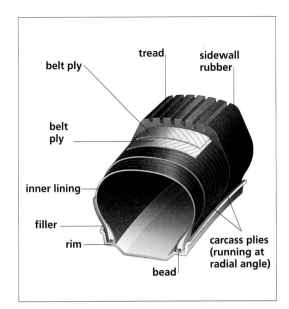

Above: A cross section of a pneumatic tyre, which revolutionized cycling by giving a faster, more comfortable ride.

In the USA alone, bicycle production reached an annual high of one million units by 1899. Women, still bound by Victorian concepts of modesty, would not think of riding an ordinary, but the safety bicycle let them ride without offending sensibilities. The new-found travelling freedom of the working classes and women made the bicycle into an almost universal tool. Suffragettes embraced two-wheel transport, with American civil rights leader Susan B. Anthony claiming that "the bicycle has done more for the emancipation of women than anything else in the world".

Meanwhile, in Europe, bike racing grew as a popular sport. Events like the Tour de France, which first ran in 1903, captured the public imagination. Into the 20th century, bikes grew in popularity and use. The pace of innovation in bicycle design slowed, until an Italian racing cyclist called Tullio Campagnolo made two significant developments during the 1920s and 1930s. The first was the quick-release wheel, which made disassembly much simpler. The second was the derailleur gear system, which is still seen on bikes today. Campagnolo's parallelogram-shaped derailleur allowed the chain to move between several sprockets on the back wheel, giving a wide range of gears so that the bikes could be easily ridden on hills, as well as along the flat.

The boom in car ownership ended the popularity of bicycles. After 1945, while car numbers grew, sales of bikes in Britain went from a pre-war peak of 1.6 million in 1935 to fewer than half a million in 1955. In the US, numbers dropped even more, but technological development continued. Utility bikes remained popular in Europe, while in the Far East, the bicycle was the main mode of transport. Racing bikes were made stronger, lighter and faster, and bikes now come with up to 33 gears.

Touring bikes were built to carry luggage and camping equipment. Bicycles started to go off-road, especially with the advent of BMX and mountain bikes, which saw the development of suspension systems for greater comfort. Efficiency was gained by the use of clipless pedals; shoes were attached to the pedals for propulsion, but would release in the event of an accident.

Sales rose again during the 1970s and 1980s. Today, with environmental concerns about the impact of driving, the bicycle stands on the cusp of another golden age.

Below: Racing bikes are among the most technologically advanced models available today.

Diversification

As technology developed, it became possible to diversify and to produce bicycles that could be ridden on rough terrain as well as on roads. This opened up opportunities for producing bikes for both leisure and sporting activities.

Until the 1970s, bicycles were functional, utilitarian and serious. Utility bikes were used for commuting and shopping, touring bikes were the ultimate in self-sufficiency and practicality, and racing bikes were honed down for speed and efficiency. In California, however, two inventions revolutionized the world of bicycles and laid the foundations for a boom in cycling as a leisure and adventure activity. The first was BMX (bicycle moto-cross), the second, mountain biking.

The rise of BMX

BMX developed out of an American craze for a Schwinn model called the Sting-Ray, which came on the market in 1963. The Sting-Ray had fat tyres on small 50cm (20in) wheels with a heavy-duty frame. By 1968, almost three-quarters of all bikes sold in the United States were Sting-Rays or similar models.

BMX, an abbreviation of 'bicycle moto-cross', came about when the opening sequence to motorcycling film *On Any Sunday* showed children racing

Above: This young BMX rider is appropriately kitted out with protective trousers and jacket, a helmet with a chin extension, visor, gloves and shoes.

Two wheels, two people

It wasn't long after bicycles were invented that creative minds made a logical leap – if a bike can carry one person, why not two? And so tandems were invented. The first try was two bicycles welded together. But a patent was filed on 4 August 1891 by H. G. Barr and F.E. Peck for a two-man velocipede with one seat above each wheel and pedals on each axle. Modern tandems have a strong wheel and frame to bear the weight of two riders. They can be faster than a single bike, because they harness the power of two riders through a single drivetrain.

Left: This Spanish couple started a 10-year journey on their tandem in 2005, encompassing more than 80 different countries.

Above: A modern BMX; solid, durable with a single gear.

Above: This American cruiser is a bike that is aimed squarely at children.

Above: A heavy-duty mountain bike, a Stumpjumper, for off-road riding.

their Sting-Rays on a dirt track. Races sprang up around the country, and the bikes became more like moto-cross bikes, with knobbly tyres and crossbars on the handlebars. Through the 1970s the BMX craze took off, first in America, then in Europe, as the sport and bikes evolved a distinctive look. By 1975, BMXers had started freestyling in skateboarding parks in California, and performing complex jumps and tricks.

In the 1980s BMX hit mainstream culture, with top stunt riders and racers earning big money.

The US television channel ESPN sponsored a televised race series with a first-prize fund that reached more than $50,000. BMX peaked in the mid-1980s, but even now, more BMXs are sold in North America than any other kind of bike.

Mountain biking
In the 1970s and 1980s, a new and innovative form of cycling followed on the heels of the BMX craze. This was to be the start of mountain biking. Its roots are obscured somewhat but it is known that a group of riders in Marin County, California, started customizing their bikes with fatter tyres and extremely efficient brakes.

In the 1970s, the first downhill race took place when riders raced down a hill known as Repack Road. Repack descended 400m in 3km (1,300ft in 2 miles), and the races grew in size, then spread to other locations. In 1977 the first purpose-built mountain bike became available, and the mainstream media began to recognize a new craze. In 1982, the first mass-produced mountain bike was developed – the Specialized Stumpjumper – and sales boomed worldwide. Technology continued to refine the mountain bike, with suspension forks, full-suspension bikes and disc brakes.

Mountain biking is now one of the biggest branches of cycling for sport and leisure in the United States and Europe.

Below: The Schwinn Sting-Ray was the first bike aimed at the youth market.

Cycling as a Sport

As soon as bicycles had evolved enough to go fast, people started racing them. Pierre Michaux's velocipede was invented in 1861, and within 10 years the first recorded race had taken place. The popularity of that event confirmed bicycle racing as a sport.

In Saint-Cloud Park, in Paris, on 31 May 1869, the first velocipede race took place – a 1,200m (0.75 mile) event, with James Moore, an expatriate English doctor, taking first place. Since 1,200m was well below the distance potentially covered by a bicycle in one day, it wasn't long before races were being run between separate towns. The inaugural Paris–Rouen race, also in 1869, covered 122km (76 miles). Moore won that race, too. Considering that pneumatic tyres were yet to be invented, then the average speed of 11kph (7mph) recorded by Moore becomes even more impressive.

Bicycle racing became more and more popular in the last decade of the 19th century, with massed-start races drawing huge crowds and competitors from all over Europe. Place-to-place events were the biggest draw, and distance was no object to the organizers of these events. Bordeaux–Paris, raced

for the first time in 1891, covered a gruelling 600km (373 miles). Another Englishman, George Pilkington-Mills, raced through the night to win the race in just over 24 hours. Although another Briton, Arthur Linton, won five years later, only one more would win the race before the final running of the event in 1988 – Tom Simpson in 1963. The same year saw the even longer Paris–Brest–Paris event, which covered 1,200km (745 miles) across northern France, and was won in 71 hours by Frenchman Charles Terront. This event still exists as a four-yearly endurance test for amateur cyclists.

Professional races

The oldest professional race that is still running on an annual basis is the Liège–Bastogne–Liège Classic, which took place in Belgium for the first time in 1892, and was won for three years in a row by the Belgian cyclist Leon Houa.

Above: Fausto Coppi, one of the first great champions of road racing. Coppi captured the heart of post-war Italy when he won the Tour of Italy in 1955.

Liège–Bastogne–Liège was run only five more times before 1919, but it then became an annual fixture and remains one of the most important bike races in the world.

The most renowned one-day classic is the Paris–Roubaix race, which first took place in 1896. To this day, it still uses the old cobbled forest roads of industrial northern France, and has the nickname the 'Hell of the North'. Racing over cobbled roads is a different proposition from racing on smooth tarmac – Paris–Roubaix is a race that tests cyclists to their limits.

At the turn of the 20th century, bike races were still organized on a place-to-place basis, but a stroke of marketing genius in November 1902 changed the nature of bike racing forever.

Henri Desgrange, a journalist for French newspaper *L'Auto*, came up with

Left: The Tour de France in 1964, going along a scenic but challenging part of the route.

the idea of a bike race around France for July 1903 – not just from one place to another, but around the entire country – as a means of promoting the newspaper. The distance – 2,414km (1,500 miles) – was massive, so Desgrange split the race up into six stages, starting in Paris, then heading to Lyon, Marseille, Toulouse, Bordeaux and Nantes before returning to Paris. The stages might have been designed to break up the race, but the distances were still huge – the longest stage, between Nantes and Paris, was 471km (292 miles). The winner of the first race was Frenchman Maurice Garin, who won the substantial sum of 20,000 francs for his efforts.

L'Auto provided daily coverage of the race, and boosted circulation from 25,000 copies to 65,000 in the space of a few weeks. The positive publicity led Desgrange to make the Tour an annual event and it quickly became, and remains, the biggest and most famous bike race in the world.

Above: Eddy Merckx, winning his first Tour de France in 1969. He set a record that remains unbroken.

Below: Crowds line a mountainous stretch of the road to see the competitors pass in the 1949 Tour de France.

The world stage

In the early part of the 20th century, more and more stage races sprang up around Europe. The Giro d'Italia, or Tour of Italy, which is generally considered to be the second most important Grand Tour after the Tour de France, was started in 1909, while the Vuelta a Espana, Spain's version, followed suit in 1935. Meanwhile, important one-day races, such as the Tour of Lombardy and Milan–San Remo in Italy, and the Tour of Flanders in Belgium, became established.

As the races grew in size, the riders themselves became famous. Before and after World War II, the rivalry between two Italian riders, Gino Bartali and Fausto Coppi, divided the nation.

Bartali, a staunch Catholic with a modest and conservative disposition, attracted older fans, while the secular Coppi, who created a scandal by divorcing his wife – an unpopular move in religious Italy – was identified with by younger, more progressive Italians. The two went head to head in the 1949 Giro d'Italia, and Coppi thrashed his older rival.

Coppi's 1952 Tour de France win is renowned as being one of the best of all time. The organizers had introduced tough stages through the Pyrenees and

Alps since the 1910 race. But in 1952 they made another important development – the summit finish. With stages to ski resorts such as

Above: Eddy Merckx, shown in 1974 in Vouvray, Orléans, is held to be the best-ever racing cyclist.

Alpe d'Huez, the final kilometres were all uphill, which made the race even harder. Coppi won at Alpe d'Huez, which has become a regular fixture on the Tour, and dominated the race.

The first rider to win the Tour five times was Frenchman Jacques Anquetil, between 1957 and 1964, while his compatriot Bernard Hinault in the 1970s and 1980s and Spaniard Miguel Indurain in the 1990s also won five Tours. The two most famous multiple winners of the Tour were Belgian cycling star Eddy Merckx and American Lance Armstrong (see boxes).

Now, the Tour is a multi-million-euro affair that captures the attention of sport fans every summer. From humble beginnings in 1869, bike racing has become a global sport.

Right: Tom Boonen rides on cobbled roads in the Paris–Roubaix race in 2004.

Eddy Merckx

Belgian cyclist Eddy Merckx was the first international superstar of bicycle road racing. During a professional career spanning 13 years from 1965 to 1978, he won a record number of races – as many as 575, according to some – including five Tours de France.

Merckx's nickname was 'the Cannibal' – he had as insatiable an appetite for being the winner of bike races as Muhammad Ali had for winning boxing fights. His racing style was aggressive, and he would often attack a long way from the finish.

Early in his career, he took victories in prestigious one-day races like Milan–San Remo and Paris–Roubaix. He also won three world championships, a record equalled, but never beaten. To add to his five Tour de France wins, he also won five Tours of Italy (Giro d'Italia) and one Tour of Spain (Vuelta a

Espana) – no cyclist in history has come anywhere close to matching Merckx's 11 victories in Grand Tours.

But it was the Tour de France that defined Merckx's career. He won his first Tour in 1969, at his first attempt, and took his fifth and final win in 1974, equalling the record of five overall wins set by the Frenchman Jacques Anquetil.

Merckx's first Tour de France in 1969 was one of the most dominant victories in the history of the race. As well as winning the yellow jersey (awarded to the rider who covers the course in the best time), he won the green jersey (for the points classification) and the polka-dot jersey of the King of the Mountains. No other rider has achieved this feat. He also won a record 34 stages of the Tour de France in his career.

Lance Armstrong

Eddy Merckx may have won more races in the course of his career than Lance Armstrong, but it is the American who has achieved more worldwide fame.

Armstrong was a precocious Texan who started his sporting career as a triathlete, but focused on bike racing in his early 20s. He exploded on to the world of professional cycling when he won the world championships in 1993 at the age of 21, but although he had won individual stages in the Tour de France, he was not considered a likely winner of the coveted yellow jersey.

In 1996, Armstrong was diagnosed with cancer, and given only a slim chance of staying alive, let alone recovering enough to resume his racing career. But he battled the disease, undergoing extensive chemotherapy, and made a comeback as a professional in 1998. He surprised many people by riding to fourth place in the Tour of Spain that year, and appeared at the 1999 Tour de France as an outsider. Armstrong went on to dominate the race, gaining time in both the individual time trials and in the mountain stages, and gained worldwide coverage for his comeback from cancer. He won the next six Tours after that, taking his seventh and final yellow jersey in 2005, establishing a record that will probably never be equalled, let alone beaten. In winning seven Tours, he established a new tactic, using his team to control the opposition before landing the killer blow himself.

In retirement, Armstrong continues to be an influential spokesman in the fight against cancer. He probably summed it up best himself when he said, "cancer chose the wrong guy".

Right: Lance Armstrong, an indomitable sportsman, who won the Tour de France a record-breaking seven times in consecutive years.

LEISURE RIDING

You don't have to start cycling with the aim of participating in the Tour de France. For most people, the simple practicalities of getting around town, commuting, or embarking on a short off-road leisure ride with family and friends are all that interests them. Even when cycling aims are this simple, just working on a few key skills and boosting confidence will enable you to get the most out of your cycling experience. Improving fitness will also make cycling easier and more effective.

Above: A family ride a three-seater bike through a national park in Oregon.
Left: Children ride through a field in the country.

The Hybrid Cycle

A compromise between the speed of a racing bike, and the comfort of a mountain bike, the hybrid bike is the perfect bike for the leisure cyclist who wants to get around town, but maybe strike out farther for rides in the countryside or on bike paths.

Hybrid bikes resemble mountain bikes. While mountain bikes are built to withstand punishing rides off-road, hybrids don't need to be so resilient. They have narrower wheels, and usually come with slick tyres, which offer less rolling resistance on the road. This makes them faster. Flat handlebars and an upright position mean that riding is both safe and comfortable. Some even have suspension, which makes them still more comfortable to ride.

Most hybrid bikes are also set up so that panniers can be attached to carry luggage, making them the perfect all-round bike for short and middle distance leisure riding.

Above: Hybrids are equally practical for off- and on-road cycling, and are built for comfort and speed.
Right: Hybrid bikes suit cyclists at all levels of achievement.

Anatomy of a hybrid bike

1 Wheels: size 700x28c, which is the same as a racing bike, slightly larger than the 26in wheel standard on mountain bikes. Slick tyres for urban riding.

2 Frame: Lighter and faster on the road than a heavy-duty mountain bike frame. Geometry is tailored for an upright position.

3 Brakes: Calliper brakes.

4 Chainrings: Either two or three, depending on the model. Three chainrings offer a larger range of gears, useful in hilly areas.

5 Sprockets: There are usually eight or nine gears.

6 Gear changers: These are mounted on the handlebars for ease of changing. Many gear changers are attached to the brake levers for good accessibility.

7 Saddle: The saddle on a hybrid bike is wide and padded for extra comfort for the rider.

8 Handlebars: Flat handlebars give the rider comfortable steering and an upright position.

Folding Bike

One of the most practical ways of getting around in big cities is using the folding bike.

For most city-dwellers, lack of storage space is a problem. Buses and trains often refuse to carry bikes, or restrict them to off-peak times. Once you have reached your destination, parking may be a problem.

These problems are solved by a folding bike, which are easy to carry on public transport, and can be stowed under a desk. However, they are not designed for long distance or fast cycling and they lose in comfort and speed over long distances.

Right: The Brompton has 40cm (16in) wheels, and collapses to a neat portable package.

Clothing for Leisure Cycling

For very short distances, in temperate weather, it is possible to cycle in any clothes, but if you choose practical, comfortable gear, suited to the prevailing environment, your cycling experience will be a more positive and comfortable one.

The farther you cycle, and the more extreme the weather conditions, the more you have to think about what to wear. Suitable clothes and shoes will help you enjoy your cycling, no matter what the weather conditions.

Summer wear

Staying cool is the most important consideration when cycling in hot weather. For the leisure cyclist, overheating will spoil what would otherwise be a pleasant ride. For the office-bound commuter, there is nothing worse than arriving at work covered in sweat with the prospect of sitting at a desk wearing formal work clothes.

Modern, breathable fabrics ensure that cycling clothes are light and comfortable, and importantly, wick the perspiration away from your skin. On a hot day, it is a good idea to wear a pair of Lycra cycling shorts, a lightweight undershirt and a cycling top.

A good quality pair of cycling shorts is one of the first things you should consider buying when taking up cycling. Cycling shorts have a padded, seamless insert, which makes a huge difference in comfort levels. Normal trousers are impractical for cycling – the seam will be very uncomfortable after only a few minutes' riding, and the weight of the fabric is also a problem. In the past, inserts were made of chamois leather and needed regular treatment from creams to prevent them hardening. However, modern cycling shorts come with synthetic antibacterial inserts that require no special care.

It is also possible to buy shorts or long trousers, which are not skin-tight but still have a chamois insert.

Undershirts, or base layers, are recommended to keep the sweat away from your skin. On hot days, when you are sweating, a long downhill freewheel or a breeze can cause you to catch a

chill. Over the base layer, you can wear a cycling jersey. These are also lightweight and help to keep the sweat away from your body. They also have pockets sewn into the lower back, which are ideal for carrying small objects such as keys and money.

Protect yourself

Wearing two tops while cycling will help to protect you in the event of a crash. The two shirts will slide against each other, protecting your skin to a certain extent from abrasions.

It is also a very good idea to wear cycling mitts, which have padding on the palm of the hand and cut-off fingers to prevent you from overheating. Mitts absorb sweat and so ensure that you can keep a good grip on the

Above: When cycling in summer, it is important to wear comfortable lightweight, breathable clothes.

handlebars. In the event of a crash, they will also protect your hands from painful injuries.

In more humid areas it is necessary to invest in a good raincoat. You can get special raincoats designed for cycling, which are waterproof, extremely light, and are extra-long in the back to protect your lower back from the rain when you are in a cycling position.

During spring and autumn, when the weather can be unpredictable, it might be worth considering a gilet, which is a sleeveless top, over your cycling top. This will help keep you warm in the cooler evenings.

Winter wear

The real test of your commitment to cycling comes in the winter months, when cold and wet weather can try the resolve of even professional cyclists. However, with the right mental attitude and a sensible choice of clothing, you can be as comfortable in the cold and wet as you are on a warm summer's day.

On your legs, you need to wear thermal leggings, available from bike shops. These often have bibs attached, which stretch over the shoulders to add an extra layer of insulation to your upper body without restricting your movement. These are ideal to wear in cold weather.

As in summer, a base layer is essential. Even in cold weather, your body can heat up while cycling, so it is even more important to wick the sweat away from your body. In extremely cold weather, a thermal base layer will help you keep warm. Over your base layer, a windproof long-sleeved jersey will protect you from the cold but still allow ventilation to prevent overheating. In freezing temperatures, a base layer and windproof jersey should keep you warm enough once you have started moving.

If you suffer particularly from the cold, or if the temperature has dropped below freezing, there are several ways of

Above: A thermal jacket is necessary for cycling during the winter.

adding lightweight layers for further insulation. Cycling shops sell detachable arm warmers made of Lycra, which can be rolled up or down according to what is comfortable. They are extremely compact, and when you are not wearing them they can be stowed in the back pocket of your cycling jersey.

In cold weather it is also essential to cover your head – many thermal cycling hats and headbands are designed to be worn under a helmet without compromising safety and comfort. The feet and hands need to be protected, too. Buy a pair of waterproof, thermal overshoes and thermal gloves, and you are ready to go.

Above: A warm and waterproof lightweight jacket over a base layer and long-sleeved jersey is essential when conditions turn very cold or wet.

Right: Safety cycling helmet.

Above: Winter gloves.

Above: Summer gloves.

Above: Thermal leggings.

Above: Waterproof overshoes.

Cycling gear

In general, the better the shoes are for cycling, the worse they are for walking. The most efficient cycling shoes have stiff soles, with shoeplates screwed in for the pedal attachments. They make you cycle faster, but once you are off the bike, at best they make you walk like a penguin.

It is inconvenient to have to carry two pairs of shoes, one for walking, one for cycling, so a solution for the leisure cyclist and commuter is to buy cycling shoes that can also be used for walking, for example, Shimano's SPD (Shimano's Pedalling Dynamics) system. These still have plates to clip to pedals, but they are flush with the sole, which is also more flexible.

Safety is paramount, especially in the city. Wear a well-fitted helmet and high-visibility gear at all times, as well as a mask if you are concerned about pollution.

General Riding Skills

It is impossible to 'unlearn' riding a bike, and just about every adult in the Western world has a head start in cycling through learning to ride when they were a child. To regain confidence, practise on a quiet traffic-free road.

Most adults who want to take up cycling again, or even those who have kept riding throughout their lives, can benefit from refreshing their skill set. The more relaxed and assured you are about your cycling and your ability to deal with challenges and obstacles, the more enjoyable your cycling will be.

The most important thing when cycling is to feel comfortable, at ease and relaxed on your bike. Nervousness makes your body tense and affects the handling of your bike, especially the steering. On a busy road, this can prove to be very dangerous.

If you have not ridden a bike for a few years, it is a good idea to find a quiet road or a car park to rediscover the feeling of balance and flow that comes from confident bike handling. You don't have to spend weeks doing this – just ensure that you can manage the basic skills of starting, riding in a straight line, riding around a corner, and stopping. The rustiness will not take long to disappear, but it is better for this to happen away from busy roads.

Moving on

Once you are confident that you are used to riding your bike again, there are still some aspects of your cycling you should take care to work on.

Cornering should be smooth, consistent and safe. Depending on whether there is traffic around, and how tight the corner is, there are several different ways of getting around a corner efficiently.

For a shallow bend, it should be possible to just keep the line you have been following already.

For a sharper corner, take a wider approach to maintain as much speed as it is safe to have. If there are cars following behind, do not swing out into their path, but if you are certain that the road is clear, you can approach the

centre of the lane before turning as you reach the corner. What you are aiming for is to be more efficient and to go around the bend losing as little speed as possible, while remaining upright and safe.

Practising skills

Riding one-handed: *Find a quiet bit of road or a car park and practise riding one-handed, using both left and right hands. For the ambitious, it doesn't hurt to learn to ride no-handed, but don't practise this in traffic.*

Left: Practise riding one-handed to improve your balance on a bike.

Two other factors need to be taken into consideration when cornering – the weather, and the road surface. In dry conditions on a smooth road, it is natural to lean with the bike as you go round a corner, though when you do this you should keep your head level. But in wet conditions, especially if there are drain covers in the road, or on loose surfaces such as gravel, leaning the bike too far will result in the wheels sliding out from under you. There is no need to slow right down unless the corner is very sharp, but to compensate for the lack of grip, try leaning your body while keeping the bike as upright as possible. This will ensure your safety, while maintaining speed around the corner.

Looking ahead: *Once you are confident of your riding skills, get out on the road and cycle. Practise predicting what is going to happen consciously, before trying to make it a subconscious part of every ride you do.*

Drills to improve your skills

Cornering 1: *Find some quiet roads, and practise riding a loop. Plan your route through the corners and learn what your safe speed is. Push your limits, but be careful and sensible.*

Cornering 2: *Find a downhill section of road with good visibility and corners going left and right. Ride down a few times, learning to look ahead and plan your route through the corners.*

Cornering 3: *Once you have ridden around the route, try getting around the corner in a smooth and consistent way. Try not to lose speed but stay upright, relaxed and safe.*

Cornering 4: *Once you have got around the corner, maintain your speed and cycle confidently on. Always be aware of other road users such as cars and buses or heavier vehicles and be prepared to take avoiding action.*

Braking: *Find a quiet downhill bit of road. Ride at various speeds and work on getting your stopping distance down to a safe minimum. Start with the back brake to check speed and maintain control, then the front brake to stop.*

Go with the flow

Once you are cornering confidently and riding at an efficient speed, you are more in control of your bike. And the good news is that the more time you spend cycling, the more natural these processes will become.

Once you have got used to the way your bike handles, and the way you react to it, you will notice that you will stop thinking of yourself and the bike as separate entities, but don't relax too much – you still need to be ready to react to surprises.

Above: The more cycling you do, the more you will be focused.

Braking, Gearing and Riding Safely

Once you have spent some time cycling on the roads, you will become aware that the average bike ride throws up hazards, obstacles and challenges when you least expect it. Learning to anticipate these things is key to becoming a more proficient rider.

Awareness is seeing what is going to happen on the road ahead a few seconds before it actually does. By watching the behaviour of others, you can learn to predict even the seemingly unpredictable. If a car is about to turn across you, it is safer to slow down. Pedestrians may wander into the road, assuming that if they cannot hear a car, there is nothing coming. Cars can pull out directly into your path. If you anticipate, you can avoid problems. Always be aware of what is going on around you.

Braking

Reacting to an obstacle can involve one of two things – evasive action, or braking. If you have the time and space to swerve around a pothole, pedestrian or other obstacle you can maintain your speed without wasting energy.

More often, you need to check your speed or even stop suddenly, and there is a technique to this. Slamming on both brakes can cause a rear-wheel skid, or worse, a front-wheel lock, which is as potentially painful as it is embarrassing. The aim is to be in control of the bike at every moment, and controlled and assertive braking is part of this.

The correct technique for braking is to rely more on the rear brake at high speed, and then the front brake as you decelerate. As weight is transferred forward during braking, there is a

Right: When waiting at a stop light, keep one foot on the pedal, ready to accelerate away.
Below: Build the confidence to ride safely in traffic – anticipate what is ahead, be aware of what is behind.

Dos and don'ts of riding in traffic

Do Make sure that your bike is in good repair – sudden breakages can cause your bike to veer or crash.

Do Wear visible clothing, especially at night or in poor light.

Do Have working front and back lights, day or night. Overcast conditions can affect visibility.

Do Concentrate.

Do Relax, even when confronted by challenges. Tensing up can affect steering.

Do Look and plan ahead. Look out for potholes, junctions, manhole covers, cars, pedestrians, stones, animals and other cyclists.

Left: Cars should give cyclists plenty of room. When one comes past, stay focused and relaxed.

Don't Listen to music while you are cycling – you absolutely need to be aware of approaching traffic, just in case they are unaware of you.

Don't Approach junctions at full speed, unless you have full visibility and you are certain there is no traffic approaching. Check your speed until the way is clear.

Don't Assume that a driver, pedestrian or cyclist has seen you until eye contact has been established. Err on the side of caution.

Don't Ride faster than your skills and confidence allow.

Don't Ride the same in the wet as you would in the dry – stopping distances are greater. Also watch out for drain covers, which are like sheet ice in the wet.

tendency for the back wheel to skid, so try and push your own weight backward on the bike to compensate for this. It is a lot to think about for something that has to happen in a split second, but practise it until it is second nature. In most cases, the anticipation you have been developing will enable you to see hazards unfolding well in advance, and you will be able to slow down while remaining in control.

Sometimes you have to perform an emergency stop. Try never to panic and just grab at the brake levers, but stay

Above: Potholes can be a danger for cyclists. If possible, look ahead and avoid them, but don't swerve into the road.
Left: When braking, maintain a firm grip on the handlebars and squeeze the brake gently to control speed.

Left: Cyclo-cross riders keep their weight far back when braking, so that they can maintain control and traction.

relaxed and calm and be confident that a well-maintained set of brakes and the correct techniques will enable you to stay safe.

Using gears efficiently

Cycling effectively is not about getting from A to B as fast as you possibly can. If you start a ride sprinting, you won't last long. The important thing is to ride

at an efficient speed. Choose a gear that you can comfortably turn at 60–80 revolutions per minute, just over one per second, or whatever feels comfortable. Racing cyclists prefer a faster rhythm, but for leisure riding and commuting the main aim is economy of movement.

If you are going up an unexpected steep hill, you need to get the timing right. Lighten pressure on the pedals so you can shift down a few gears. Change up if you are going downhill. On varied terrain; uphills and downhills, the aim is to keep the same cadence.

Urban Cycling

The bicycle is the perfect mode of transport in an urban environment. A bike can squeeze through a gap when the road is blocked with traffic. There are health and fitness benefits too, and cycling is a great stress reliever.

Cars get stuck in traffic jams, and once they arrive at their destination, there is scarce space for parking. Buses and trains and even underground systems are better, but you are forced to go where they go. You also have to pay for the privilege.

If the closest train station is a 10-minute walk away from your destination, you often have no option but to walk. Cabs? More flexible, but the costs quickly mount up.

Cycling offers the best of all worlds – it's free, once you have bought a bike. It's fast. You can go exactly where you want to. And it is environmentally friendly.

More and more big cities around the world are starting to realize that congestion is a major problem, both economically and practically. It is also suspected that there are major health risks involved in having to breathe the emissions from cars stuck head-to-tail on the city's streets. So, following the lead of cities like Amsterdam in Holland, bike lanes are being laid and provision for bikes is being included in many metropolitan transport plans.

Getting around

So why not go by bike? For city dwellers, most journeys are made within a small radius, well within cycling distance. If you calculated the typical journeys you make in the course of a week, along with the mode of transport you use, you might realize that many hours spent on buses or trains could be spent cycling instead. You'll save money as well as getting fitter. It's not just going to and from work that might be

Left: Panniers fit on a bike and let commuters and urban cyclists carry their gear without a destabilizing backpack.

Above: Finding a parking space for a car if you want to go for a coffee is difficult in most cities, but cycling can take you right to the door of the café.

better by bike. Weekend day trips to a museum or exhibition could be even more fun by riding there and back. If you are a member of a sports, music or social club of any description, the act of cycling could become part of the routine of your hobby.

For a night out on the town, though, the bike is not the best mode of transport unless you stick to non-alcoholic drinks.

Shopping by bike

While it is easy to imagine travelling more within cities by bike, the idea of shopping by bike still puts some people off. Getting to the shop on a bike is straightforward, especially when it is not too far away. But getting back laden down with food or fragile goods can be difficult, or even dangerous, if you're not properly equipped.

The main problem is how to transport heavy shopping on your bike without affecting your ability to ride safely. With small loads it is possible to ride with a comfortable backpack. Backpacks are not ideal for cycling – they over-insulate your back and make you sweat uncomfortably. They also affect the handling and balance of your bike. If they are not fitted correctly, it's possible for them to slide off to one side and unbalance you. If you are riding with a backpack, make sure it is secure.

Left: Cyclists can conveniently carry light shopping in a basket fixed to the handlebars of the bike.

With most hybrid and leisure bikes, there are attachments on the frame for panniers, and for heavier loads, these are ideal. A pair of bags on a rear pannier should be able to accommodate a substantial amount of shopping. You can also attach an ordinary bag to the top of the rack with bungees, but check it is secure. The weight does affect the handling of your bike, but it is easy to get used to, and once you adjust to the extra weight, it won't slow you down too much.

Once you have got used to this, it is by far the easiest way to go shopping. Your bike is taking the load for you – even when you drive to the shops, you have to carry your shopping to the car, and then again at the other end. For very large loads, it is worth considering a detachable trailer. These hook on to the back of your bike, and can be pulled along. If you are cycling to keep fit, the extra work involved in pulling a laden trailer will have a substantial effect on your fitness levels.

When you start to cycle more, the planning of journeys becomes a major part of the exercise. Plot an interesting route down roads that avoid the main traffic arteries of the city, and you will discover new areas, streets and buildings. Exploration doesn't have to take place in the wilderness to be fun.

Above: Bikes are the ideal form of urban transport – cities are too congested for most people to consider driving.
Right: A young child can be transported by bike, strapped in a seat on the back. You may not want to risk cycling in heavy traffic, though.

Commuting by Bike

If you live close to your office, there are many reasons to choose cycling as your method of transport. Door to door, cycling to work can save you time and you also do not have the expense of a bus or train ticket.

Cycling 16km (10 miles) a day will have a massive effect on your fitness level if you have been leading a sedentary lifestyle. If you cycle five times a week, there is no need to take out an expensive gym membership, which will save you time and money. Add this to the saving on travel tickets, or petrol and parking, and you will have substantially more money in your pocket. You will arrive at work fresh and invigorated from the exercise and the fresh air, even when it is raining. This will have a positive effect on your performance at work.

There is evidence suggesting that cyclists are less affected by pollution from car emissions than the drivers of the cars themselves. Cyclists' heads are above the level where the air is most polluted, while car ventilation systems take in all that polluted air and feed it straight into the vehicle. Of course, vehicle emissions are still a problem for cyclists, and you can buy lightweight face-masks that cover the mouth and nose and filter out pollutants and dust.

If you live up to 16km (10 miles) away from your office, commuting by bike is worth trying – your journey time might increase to somewhere between half an hour and an hour, but this is still less time than many people spend on public transport.

If you are starting from scratch, it is advisable not to try cycling to and from work five times a week. Suddenly going from no exercise to 160km (100 miles) in five days is a big jump. It is a good idea to plan a system whereby you ride to work one day, then get the train home. The next day you take the train in, and cycle home. You can build up from there.

If you live farther than 16km (10 miles) away, commuting by bike is still a viable option. Build up to the greater distance

Left: By riding to work you can save money on transport and gym membership – you'll get all the exercise you need.

Above: Cycling to work keeps you fit, is faster than driving and allows you to enjoy the fresh air.

slowly, and take days off if you are tired. You could consider splitting your journey by cycling part of the way and using public transport for the other part.

Arriving at the workplace
Once you have taken the decision to start commuting by bike, it helps if your office or workplace has a shower so you can wash and change before work. Many employers provide showers these days, which is the first concern of many would-be bicycle commuters. If yours has not, start to press for one to be installed. The practical benefits for the cyclist will far outweigh the initial investment in time and money. Second, you will need somewhere secure and preferably dry to store your bike during the day. Some workplaces have bike-locking facilities. If yours does not, ask

for some to be installed. If you have a folding bike, however, you can fold it quickly and store it neatly out of the way under your desk.

Lock it up

Finally, invest in a heavy-duty bike lock. The thicker and stronger your lock is, the harder it is for thieves to cut through it. Cable locks, or simple chains, will deter some attempts at theft, but a rigid D-lock is more secure. These items are bulky, but bike security is essential. Leave a lock at work if you don't want to carry it back and forth every day. For peace of mind, some cyclists even use two locks.

Make sure you lock your bike to something secure – a set of railings or a purpose-built bike stand. Some bike stands have brackets screwed to the wall – beware of thieves unscrewing the brackets and taking away your bike, heavy-duty locks and all.

All change

Now that all the facilities are in place for you to cycle to work, the key thing is to be organized. Given that arriving at work in sweaty cycling gear and then doing a day's work is probably unviable

Below: Parking problems will become a nuisance of the past when you commute by bike. Just lock up your bike at a dedicated cycle rack and go.

in most offices, you'll have to make sure that you have clothes to change into. Some bike commuters carry enough clothes for a week in on a Monday morning, then take it all home again on Friday. Others prefer to take fresh clothes in every day.

If you take fresh clothes in to work every day, experiment with the best way of folding your shirts to keep them pressed and the rest of your clothes crease-free. Carefully fold ties, or pay the consequences.

The less you have to carry, the easier your cycle ride will be. Pack a spare set of clothes, perhaps a laptop computer and diary. A good idea is to pack all your clothes and other items in plastic bags within your panniers or backpack to keep them dry in wet conditions.

On your bike

Now you are ready to go. In time perhaps you can start experimenting with different routes – a short deviation might add a mile or so to your journey, but may lead you to discovering new areas and finding a more scenic route. How many people who take the train get that opportunity?

Above: What to pack when commuting to work by bike: clothes, your laptop, bike lock, and plastic bags (top) and work papers and notebook (above).

Above: A light backpack.

Checklist
What to wear
Cycling shoes
Cycling shorts
Base layer
Cycling jersey
Helmet
Mitts
What to pack
Laptop
Diary
Papers
Underwear
Trousers/skirt and shirt
Tie
Secure bike lock
Plastic bags
What to keep at work
Shoes
Towel
Toiletries
Spare cycling kit in case of rain during ride

Mountain Biking: Getting Started

At some point, the ambitious leisure cyclist will want to broaden his or her horizons and take on the challenge of going for an off-road ride. Mountain biking is fun and user-friendly: you can ride the bike on and off the road.

Mountain biking off-road confers two immediate benefits. First, there is no traffic, save other cyclists, walkers and horse riders, and in general these three groups of people have learned to coexist harmoniously. (When riding on the trails, ride with tolerance and consideration, and everybody else should do the same.)

Second, in the unfortunate event of a crash, there is a higher likelihood of having a soft landing.

Unless you are riding on steep terrain, the same rules apply to off-road riding as to riding on the road. The specific skills of trail riding will be explored later in the book, but the main skill set is the same as for road riding, with the loose surface of most off-road paths taken into account.

Mountain biking in the countryside is one of the greatest pleasures of cycling, and it is a genuine social activity. If you are a recent convert to leisure cycling or commuting, mountain biking is a great way to get even more out of your bike.

Getting started is as easy as it is for road cycling. You need a bike and a healthy dose of enthusiasm. You can even use the same clothes and equipment, although you will need some proper mountain-biking shoes, which are good for walking, but that also clip in to your pedals.

The rough and the smooth
The biggest difference between road cycling and off-road cycling is obviously the surface on which you ride. Gravel and potholes aside, roads are uniform as well as predictable, while country paths are precisely the opposite. On a single ride, the surface can be soft mud, hard earth, gravel, rocks, grass or any combination of these surfaces. Learning to cope with the change in the surface, and the way it affects the handling of the bike, is important if you want to improve.

On most surfaces, the thick knobbly tyres on mountain bikes are capable of offering more grip than slick road tyres. On gravel, rocks or soft wet surfaces, however, cornering can still be hazardous. Approach bends with caution, and treat them as you would on a road bike, maintaining as much speed as possible, while staying within the bounds of safety.

Because of the bumpy surface on most off-road bike rides, mountain biking is more tiring. It is important to save energy by relaxing as much as possible, holding the handlebars in a firm but relaxed grip, and allowing the arms to be used as shock absorbers. If your bike has suspension forks, or is a full-suspension model, your ride will also be far more comfortable.

Braking also has to be treated with more caution, because of the tendency of wheels to lock up on loose surfaces. The front brake is the more powerful,

Above: The benefits of mountain biking are clear: it's just you, your bike and a spectacular landscape.

but use the back brake to control your speed, and the front brake to slow down more quickly.

Lastly, gearing is an important consideration. Because the hills tend to be steeper and more unpredictable, you can easily grind to a halt if you don't change down soon enough. If you see a hill coming, try to assess the steepness, and as you hit the bottom, change into a gear you know you will be able reach the top in. It's much better to err on the side of caution – if you stall, it is hard to get going again.

Above all, the best way of improving your cycling technique and to enjoy off-road riding more is to practise regularly and get used to the way your bike reacts on the different terrain.

Drills to improve your skills

Braking 1: *Find a slightly downhill section with a loose surface. Build up a little speed, then bring yourself to a fast but controlled stop using both brakes.*

Braking 2: *On a steeper downhill path, repeat. Push your weight back, start to slow down with the back brake then the front brake once deceleration is controlled.*

Reactions: *Riding on a downhill path with a loose surface and corners, keep the same speed and avoid rocks. Be sensitive to the way the bike reacts.*

Gearing: *Find a section of path that goes up and down hills in quick succession. Change gear for the uphill section as you reach the bottom, and continue with no loss of momentum.*

Balance 1: *Ride along a camber, that is, across the slope of a hill, holding out your 'uphill' leg for balance if necessary. Prevent your bike from slipping downhill as you ride along the camber.*

Balance 2: *Ride on a very loose or unpredictable surface, making quite exaggerated turns on corners to test your reactions and balance. Try this on a flat surface first.*

Cycling for the Family

Riding a bike needn't be a solitary activity – it is one of the cheapest and most sociable ways of enjoying an outing for families and friends. In fact, if children get involved in cycling it will help them to learn a new skill and enjoy a healthy lifestyle.

Children enjoy cycling, both when they are very young and can ride as a passenger on their parents' bikes, and later, when they learn to ride themselves. The speed, freedom and fun of cycling gives children all the stimuli they need to develop, and it encourages them to explore other places.

All it takes is the attachment of a child seat, and you and your family are ready to ride. Once your children are riding their own bikes, the family ride takes on a new dimension – they can learn about independence, within the boundaries of spending time with the family.

Right: Cycling is a fun way for a child to learn independence.
Below: Going out on a ride is a cheap and enjoyable activity for a family.

Above: A flag warns that there is a child on the back of an adult's bike.

Above: A child can gain confidence by riding a bike attached to a parent's bike.

Above: Cycling is a healthy activity that families can do together.

Starting young

If you have young children who are not old enough to ride bikes, there are several ways of including them in your cycling activities. One way is to attach a child seat to your bike. Most of these fit above the back wheel, but models exist in which the chair attaches to the top tube and the child sits between your arms. Both are safe, but handling and steering are affected by the weight above the back wheel with a rear-mounted seat. The main consideration, however, is safety. First, children should always be fitted with helmets and must wear them when they are cycling.

Rear-mounted seats should have safety guards to prevent the child's feet from touching the back wheel. Another way is to get a trailer with child seats. These are designed for one or two children, and can take a great deal more weight than a bike-mounted seat. If you use one of these, visibility to other road users is very important. Attach high-visibility strips and lights to the rear, and a flag to draw attention to the presence of a trailer.

Always check the manufacturer's guidelines for the minimum age for children to be carried in their products.

For older children, who are already competent at cycling and aware of the dangers on the road, you can buy a half-wheeler, which adds an extra wheel, seat and frame to the back of your bike. Your child can even help with the pedalling!

Left: Stabilizers attached to a child's bike will help him or her to achieve good balance before attempting to ride a two-wheeler bike.

Cycling for Kids

To children, the urge to explore, test their boundaries and broaden their horizons is as natural as wanting to eat or sleep. A bike is an ideal way of allowing them to do this. And once cycling is mastered, there is a satisfying sense of achievement.

It is important to give children their independence, but at the same time teach them that safety is paramount. Children should be encouraged to get around by bike, but responsible parents should explain which roads are safe to cycle on and which are too dangerous. They should be taught not to expect danger, but to be able to deal with it on

Above: Taking children on bike rides will keep them healthy and eager to explore their surroundings and the wider world.

the rare occasions it does come. The two most dangerous hazards are other road users, and children themselves. Children should be taught to be aware of approaching traffic and to avoid busy roads. Most car drivers will adjust their driving to take into account a child or indeed any person on a bike. But for the small minority who behave unpredictably, children need to be able to anticipate danger before it happens.

Once all the safety issues have been explained to children, most of the danger comes from their desire to find their limits. In doing so, they may pass their limits and crash, or fall off. In most cases, a few painful cuts and grazes are the consequences, as well as a more definite knowledge of their skill level.

For family rides together, it is best to avoid busy roads. Keep to quiet roads with good visibility, or take the children off-road and ride on designated bike paths.

For children below the age of 13 or 14, be particularly careful about planning a ride, and make sure the

Above: Get involved in teaching your child to ride a bike. Giving a helping hand can help instil confidence.

distance is manageable. A few miles at a time is enough. Plan plenty of rest stops with healthy snacks, and don't forget to take food and water.

Learning to ride

There are two ways of learning to ride a bike. The first is by experience. The second is by analysing the techniques and attempting to explain them verbally. Experience wins every time. Take your child, along with his or her new bike, to a park, preferably with grass to ride on. Explain how the brakes work, and warn them not to turn the handlebars too sharply. You can then sit back and watch as they experiment with how to keep

Above: Take children on rides away from roads to build their confidence and develop their skill at cycling.

Above: Encourage your child to wear a helmet to protect his or her head.
Below: Once your children are proficient at cycling, take them on longer, more adventurous rides.

the bike upright. Only help if they ask for it, and be willing to hold them upright as they start, but otherwise, cycling is a skill best learned by trial and error. It will take a few goes, sometimes a few days, but eventually they will get the hang of it. Once they have mastered wobbling along in a reasonably straight line and can work the brakes well enough to stop, you can encourage them to work on more advanced techniques – turning left, turning right, speeding up and slowing down. Before long they will be fully fledged bike riders, and there will be no holding them back.

BMX for Kids

BMXs are ideal for children. They are designed for getting around without looking in the slightest bit sensible, for riding fast and for having fun on. They are perfect for riding on specially designed BMX dirt tracks, which will improve the child's bike handling ability.

Several Tour de France riders, including some of the best sprinters in the world, grew up riding BMX bikes.

BMXs are also great for stunts and tricks, either in BMX parks, which are similar to skateboarding parks, or on the street. Doing stunts is fun and safe, within certain boundaries, for kids. It is also great for learning co-ordination and balance, and building strength.

BMX tracks

It will take a while for your children to develop the appropriate skills. Encourage them to ride the BMX as much as possible without trying stunts. Once they are used to the way it handles, you can take them to a BMX track to start developing the skills to ride around it fast and safely.

Above: You can maintain a high speed riding around berms on the race track.

BMX tracks have a dirt surface and consist of a series of jumps, bumps, sloping corners or 'berms' and straights.

Good technique and balance are needed. When riding fast, the steepness of the jumps causes the bike to become airborne. Keep the BMX straight on the approach, stay straight on the jump, and land straight. Landing at an angle will cause the bike to veer and it may crash. Bumps should be ridden over, with the legs and arms bending to absorb the shock. The BMX should stay on the ground or it will lose speed.

Riders should aim for the centre of the berm for maximum speed. It's sometimes possible to pedal all the way through, but you may need to keep the outside foot at the bottom of the pedal stroke, or even to put the lower foot down, for balance.

Left: BMXs are good for developing agility, strength and balance.

Jumps and tricks

The easiest trick to perform on a BMX is a bunny-hop. These can be practised at low speed.

Stop pedalling, in a position where both your feet are at the same height, and 'crouch' over your BMX. The momentum for the bunny-hop comes from the action of the arms pulling up. Pull the arms up first, so that the front wheel comes off the ground, then pull the heels back and up (without coming off the pedals), and the back wheel will also come up. With practice, it is possible to co-ordinate these two movements so you can make them almost simultaneous.

Pulling wheelies is also fairly straightforward. As with learning to ride in the first place, trial and error is the best way to work out and maintain the correct balance.

Sitting down, pull up on the handlebars while pushing down on one pedal (this is called a power stroke). On an adult bike, the gears are generally too high to generate enough momentum, but BMX bikes have low enough gears to allow you to carry out the manoeuvre.

Extend the arms, and pull the handlebars up towards the chest. If you go too far, you can fall backwards. If you don't go far enough, the front wheel will come back down.

Bunny-hop

1: *To bunny-hop the bike, pull the arms up so that the front wheel comes up off the ground.*

2: *Pull the heels back and up. Pedal, and be prepared to jump the back wheel up.*

3: *Pull heels back and down to attempt to bring the back wheel into the air.*

4: *Land back on the ground with the handlebars straight.*

Wheelies

1: *To pull a wheelie, pull up on the handlebars and push down on one pedal.*

2: *Next, pull up the handlebars in the direction of the chest.*

3: *Keep pedalling while the bike is balanced on the back wheel.*

Improving Your Health by Cycling

Riding a bike is a healthy activity. Regular exercise in the form of cycling will make you fitter and stronger, help you reduce your fat levels and look in better shape, boost your energy and generally improve your mood.

Most everyday cycling is an aerobic activity, when muscles generate energy for movement using oxygen. Sprinting or riding up hills is anaerobic exercise, when the muscles burn energy supplies without using oxygen, because not enough is available. Aerobic activity is sustainable for long periods; anaerobic exercise is only possible for short bursts.

Unless you are training to race your bike, it is best not to get too hung up on whether you are exercising aerobically or anaerobically. Just getting out and riding will be enough to boost your fitness levels far above those of the average member of the population. You may want to push yourself sometimes, but be careful not to overreach yourself.

Effects of cycling

Cycling mainly works the legs, but the arms, back and core muscles also get a significant workout during a ride. More importantly, the cardiovascular system works hard and becomes more efficient. After just a few weeks of regular cycling, you will be less out of breath when you climb stairs, and able to sustain longer periods of activity.

Depending on how hard you go, an hour-long bike ride can burn between 300 and 800 calories. If you ride at a moderate intensity, your body will gradually burn its fat stores. If you are

Top: Regular training and riding has a beneficial effect on health and fitness.

overweight, you will lose weight cycling, but the most important thing is not necessarily to lose weight, but to reduce fat to a healthy level. Cycling burns fat, but also builds muscle, so your lean body mass may increase after a few months' cycling. This is perfectly healthy.

Incorporating the bicycle into an organized exercise routine is easy. You may wish to ride 8km (5 miles) to and from work every day, which takes no organization. Or you can set aside two evenings a week and go for an hour-long ride, plus an extra ride at the weekend. The only limiting factor is your schedule, so work with it, not against it.

Far left: Bananas are easily eaten while cycling and are a good energy source.
Left: The faster and harder you ride, the fitter you will become.

Above: Use plenty of fresh vegetables and grains to make your meals varied, interesting and tasty.

Above: Nuts, pulses and cereals will provide you with energy to keep cycling.

Above: Eat a variety of fresh fruit regularly as part of a healthy diet.

Cycling is great exercise, but it will have a far more positive effect on your body and health if you eat and drink properly as well. A balanced diet, with natural foods and sensible levels of hydration, will fuel your body much more effectively than TV dinners and junk food. By putting better fuel into your body you will have enough energy to continue cycling and also reap the health benefits.

If you are commuting to work, or planning on a leisure ride, it's essential to have a healthy breakfast, with cereal and fresh fruit.

If you can find a cheap source of fresh fruit, it can become extremely economical to make your own juice or smoothies. Bananas are perfect fuel for cycling. Dried fruit is good, too.

While you are cycling, it is important to eat extra food on rides longer than about an hour, to prevent an energy crash. Bananas, sandwiches, dried fruit, and cereal bars are practical. If you want to stop for a cake, go ahead – you've earned the privilege.

Eat well

After a long bike ride, replenish your body's energy supplies, or the tiredness will discourage you from going out again. There are more tasty and healthy combinations of lean meat, poultry and fish, eggs and cheese, or nuts and pulses, along with carbohydrates in the form of rice, bread or pasta, and steamed or raw vegetables than there are days in a month. Go for variety, fresh ingredients, seasonal produce and home-made sauces and dressings.

Finally, hydration is important for your general health. Cycling can dehydrate you quite badly on a hot day, so drink plenty of water. There is no correct amount of water to drink in a day – it varies enormously depending on the temperature and how much you exercise – but in hot weather, when you

Above: Make your own juices and smoothies from fresh fruits.

have been out for an hour-long ride, you may need at least 2 litres (3.5 pints) of water. If you are not urinating often, you are dehydrated, but there's no need to consume huge volumes of water in a day if you're not thirsty.

Getting fit

As we have discovered, cycling has beneficial effects on your fitness levels. Regular cycling makes you fit and healthy, and for many, this is enough. But why stop there? If you design a long-term training plan and work on improving steadily in the long term, your fitness will continue to improve, with all the benefits that involves. It is a good idea to build a strong foundation of fitness, then progress further by adding time on the bike, or going a little harder.

The main principle involved in gaining fitness is overload. By stressing your body's muscles the cells within the muscles break down on a microscopic level, which explains the tiredness and stiffness you feel after exercise. However, your body will rebuild those cells stronger than they were before. You will become fitter.

In turn, as time progresses and you continue to ride, you will be capable of going just a little bit harder or faster than you could before. The muscle cells will break down again, and be rebuilt stronger than before.

The fitter you get, the closer to your capacity you will get, and the rate of improvement may slow. If you are just starting out in cycling you will be amazed at how fast your body adapts to the workload you are placing on it.

Above: Use the stairs at work whenever you possibly can, to give yourself a free daily workout.

It is easy to get carried away with an exercise regime when you first start out. The training plan below will suit anyone taking up cycling for the first time, but for unfit or overweight individuals, it is best to consult a doctor before taking up physical exercise. If the most you can handle is half the time on the schedule below, then that is the correct level for you to start at.

Above: Instead of taking public transport, briskly walk – this will burn calories and raise energy levels.

In only two months it is possible to make big changes in the level of your fitness, but at this stage the most important impact on your life will be to create the long-term habit of regular cycling. If you look on a training plan as a closed period of time that is only done once, you run the risk that when it is over you will sit back, relax and let your hard work go to waste.

Stick to the programme

Follow the training plan. Swap days around if urgent appointments get in the way of the schedule. Be flexible, and keep a record of each successful ride to spur you on. After one month, assess your progression, move on to month two, and then plan month three. This way, you will have the motivation of knowing that you are fitter than you were when you started, and you have a long-term plan beyond the initial two-month period. The most important thing is to establish cycling as a regular part of your life. The fitness benefits will come hand-in-hand with that.

Left: By gradually making your training harder, your body will adapt to become fitter, stronger and more flexible.

Basic two-month training plan

Day	Weeks one to four	Weeks five to eight
Monday	Rest day but if you wish do some gentle walking	Rest day with some gentle stretches or walking
Tuesday	Ride for about 30 minutes, slow and steady	Ride for about 1 hour at a moderate pace
Wednesday	Rest day, take it easy but if you wish do some gentle stretches	Rest day but do some gentle walking
Thursday	Ride for about 45 minutes, slow and steady	Ride for 1 hour at a moderate pace; go harder up the hills
Friday	Rest day with some gentle stretches and walking	Rest day but do some gentle stretches or walking
Saturday	Ride for about 1 hour, slow and steady	Ride for 1½ hours, slow and steady
Sunday	Ride for up to 1 hour, slow and steady (optional)	Ride for 1 hour, slow and steady (optional)

Left: Make cycling part of a healthy life by riding three or four times a week.

Lifestyle choices

In our basic two-month training system, there are three or four rides a week. Just this much exercise will help you reduce fat in your body to a healthy level. The maximum amount of time you will be on your bike in a week is only 3¼ hours at the start, which still leaves more than 164 hours over the rest of the week to sleep, eat, live and work!

There are some very easy changes you can make to your daily routine to make the most of your improved fitness levels and ensure that your healthy lifestyle doesn't stop when you get off the bike.

Stretch regularly to help to loosen muscles and improve flexibility.

Walk a little faster Pick up the pace a little, so you are conscious of your body working harder.

Take the stairs Cycling builds strength in the legs – make the most of it by taking the stairs whenever possible. Yes, even if you work on the 10th floor! Walk down, too, adding to your daily exercise.

Don't use motorized transport Popping to the supermarket for some shopping? Go by bike. Attach a basket or panniers to your bike to carry the shopping.

Right: Training regularly will reduce your vulnerability to injury.

TOURING

Touring on a bike is a rewarding cycling experience. Whether it is a day-trip, a weekend away, a week-long tour in a foreign country or a full-scale off-road expedition, bicycle touring is the ultimate in self-sufficient, independent and environmentally friendly tourism. Planning a trip is part of the fun, and designing an interesting route can add to the enjoyment. Keeping your baggage light is also an important part of touring. And for those with a spirit of adventure, there is the challenge and fun of camping with the bike.

Above: Travelling light is essential when touring for long distances.
Left: Touring is one of the best ways to explore the countryside.

The Touring Bike

It is technically possible to go cycle touring on any bike. The fact that you own a mountain bike or hybrid bike should not prevent you from planning short-distance tours. However, it will be better to invest in a fully equipped touring bike.

For touring, especially long distances, buying a specialized bike is a great idea. Touring bikes are light but strong: self-sufficiency is the basis of cycle touring, and the bike must be durable enough to carry a heavy load for long periods of time.

The classic touring bike resembles a racing bike, but with several subtle differences that make it ideal for the purpose. The frame has more relaxed geometry than a racing bike, which makes it more comfortable over long distances. This sacrifices a bit of speed, but bike tours are not races. The wheels are strong, with heavy-duty tyres to prevent punctures. The fewer punctures you have on a long tour, the more you can enjoy the experience of the trip.

There are fittings for panniers over the rear wheel, and often over the front wheel as well. For a long tour, it's sometimes necessary to carry a lot of equipment, and if the load is spread evenly, it is easier to carry. Many cycle tourists attach bags to the handlebars, for maps, money and anything you need easy access to, with a basic toolkit in a bag under the saddle. Mudguards are essential – they add very little to the

Above: A mountain bike is also suitable for a touring trip.
Right: Planning your route and following it is one of the enjoyable challenges of cycle touring.

weight of the bike, but keep you and your clothes drier in the case of rain (and your spare clothes will be limited).

When buying a touring bike, take time to think about which model will be best. If the longest tour you are going to do is a weekend of 50km (30 mile) rides, a hybrid bike with pannier fittings will be adequate, and good for riding around town as well.

If you are planning full-scale expeditions, covering up to 160km (100 miles) a day for a week or two, it is important to invest in a resilient, reliable and comfortable bike.

Make sure you give the bike a good test ride before you buy it, to see whether the saddle is right for you.

If your tours will include off-road riding, choose a hybrid or mountain bike, adapted and equipped so you can carry your luggage.

Above: Panniers fitted over the rear wheel can store your equipment on tour.
Top left: It's practical to keep money and maps in a handlebar bag.
Left: Allen keys, chain breaker and pump.

Anatomy of a touring bike

❶ **Wheels:** Strong and durable, with 36 spokes to help take the weight of luggage and rider. The tyres are thick, with a good tread that will help to prevent punctures.

❷ **Frame:** Comfortable, light and strong with relaxed geometry for riding long distances. The frame has attachments for rear panniers, pump and water bottles.

❸ **Brakes:** Cantilever brakes for general touring. Some models have disc brakes, although maintenance is difficult with these.

❹ **Chainrings:** A triple chainset offers low and high gears. With a heavier load, lower gears are needed to climb hills.

❺ **Sprockets:** Nine gears at the back for all gradients.

❻ **Gear changers:** These are attached to the brake levers to allow for good accessibility.

❼ **Saddle:** Wide and padded for comfort during long rides.

❽ **Handlebars:** Drop handlebars give a wide variety of hand positions, for comfort.

❾ **Pedals:** Clipless pedals for combined walking/cycling shoes.

Touring Equipment 1

Develop the art of travelling light when touring on a bike. If you limit yourself to the bare essentials, you can go anywhere. Stick to a few guidelines and eliminate all the heavy unnecessary gear that will just weigh you down.

The number one rule in bike touring equipment is to take as little as you possibly can. That's not to say that you can leave the sleeping bag or map book at home, but superfluous equipment and items in your panniers have to be hauled everywhere – if you don't need to use something, leave it at home.

Pack a tool kit

For every trip, whether it's a day-long ride or an expedition, a toolkit is essential. You will need spare inner tubes and a patching kit in case of punctures. Allen keys for loosening and tightening bolts on the bike are useful.

A chain breaker is also necessary – breakages are rare, especially if you maintain your chain properly, but when it happens the only way to repair the chain is with a chain breaker. Perhaps more importantly, you will also need it every time you have to remove a wheel. Optional extras include a spare spoke, spoke key, screwdriver, spare cables and brake pads. It would be possible to carry a great deal more, but the compromise

Right: Always take a map on tours to keep track of where you are.
Below: If you're well equipped, you can relax and enjoy your tour.

between travelling light and covering all possible eventualities has to be made. As a self-sufficient cyclist, you are responsible for deciding how to manage the risks of mechanical failure. But never go anywhere without a chain breaker.

Cycling clothing

Sensible clothing will make touring easier. Ordinary cycling clothing is perfect – it is light, warm, and keeps the sweat away from your skin. Shoes should be combined walking and cycling shoes, with a cleat to clip into the pedals. You will need clean clothing every day for cycling, and clothes to wear in the evening when it is cooler and you are not cycling. The longer you spend away, the more you have to consider how to ensure clean clothes every day. Hardened cycle tourists work along the principle that two sets of clothing will suffice – one to wear, one to wash. This keeps weight down, but it is worth considering a small number of spare garments in case washing facilities are impossible to find.

If you are washing your cycling kit on the go, remember to bring detergent. Clean kit is essential on a long tour, because riding in dirty shorts increases the chances of a nasty and probably painful infection. Some cycle tourists wash their clothes, then they attach them securely to the outside of

Above: Bike touring is one of the best ways to see and understand other countries and cultures.

their panniers, so they don't flap into the wheel. The motion of the bike wheeling smoothly along through moving air, combined with the heat of the sun, dries and freshens their clothes in no time.

Books and other essentials

Purists would say no to carrying books – after all, they're not essential. But a little extra weight for the sake of sanity and something to do in the evening is a payoff that most people would find reasonable.

You will also need a few essential items. Buy a detailed map of the area you are visiting before you leave home. In order to save weight, rather than taking an entire map book, you can detach the pages you need and only carry them. It's also a good idea to put map pages in waterproof sleeves, to prevent damage in wet conditions. Take a wallet with credit cards, identification and spare cash. Lastly, pack a mobile phone in case of emergencies. If you are staying in hotels or hostels, that is all you will need. If you are camping, you will also need to make space in your panniers for a tent, roll mat, sleeping bag, camping stove, plate, cup and cutlery. Suddenly the third set of clothing looks like a less practical idea.

Left: Touring bikes are heavily loaded with conventional panniers at the back, as well as having capacity for extra baggage over the front wheels.

Touring Equipment 2

Modern cycling and camping gear means that you can go on a full-scale expedition without hauling several kilograms of extra weight up every hill. Over the course of an 800km (500 mile) tour, this makes a huge difference.

If you are going away for fewer than five days or if you are staying at hotels or hostels there is no need to attach front and back panniers to your touring bike. Back panniers and a handlebar bag have enough space for all the equipment you might need for a few days' cycling. If you cannot fit it all in, unpack and try again!

Panniers and tents

Front panniers become useful when you are carrying camping equipment. The main challenge is to balance all your kit equally on both sides of the bike. If your bags are heavier on one side, it will affect the handling of your bike.

A lightweight one-person tent generally weighs about the same as a sleeping bag, so a good idea is to put these on opposite sides at the back. Then cooking equipment can be split,

Below: A winding road in the Rocky Mountains, through beautiful scenery, is ideal for cycle touring.

Above: A fully loaded bike with a handlebar bag, panniers, tent, sleeping bag and water bottles.

with spare clothes going in the front panniers. Roll mats are bulky but don't weigh much – they can stay on the outside, in a waterproof bag in case of wet weather. Sometimes tents are heavier than any other piece of equipment, but it should be possible to carry tent poles on one side, and the body of the tent on the other, then various items can balance.

Try to keep heavier items at the back, while light but bulky things are fine in front. Too much weight at the front will make steering more difficult.

Things become more efficient if you are camping with a group of people. Communal equipment like tents and cooking utensils can be shared out between everybody, with individually owned items such as sleeping bags and clothes in one's own panniers.

What if it rains?

Bad weather is the last thing the cycle tourist wants to experience but it is always a possibility. Soaking wet kit will cast a real dampener on a holiday, especially if you are camping and have

no means of drying it out. Unless the weather forecast is for an immovable ridge of high pressure over the area you are camping in and bright sunshine

Below: On a cycling tour, a global positioning system (GPS) will locate your position accurately. It is ideal if you are travelling long distances.

Panniers

Plastic picnic utensils

Binoculars

Collection of maps

Camera and film

Sunscreen

Water sterilizing tablets

Compass

Flashlight

Above: A selection of equipment that would be useful when touring includes panniers to fit on a bike, plastic picnic utensils, a pair of binoculars, a collection of maps to cover the area, a camera and film, a sunscreen of SPF25, water sterilizing tablets, a compass as an aid to navigation and a waterproof flashlight.

every day, it's best to bring plastic bags to put inside your panniers, to keep the contents dry. A raincoat will repel all but the heaviest rainstorms and keep your cycling clothes dry.

If all your kit is damp, and there is no prospect of a dry day's cycling, try to include an extra long stop at a friendly roadside café. While you enjoy a warming hot chocolate and cake, ask permission to hang your wet kit on a radiator or chair. The psychological boost of warming up and having dry kit to change into will make the difference between an enjoyable trip and the holiday from hell.

Touring checklist

Equipment	Day trip	Weekend away	Week-long tour	Expedition
Rear panniers	-	Y	Y	Y
Front panniers	-	-	(Y)	Y
Cycling shoes	Y	Y	Y	Y
Cycling clothes	Y	Y(2)	Y(2)	Y(2-3)
Raincoat	(Y)	(Y)	Y	Y
Spare tubes	Y	Y	Y	Y
Allen keys	Y	Y	Y	Y
Chain breaker	Y	Y	Y	Y
Spare spoke, cables and brake blocks	-	-	-	Y
Sleeping bag	-	(Y)	(Y)	Y
Tent	-	(Y)	(Y)	Y
Roll mat	-	(Y)	(Y)	Y
Cooking equipment	-	-	(Y)	Y
Plate, cup and utensils	-	-	(Y)	Y
Map	Y	Y	Y	Y
Money	Y	Y	Y	Y
Torch	-	-	(Y)	Y
Book	-	-	Y	Y

Above: It may be useful to copy this list and tick off items as you gather them together before packing your panniers.

Planning a Tour

For some cycle tourists, half the fun of a good cycling tour is in the planning. If you take some time and effort before you leave to make sure that your bike and equipment are in good order and that you have everything you need, the tour is likely to run without hitches.

It is fun to design an itinerary using maps and guidebooks. You don't have to carve a route in stone and adhere to it religiously – you may be tired one day, or you may want to stay an extra day – but if you have a plan of your route, your tour is likely to be rewarding.

The morning of your departure is not the time to organize your cycling holiday. The first decision should be made days, weeks or even months in advance – namely, where to go. There may be a particular area whose scenery you are attracted to, or a place you want to visit for cultural reasons. You might want to go to a quiet area away

Below: Spectacular scenery is one of the many joys of cycle touring.

Above: A well maintained bike is essential: breakdowns can ruin a bike tour if you are miles from help.
Left: Before leaving for a tour of any distance, do pump up your tyres.

from the beaten track, or a region that is popular with tourists. Flat or mountainous? At home or abroad? The main thing to realize is that within limits, you are free to go cycle touring almost anywhere in the world.

Know your route

Once you have decided where you are going, you should buy a detailed road map of the area. If you are planning to stay in hotels, can you guarantee that the next town is close enough to reach in one day's cycling? You should plan your route using your map and according to your ability to cover the distance, with the emphasis on quiet roads and scenic routes. If you are capable of riding 65km (40 miles) a day, don't plan to stay in a hotel that is 95km (60 miles) from the last one. If you want to ride 160km (100 miles) every day, make sure to plan your accommodation accordingly.

If you are cycling in a mountainous area, gradients and altitudes are sometimes indicated on maps. Chevrons on the road indicate that the road is

going uphill, and in high mountain ranges such as the Alps or the Rockies, hills can go on for many miles. Ensure that your gearing is low enough for you to pedal with all your equipment in tow.

Most importantly, be flexible. If you are more tired than you anticipated, stop at the next town and stay there. You are free to do whatever you want.

Preparing for the tour

Your bike should be in perfect running order before you leave. Mechanical failure could stop your tour right where it happens, so look after your bike and give it a service before your departure. After the service, take it out for a ride to test that it is running well. If you are camping, it pays to double-check that none of the tent poles have gone missing or are damaged. Erect the tent in your garden, then pack it immediately and put it into your panniers. The day before you leave, wash and dry all the clothes you are taking with you, and pack them into your bags, along with all your other equipment. You are now set for the journey of a lifetime.

Above: Touring doesn't have to follow roads – with mountain bikes it is possible to strike out across country. Many countries have trails for bikes, but it is always best to check first.

10 steps to a successful tour

1. Decide which region you are going to cycle in.
2. Plan your route, including daily distances and stopping points.
3. If you are travelling farther afield, you may need a visa. Check for any restrictions or requirements for taking your bike on to trains, ferries or aeroplanes.
4. Plan accommodation, book if necessary.
5. Clean your bike, ensure it is running well, test brakes and gears, pump up tyres.
6. Make a list of equipment to take.
7. Check that the tent has all poles and fittings. Put it up to make sure it is in good working order.
8. Wash your clothes.
9. Get new batteries for lights.
10. Pack your panniers.
Enjoy the ride!

Camping by Bike

Cycle touring is a great way to enjoy an independent holiday. When you add camping into the equation, it becomes the ultimate in self-sufficiency. There is no need to worry about finding accommodation or a suitable place to eat supper.

Modern tents are lightweight, very easy to erect and pack down to take up very little space. You can buy single-person tents that are big enough to fit one person in a sleeping bag, and they weigh less than 1 kilogram (2 pounds). Modern synthetic sleeping bags are warm and light.

Camping does make a cycle tour more challenging. A roll mat on a hard surface is not as comfortable as a hotel bed. Nor is it as warm. If it rains, your tent is waterproof, but every time you go in and out with wet clothes on, everything becomes a little damper. Sleep might not be as deep as it would be in a bed, so you will be more tired, an important consideration when you are cycling a long distance the next day.

On the plus side, you are closer to nature when camping. If you are pitching wild, rather than staying at an organized campsite, the sense of escapism is hard to equal. Away from towns that are crowded with tourists and traffic, you can discover solitude, peace and tranquillity.

It is easier to plan your route around campsites, which allow you to pitch your tent in their grounds. This costs money, but not much, and if the idea of a week without human contact intimidates you, campsites are far more sociable.

Right: When camping, stay organized and keep the campsite tidy.
Below: Camping by bike doesn't have to be a solitary pursuit.

Left: A trailer can help take the strain.

Before you even get to the campsite, you should have planned your evening meal. Many campsites serve food, but you shouldn't rely on that unless you've checked in advance. If you are looking to save money, or are not at an official campsite, you have to provide your own food. Buy it en route, so you don't have to carry it all day. This means that when you arrive at your campsite, you don't have to go on last-minute shopping trips.

Making camp

As you have practised pitching your tent before your trip, it should present no trouble once you are on the road. If you have had to split the components of your tent between panniers, remember where everything is, and have it ready so that you are not missing the tent pegs just as your tent is about to blow away.

Roll your ground mat out, put your sleeping bag into the tent, stow the panniers, and your bed is ready for the night. Usually this can be done in less than 15 minutes, leaving you plenty of time to relax. If there is more than one of you, share the work out. One person

could pitch the tent, while the other starts to prepare and cook dinner. Dinner can be heated on portable stoves available from camping shops. The most convenient ones use gas cartridges, and it is important to carry a refill for longer trips. After your meal, clean all your equipment and keep it somewhere dry. In the morning, pack your things away, and be sure to dry the inside of your

Above: Camping wild can be an enjoyable experience – but be careful to always leave sites as you found them.

tent with a dry cloth – it will have got damp from condensation and will become musty if packed away when damp. If you are camping wild, try to remove all evidence that you were ever there, especially litter.

Touring in Northern Europe

Cycling is a popular activity in the UK and northern Europe, especially in the low-lying countries of the north – Belgium and the Netherlands. The flat terrain makes it especially easy and relaxing to get around and just enjoy the scenery.

The United Kingdom is generally good for cycling tours, apart from the crowded south-east, where traffic congestion spills on to even the country roads. Luckily, outside this area, and the industrial Midlands, there are areas of quiet countryside and even wilderness. Scotland is sparsely populated and extremely hilly, even mountainous, and would be suitable for a camping

A mini tour of Devon, UK			
Day	**Route**	**Distance**	**Highlights**
Day 1	Exeter–Tavistock	48km/30 miles	Quiet roads through the wilderness of Dartmoor
Day 2	Tavistock–Barnstaple	105km/65 miles	Lydford gorge and waterfall
Day 3	Barnstaple–Minehead	80km/50 miles	Exmoor forest and moor
Day 4	Minehead–Exeter	80km/50 miles	The view from Exmoor over the Bristol channel

expedition. The farther into the Highlands you go, the more wild the terrain. North Wales is similar, with quiet roads and spectacular scenery. The Pennines, Lake District, Peak District and North Yorkshire Moors in the north of England are perfect cycling terrain. Devon and Cornwall are good cycling country, while in between all these areas are stretches of picturesque countryside waiting to be explored.

Planning a tour in the United Kingdom can spoil you for choice. Choose an area, buy a map and find the

Left: Touring cyclists pause to admire the view at Noirefontaine, Belgium.

Above: With cycle touring you can stop for a break whenever you feel like it.
Top: When you are touring on a bicycle, head for smaller, quieter roads.

extensive network of cycle paths. Most main roads also have bike lanes running parallel, which in some cases are mandatory to use, but are safe and smooth. If you are embarking on your first cycle tour, and are worried about your fitness levels, the Netherlands and Belgium are perfect – the terrain is flat, and the towns are fairly close together, so that some days you can reduce the mileage between stops. Northern Germany and France are also ideal countries for novice and intermediate cycle tourists.

Left: The unmistakable scenery of the Netherlands, one of the most cycle-friendly countries in the world.
Below: Most cities are not ideal for cycle touring, but Amsterdam should be on everyone's cycle tour itinerary.

many ancient minor roads leading between villages and towns. Take a history book, too – hidden away in unpredictable nooks and crannies you can sometimes stumble on cultural and historical treasures.

In mainland Europe, cycling is a part of everyday life, which makes cycle touring much easier. A cycling tour in northern Europe offers more in the way of cultural variety than possibly anywhere else in the world. From Belgium, it would be possible to cover four more countries – Luxembourg, France, the Netherlands and Germany – in just a few days, each with a distinctive culture and landscape. The Netherlands and Belgium, especially, are geared to cycle touring, with an

Cycling in northern Europe

Country	Terrain	Language	Climate	Notes
Belgium	Flat/hilly	Flemish/French	Warm in summer	Wind and rain common. Towns are close together – makes it easy to find accommodation.
Denmark	Flat	Danish	Warm in summer	Denmark is renowned for being expensive.
France (north)	Flat	French	Hot in summer	Beautiful cycling country.
Germany	Flat/hilly	German	Hot in summer	Hotels are expensive, but camping is cheap and popular.
Holland	Flat	Dutch	Warm in summer	Very accommodating of cyclists.
Luxembourg	Hilly	Luxembourgeois/French/German	Warm in summer	Good camping country, and lots of very quiet minor roads.
United Kingdom	Flat/hilly	English	Warm in summer, prone to rain	Many minor roads make for good cycling.

Touring in Europe's Mountains

Mountainous regions are a challenge for the bicycle tourist, but the hard work of getting to the top of a mountain pass is usually compensated for by the sense of achievement and by the glory of the view once you get to the higher peaks.

The mountainous areas of Europe are tough terrain for cycle tourists, but offer some of the most spectacular scenery in the world.

In the French Alps, the highest mountain passes crest at almost 3,000m (10,000ft) above sea level, with climbs of up to 30km (18 miles). With a fully laden touring bike, it takes a great deal of fitness, stamina and determination to reach the top.

The Italian Dolomites and Swiss Alps are equally as hard. In Spain, desert-like conditions make for a challenging ride. There are also some very tough mountainous routes in the Apennines, in Umbria.

Training

When planning a touring trip in the mountains, preparation is even more important than on other trips. If you are new or relatively new to cycling, or are a little rusty, it is a sensible idea to undergo some training to prepare for the tough climbs. Be realistic, not optimistic, when planning your route, so that you won't spend the entire trip wishing you were anywhere else but on your bike.

In fact, training will add a new dimension to your tour and add excitement to the build-up. By acknowledging that your tour is both a bike holiday and a physical challenge, the feeling of achievement at the end of a trip will be all the more fulfilling.

Plan your pit stops

During the planning phase of your trip, look for towns along the way where you will be able to refill your water bottles and buy food.

In the mountains, towns are generally farther apart, and forward planning will ensure that you don't run out of supplies. As you are expending more energy than usual cycling up hills

A tour of the Alps, France			
Day	**Route**	**Distance**	**Highlights**
Day 1	Grenoble–Gap	113km/70 miles	Souloise Gorges
Day 2	Gap–Briancon	120km/75 miles	Col d'Izoard
Day 3	Briancon–St Jean de Maurienne	80km/50 miles	Col du Galibier
Day 4	St Jean–Bourg St Maurice	129km/80 miles	Col de la Madeleine
Day 5	Bourg St Maurice–Chambery	113km/70 miles	Cormet de Roselend
Day 6	Chambery–Grenoble	80km/50 miles	Chartreuse Mountains

(although the descent down the other side is a little less strenuous) regular refuelling is important. Almost every corner offers a spot with a fantastic view to rest for a few minutes and have a bite to eat and a drink.

Although the weather in southern Europe is generally warm, the conditions high in the mountains can change quickly. About every 100m (320ft) of altitude gained results in 1°C (2°F) of temperature lost. A 2,500m (8,000ft) pass can be 15°C (30°F) degrees cooler than the valley floor.

Below: Cyclists touring on the Lofoten Islands in Norway enjoy quiet roads and wonderful scenery.

While climbing, you will be working very hard and sweating a great deal. As soon as you start descending, the air is cool and it is possible to catch a chill. Stop at the top to put on an extra layer to protect you from the cool air before you begin your descent. However, you've worked hard to get to the top so enjoy the descent and remember to brake carefully into the bends.

Above: Mountain passes such as that through Wengern Alp in Switzerland are a big challenge in cycle touring.
Above left: Two cyclists ride along a road through mountains in Switzerland.

Cycling in southern Europe

Country	Terrain	Language	Climate	Notes
France	Mountainous	French	Hot in summer	Well-surfaced roads through the Alps
Italy	Mountainous/hilly	Italian	Hot in summer	Beautiful cycling country
Portugal	Hilly	Portuguese	Very hot in summer	A high level of traffic accidents – be careful
Spain	Mountainous	Spanish	Very hot in summer	Long distances between towns
Switzerland	Mountainous	French/German/Italian	Warm in summer	Not many flat areas

Above: Stop and take a break when you need to orientate yourself.
Left: When cycle touring in the Mediterranean, it can be very hot.

Touring in North America: West Coast and Midwest

Cycle touring is still in its infancy in North America, compared with Europe. On a typical day's touring in Europe, you will see tens if not hundreds of cycle tourists. However, North America has much to offer – fantastic scenery and a challenging terrain.

In North America, long distances between towns ensure that the primary means of getting around is the car. Bike touring is unusual. Why carry your equipment and luggage about on the back of a bike when you can carry far more in the trunk of a station wagon?

However, that attitude is gradually changing. Green issues are becoming more important, and Americans are becoming conscious of the low environmental impact of cycle touring.

Cycling is enjoying a boom in the States, thanks to public awareness of Lance Armstrong's seven Tour de France wins. It is now no longer a rarity to see bikes hooked on to the back of camper vans and motor homes so that when people set up camp, they can use their bikes to go and explore the surrounding area. It is only a small, logical step away from doing the whole trip on bikes.

Below: A group of cyclists on mountain bikes set off on a touring trip around Kentucky, in the United States.

Above: Big sky, big landscapes and a big adventure – touring cross country in North America.

Where to go

The west of the United States is superb cycling terrain. Whether you like hot or cold weather, arid desert or humid forest, mountains or lowlands, densely populated areas with plenty of hotels and campsites or wilderness, you will find that the western states have it all.

One of the most popular areas for cyclists, and the most rewarding and enjoyable for cycle tourism, is California, where the climate is suitable for year-round cycling.

Central Los Angeles is no place for a bike, but even just an hour out of the city, the conditions are perfect – quiet roads, stunning scenery and varied terrain. Californians need not travel to France to cycle through vineyards, when there are vineyards on their own doorstep.

Farther up the Pacific coast, Oregon and Washington both offer good opportunities for cycle tourism, although they are cold and wet during winter.

Colorado has become a cyclists' Mecca – the Rocky Mountains are very tough to cycle in – while Montana and Wyoming are extremely challenging for wilderness expeditions.

The Midwest mountain states are generally hot in summer, and the terrain is very difficult, with long distances between towns. The planning for trips around these states should

Cycling in North America

Region	Terrain	Climate	Notes
California	Hilly–mountainous	Hot	Coastal highway is a must. Go inland for hilly rides.
Canada (Rockies)	Mountainous	Cool	Wilderness, be prepared for long distances between towns.
Colorado	Mountainous–extreme	Cool	Sparsely populated, and altitude a challenge in the mountains.
Montana/Idaho	Mountainous	Cool	Long distances between towns, and challenging hills.
Oregon/Washington	Hilly	Temperate	Be prepared for wet conditions, but beautiful scenery.

take into account that it will be necessary to carry more food and plenty of water. Self-sufficiency is vitally important, as you may find yourself a long distance from the next town and source of water. You may need to camp or sleep out if it's warm enough.

Left: Many Americans take short daily excursions, rather than embarking on a full cycle tour complete with luggage.
Below left: When cycle touring in North America, you can enjoy some truly amazing scenery.
Below: Always ensure that you carry plenty of equipment and supplies on a cycle tour when there are long distances between towns.

Touring in North America: East Coast

While the West Coast and Midwest are hard touring country, the eastern half has a broader appeal. Parts of New England are remote, with tough cycling and unpredictable weather, but the East Coast and the southern states offer an easier ride.

It is impossible to generalize about such a large geographical area, but the variety of terrain around the East Coast of North America is such that the cycle tourist will be able to find something that suits his or her level. There are diverse touring experiences available, with something to appeal to everyone, ranging from deserts, plains and mountain ranges to woods. An added attraction are the roads, which are well maintained just about everywhere. There are many parks which extend for miles and which are well organized with extensive services for people who are bicycle touring. To make it perfect for the cyclist, cycle lanes abound in many states and provinces, and there are also special bicycle trails.

Bicycle touring is also made easier in North America because there are so many campgrounds that are ideal for cyclists, which are either run privately or by the government.

Mountainous terrain

If you are looking for more challenging terrain, it is well worth considering planning a bicycle tour through the Appalachian Mountains. The mountains

Above: Some of the roads on the east coast are empty, which is ideal for touring. Below: When cycling in a hot area, particularly in summer, you'll need to take plenty of water.

Flat terrain

The easiest cycling is to be found in Florida, which is very flat, with almost imperceptible undulations inland. When the highest point in the state is only 105m (345ft) above sea level, even novice cycle tourists can be confident that there will be no hills they can't manage. Although parts of the state are densely populated, it is easy to avoid the crowded areas. The weather will be the biggest challenge to a cycle tour – while winter temperatures are pleasant and temperate, the summer is scorchingly hot and prone to frequent thunderstorms.

When you plan your cycle tour holiday, always research the typical weather patterns for the time of year in which you are planning to travel.

run for more than 1,600km (1,000 miles) from Alabama, which is in the southern United States, all the way to Newfoundland in Canada.

The Appalachians are a middle-mountain range – the roads are approximately half the altitude of a typical Alpine or Rocky Mountain pass.

The Blue Ridge Mountains in Virginia are ideal cycling country for the cycle tourist who has ambitions for a challenging tour, but who does not want to endure the extreme physical exertion of a route through a high mountain range. The roads in Virginia are quiet and rolling, with forests to shelter you from the midday sun. In high summer, Virginia is humid, but apart from this time, and winter, the weather is perfect for cycle tourism.

New England

A popular destination for cycle tourists in the United States is New England – the quiet backroads, moderate terrain, attractive scenery, temperate climate and the friendliness of the people make for good cycling country. You can choose between forested areas, farmland and New England villages. Summer and the famous New England Fall, when the foliage is at its resplendent best, are good times of year to explore.

Where to go?

With such a wide choice of destinations in North America, it can be difficult to make a decision – you may feel you want to go everywhere! The best starting point is to look at yourself and your touring companions. Ask yourself what you want to experience, and assess your ability to cover long distances or hard terrain. Factor in whether you want to ride through woods, towns or farming country, and if mountainous or flat terrain is preferred. This approach may seem coldly scientific, but your tour is much more likely to be a fun, rewarding experience.

Right: This tranquil road, which is perfect for cycle touring, goes through beautiful pastures in the Great Smoky Mountains National Park in Tennessee.

Above: Touring through New England is a great experience; it is fantastic cycling country and the scenery in the fall is particularly breathtaking.

Cycling in North America			
Region	**Terrain**	**Climate**	**Notes**
New England	Hilly–challenging	Temperate	Very enjoyable cycling with a range of difficulties
Southern States	Flat–hilly	Hot	More densely populated and be prepared for hot temperatures
Virginia	Hilly	Temperate	Perfect cycling country, in Blue Ridge Mountains

Touring Farther Afield

Africa, Asia and South America are a good challenge for the more experienced cyclist. They present more difficulties than Europe and North America, but, with a little foresight and packing the appropriate equipment, the result can be a holiday to remember.

A great deal of the enjoyment and challenge of cycle touring comes from the self-sufficiency involved in completing a tour. Whether you have ridden for two short days between hotels or three weeks in the Alps, the sense of achievement comes from having relied on your own horsepower to get from the start to the finish.

For an even more challenging cycle-touring experience, Africa, Asia and South America are as tough as it gets. The climate is hotter, the roads are less well maintained and the distances between towns are potentially huge.

Right: Cycle touring can be your passport to scenery like this.
Below: Conditions can be challenging when touring in remote areas – be prepared and plan carefully.

Above: Should you have a puncture en route, carrying a spare tyre is essential.

Above: A GPS phone is useful to help with navigation.

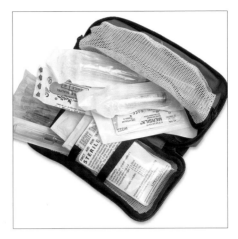

Above: Always take first aid supplies when touring off the beaten track.

You don't just have to be self-sufficient in terms of covering the distance, you have to take into account that you may need to carry more food and equipment. If your maps are inaccurate, you may even have to navigate yourself in order to get to your destination.

Remote areas

It is important to plan for every eventuality when organizing a cycling expedition to Africa, Asia or South America, from picking your destination, through making contingencies for mechanical failure, to researching the geography, roads and local people. Parts of south-east Asia have extremely busy roads, with the occasional erratic driver, but escape from the built-up areas and you will experience friendly hospitality from the people you meet.

A cycling tour in northern India should take into account the monsoon season, and the extreme terrain of the Himalayas. Avoid cycle touring during the monsoon – touring in pouring rain and extremely high humidity is no fun.

Touring in the Himalayas, or Andes, is a different proposition from the Alps. The roads suffer from weather damage in the freezing winter, and from landslides, so surfaces are unpredictable and difficult to ride on. The altitude is higher than the Alps, with the highest road pass in the Himalayas, the Karakoram Highway, tops out at almost 5km (3 miles) – the thinner air makes exertion extremely tough. The roads can climb for around 50km (31 miles), so good

physical fitness is essential. In the southern half of India, the heat is not ideal for touring, but the terrain is less mountainous. In any country, assumptions about the weather can make or break your cycling holiday – find out the typical rainfall, humidity and temperature of the month you are visiting.

Cycle touring in China is also varied. Avoid industrial areas and the arid west – there's plenty to see elsewhere. Beijing is less cycle-friendly than it used to be, but once you are out of the city, avoid the expressways and keep to old minor roads.

Africa, on the other hand, offers wild, hot and challenging terrain. The roads range from good to non-existent. And South America is a continent of contrasts

---

Respect local culture

In some regions, the locals are not used to seeing western tourists, let alone a group of them on bikes. In most parts of the world, hospitality to strangers is a common trait, and you can find yourself being treated like a celebrity for the duration of your stay. However, it is important to respect local traditions. If local people have their legs and arms covered, cycle tourists should be aware of the impact of cycling into town in shorts and a teeshirt. It is rare, but the locals may take exception to westerners, in their eyes, dressing immodestly or behaving disrespectfully. Common sense is the best way to decide how to behave. A friendly and generous manner will get you a long way with most of the world's people.

---

for cycle tourists. The Andes are extremely challenging, while the wide open spaces of Brazil and Argentina make a more leisurely tour possible.

One more note – touring in Australia is fairly straightforward when keeping to the more densely populated coastal areas. But crossing the centre needs careful planning. Water stops are few and far between, and the weather is extremely hot. Self sufficiency is the key to all cycle touring, but especially in conditions like these.

Be prepared

Self-sufficiency is important for both you and your bike when cycle touring off the beaten track. If there is a problem, you cannot ride to a town and buy a replacement part. You have to carry a few more tools and replacement parts to deal with any mechanical failure. If there are long distances between towns or stops, carry your own food and water, plus water purification tablets in case you have to use a local source.

Extra equipment for touring

As well as all the general equipment you will need for touring, planning for certain eventualities involves carrying more equipment. It is worth taking the following items, the extra weight will be well worth it: GPS phone, first-aid kit, water purification tablets, freewheel remover, lubricants, spare tyres, various dried foods and/or canned foods.

BIKE TECHNOLOGY

Maintaining a well-running bike is part of the enjoyment of cycling. It is easy to forget to look after your bike – they are so well-designed and engineered that it is possible to run them for long periods without maintenance or even cleaning. However, failing to look after your machine could lead to breakages, inefficient running and possibly even crashes. If you do a few small jobs regularly – some every time you ride, some on a weekly basis, and some once a month – your bike will continue to run as well as it did when it was new.

Above: Set aside an area in which to work on cleaning and repairs.
Left: To ensure its smooth running, learn how to maintain your bike.

Frames and Forks

The frame and forks are the heart of your bike. The material they are made out of, the angles of their design and the quality of the joins have more of an effect on the way your bike rides than any other component.

Bicycle frames need to be light and strong. The lighter the frame, the easier it is to ride up hills. The stronger the frame, the more reliable it will be. Both these factors depend on the material used and the thickness of the tubes. There is a third attribute, which affects how efficiently power is transferred from your legs into forward motion: stiffness. A stiff frame will respond better to accelerating forces, because less power is lost in the tubes flexing, but it can sometimes mean an uncomfortable ride over long distances – there is no shock absorbency, and the rider feels every bump and rut.

The geometry of the frame also affects the way the bike handles. The relaxed geometry of a touring frame makes for a comfortable ride, but acceleration is more sluggish. A steep-angled racing frame is much faster and more responsive, but over long distances is not as comfortable.

Above: Modern bike frames are available in all shapes and sizes. This one is a lightweight mountain bike with full suspension for shock absorbency.

Above right: Wipe your frame clean every few days to prevent dirt building up.
Above left: It's important to inspect your frame and forks regularly to check for damage and denting.

Frame care		
Task	**Frequency**	**Time taken**
Wipe frame clean	Every 3 days	2 minutes
Check frame and fork for damage	After a crash	3–5 minutes

Above: A full-suspension mountain bike frame.

Above: A mountain bike frame with the suspension at the rear.

Above: A carbon fibre racing frame, which is stiffer than frames made from other materials.

Above: A steel racing frame, which is more comfortable than carbon fibre.

Looking after the frame and fork

Unlike many parts of your bicycle, which can be stripped down into their constituent elements, the frame and the fork require very little in the way of maintenance. It is impossible to take the frame apart and put it back together again.

It is important to keep your frame clean because dirt and grit can quickly build up where the tubes join, and this can lead to scratches on the paintwork. After every ride in the wet, or every few days if the weather is dry, wipe your frame and forks with a damp cloth. This takes about two minutes and is well worth the time.

Another important task is to inspect your frame and fork regularly, especially if you have had a crash. Small dents and misalignments can eventually result in structural failure.

Materials

Frame materials have come a long way since the 1980s. Steel was the most popular and the best material for bike frames for most of the 20th century. Then, in the 1980s and 1990s, bike manufacturers started using carbon fibre, aluminium, titanium and even magnesium to make frames.

Steel is strong and easy to work with. Frames made of steel are very durable – if you avoid damaging them in crashes, they can last for a lifetime.

Aluminium is a more popular choice for racing bikes and serious tourers – it flexes less than steel, weighs far less and is cheap and easy to work with but it is not as durable. Aluminium frames seem to have a 'sell-by' date after which they wear faster than steel frames.

Carbon fibre is a popular material for high-end racing frames. It is as strong as steel and aluminium, and weighs even less than aluminium. Carbon fibre is moulded into shape, so that unusual frame designs such as monocoque time-trialling bikes can be made.

Titanium is strong and light, but is expensive and therefore a less common material for bike frames.

Suspension

For mountain bikes, it is not just the materials used for the frame and fork that have changed over the years. The development of suspension has radically altered the design of mountain bike frames and the way they handle. A suspension frame will be significantly more comfortable to ride on bumpy surfaces, but the suspension absorbs energy from the rider, resulting in a slower ride. There is also a payoff in having to maintain extra moving parts.

Wheels

Your bike is not going to get very far without these vital pieces of equipment. As with frames, the lighter and stronger the wheels are on your bike, the faster you will go. A little bit of maintenance of the wheels will give you a smoother ride.

Most wheels are designed along an arrangement of spokes radiating outward from the hub to the rim. The spokes are kept in tension, which makes the structure extraordinarily strong for its weight. Some specialized bikes for time trialling use solid carbon fibre bodies for superior aerodynamics, but the basic design of bike wheels has remained remarkably constant.

The two attributes of wheels that will affect the speed of your cycling the most are aerodynamics and weight. Even on a thin racing wheel there is a significant slowing effect from the spokes passing through the air. Manufacturers try to get around this by making the rims deeper.

Bike wheels are not particularly heavy compared with other parts of your bike, but the rotational movement increases their 'weight' through a phenomenon called gyroscopic inertia, whereby the momentum of the wheel resists changes to its orientation. In short, the less material there is in the wheel, the less energy it takes to brake and accelerate.

Racing-bike wheels are narrow and light, often containing 32, 28 or even 24

spokes – weight saved by cutting the number of spokes is significant, but the compromise is in the strength of the unit. Touring bikes, which carry much heavier loads, have 36- or 40-spoke wheels. Mountain bike wheels have a slightly smaller diameter, and they range between 28 and 36 spokes.

Spokes can be arranged in different patterns, which maintain lateral stiffness.

Above: Hybrid bikes need stronger wheels – they have an increased number of spokes, which add strength.

Looking after your wheels

Wheels are your bike's point of contact with the road and they consequently take a great deal of abuse, especially from rough road surfaces. Potholes, ruts and bumps in the road can put your

Above: Narrow-section racing wheel.

Above: Carbon fibre racing wheel.

Above: Solid wheel for time trialling.

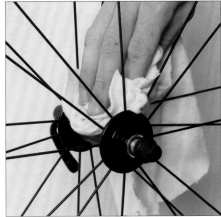

Above: Check your wheels for alignment by spinning them and watching the rim – if it moves, you may need to straighten your wheels.
Top middle: Prevent dirt building up on the hubs by wiping them every few days.
Top right: Apply grease to the axles on a regular basis.
Right: Wipe spokes down regularly.

wheels out of alignment, which affects your speed and leads to uneven braking. Learning to make wheels straight again is one of the great arts of bike maintenance. It involves mounting the

Wheel maintenance

Task	Frequency	Time taken
Clean rims, hubs and spokes	Once a week	5 minutes
Check alignment	Once a week	30 seconds
Take axles out to clean and lubricate	Once a month	3 minutes
True your wheels (if you know how)	When misaligned	30 minutes+

wheel on a jig and tightening or loosening the spokes with a spoke key – called 'trueing' the wheel. When all of the spokes are at the correct tension, the wheel will be true, or straight, again.

Tyres

The fatter your tyres, the more comfortable the ride. The thicker your tyres, the less likely you are to suffer from punctures. But these benefits come at the cost of speed.

When choosing tyres for your bike, you must decide which kind of tyres best suit your needs. A racing bike needs slick, narrow tyres, although

Left: Thick tyres with a deep tread are used on mountain bikes.

punctures are more frequent. A touring bike needs slick tyres too, but wider, to fit wheels designed to take heavier weights. Mountain bikes need knobbly, thick tyres. These are good for puncture resistance, but much slower on a smooth surface.

Tyres are designated by size. Racing and touring tyres come in sizes between 700 x 20C and 700 x 28C (where 700 is the diameter of the tyre in millimetres and the second figure the width of the tyre in millimetres). But mountain bike wheels are generally 26in in diameter. Tyres are designated 26 x 1.5 (26in diameter x 1.5in wide) and upwards.

Always make sure you are buying the right size of tyre for your wheels, and choosing the right tyre for your needs.

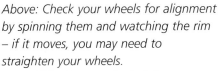

Drivetrain and Gears

The first bicycles had a single gear – good for riding on the flat but hard going up hills. Gears can make all the difference to whether your bike ride is easy or difficult. Understanding your gearing system will help you improve your cycling efficiency.

Racing bikes from the early 20th century managed to add a gear by putting one sprocket on either side of their back wheel – one for uphill sections, the other for flat roads. To change gear, the riders would dismount, unbolt their back wheels and turn them around.

Then Tullio Campagnolo, an Italian racing cyclist, came up with the idea of the derailleur gear, where the chain runs through a movable device and can change on to different sprockets while the bike is in motion. This is the gearing system used on most leisure bikes today.

The early derailleur gearing system had two or three sprockets on the back wheel. As technology evolved, it became possible to have two, then three chainwheels at the front, and in the case of modern bikes, 10 sprockets at the back, giving 30 possible gear ratios.

Gear ratios are what make it possible for you to ride your bike efficiently.

In a big gear, one revolution of the pedals causes more revolutions of the wheel, but it is correspondingly harder to push the pedals around. Smaller gears make it easier to ride up hills.

The more teeth on the chainwheel (at the front), and the smaller the sprocket (at the back), the bigger the

gear. On a typical racing bike, the front chainwheels have 42 and 52 teeth, although depending on the terrain, many riders change these for slightly smaller or larger numbers of teeth. At the back, sprockets range from 11 teeth (a high gear used only on steep downhills and in sprints) to 23 or 25 teeth, enough to get up long, steep hills. When selecting a gear, keep the chain as

Above: The drivetrain consists of chainrings, which are attached to the pedals and cranks at the front, and a range of sprockets at the back.

straight as possible. Riding in the big chainwheel, which is on the right-hand side, with the largest sprocket, which is on the left-hand side, puts the chain at an angle, which will quickly wear out both chain and cogs. On a 30-gear bike, there is enough crossover between gear ratios that you can change to the middle chainwheel and a smaller sprocket to find a similar gear.

Try to avoid overgearing – professional racing cyclists can cruise along in a 52-tooth chainwheel and 14-tooth sprocket, but trying to push big gears puts a strain on the knees. Aim instead to spin the pedals faster.

Looking after your drivetrain

The chain, chainwheels, sprockets and front and back gear changers are the parts of your bike that are most prone to dirt accumulation.

Hub gears

Shopping and town bikes sometimes come with three- or five-speed hub gears, where the changing mechanism lies in a sealed unit within the back hub. These do not offer as many different gear ratios as racing or leisure bikes and they are not as power efficient. If you are too busy to maintain your bike regularly, and only want your bike for riding around town, it is worth considering buying a bike with hub gears.

Left: Hub gears require just a squirt of lubricant every few weeks.

Above: The rear mech shifts the chain from side to side along the sprockets on the back wheel.

Keeping a smooth-running and clean drivetrain is crucial for the efficient performance of your bike. If you do not clean your gearing system, dirt and grit sticks to the lubricant and forms a thick, sticky black coating that wears down moving parts, makes changing gear inefficient and generally gets everywhere. Once this has built up, it takes a lot of time and effort to clean it off. It is far better to spend 15 minutes once or twice a week to clean and lubricate your gears than to leave it for a month, then have to spend an hour up to your elbows in dirty grease while

risking damage to your drivetrain. To clean the chain, you can use a chain-breaking tool to take it off the bike. An easier way is to attach a chain-cleaning bath to the bike. These are made of plastic and contain brushes and a reservoir of cleaner. Bike shops sell degreasers and solvents that will loosen the dirt on your chain.

To clean sprockets and chainwheels remove them from the bike and scrub out the dirt with a hard brush and cleaner. When cleaning sprockets that are still on the back wheel, be careful not to let grease drip on to the rims. You can buy a brush called a cassette scraper to clean between the sprockets. Finally, the derailleurs also need careful cleaning and attention. You can

Above: The front gear mechanism shifts the chain from one chainring to another.

generally wipe a front derailleur clean, but most dirt build-up occurs in the rear derailleur. Remove it from the bike and clean all the moving parts, paying special attention to the jockey wheels.

Once everything is clean, use a light lubricant. Too much lubricant will result in more dirt build-up.

Cleaning little and often, with a major stripping-down every month or two, will keep your bike in perfect, efficient working order.

Below: Modern racing bikes have their gear changers built into the brake levers.

Drivetrain care		
Task	**Frequency**	**Time taken**
Clean chain using a chain bath	Once a week (more in wet conditions or winter)	5 minutes
Clean sprockets	Once a week	15 minutes
Clean rear derailleur	Once a week	15 minutes
Clean front derailleur	Once a week	5 minutes
Take entire drivetrain apart for deep cleaning and lubricating	Once a month	30 minutes
Clean hub gear	Once a month	10 seconds

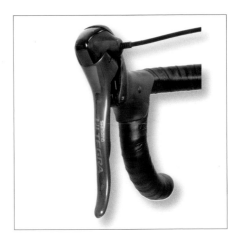

Brakes

A well-maintained set of brakes is one of the most important components of your bike. While an inefficient drivetrain or slightly untrue wheel will affect your speed and make cycling hard work, a badly worn set of brakes is potentially a killer.

Until the advent of mountain bikes, most bikes came with simple calliper brakes. By pulling a cable attached to the brakes, the brake blocks came into contact with the rim of the wheel, and the friction slowed the bike down. With narrow rims and lightweight wheels, not much surface area is needed on the brake blocks, meaning stopping performance with calliper brakes is generally very good.

Calliper brakes come in a variety of designs. Dual-pivot brakes are common on racing bikes and leisure bikes, and consist of two arms, one of which pivots around a point above the wheel, while the other pivots at the side. The arms grip the rim. They are light and useful for around-town use and longer rides, but should not be used on mountain bikes, where greater stopping power is needed, and the thick tyres get in the way.

Above: Racing bikes are fitted with dual-pivot calliper brakes, which are lightweight and provide good stopping power.

Cantilever brakes have each arm attached to a pivot point on the forks or seat stays. These have greater clearance than side-pull brakes, so they can be used on mountain bikes for riding around town, or light-duty off-roading. These brakes have generally been replaced for urban use by V-brakes, which have the cable housing on one arm, and the cable wire on the other. The longer arms of cantilever brakes provide more stopping power than V-brakes: they are also easier to maintain.

For serious mountain biking, especially on steep hills, traditional cable brakes are not strong enough to control speed effectively. Mountain bikes have heavier, wider wheels, and disc brakes, similar to those used in motorbikes and cars, can be used for greater stopping power. Disc brakes are heavier than traditional calliper brakes, but they work far better, and are easy to look after.

Above: Cantilever brakes are a good option for mountain bikes if disc brakes are not practical.
Above left: Modern mountain bikes are fitted with disc brakes, which provide good stopping power in poor conditions.
Left: V-brakes are fitted to hybrid bikes, and mountain bikes for urban use.

Brake maintenance

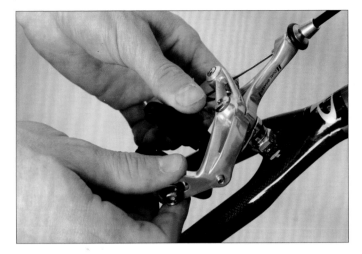

Alignment: *Check brakes for alignment regularly.*

Cables: *Maintain stopping power by keeping cables tight.*

Blocks: *Replace worn brake blocks.*

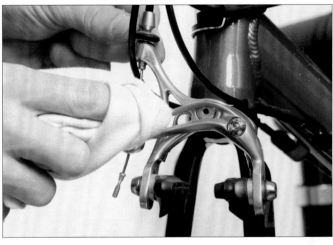

Clean: *Keep your brakes clean and oil-free by wiping often.*

There is a metal disc attached to the hub, and brake pads squeeze the disc to slow the bike down. The benefit of disc brakes is that they work as well in wet as in dry conditions. Disc brakes are used for touring, when heavier loads make stopping difficult.

Brakes wear out fast, especially calliper brakes in poor conditions, and it is important to keep an eye on the rate of wear of the rubber brake blocks. When you notice blocks getting worn, replace them – unscrew the old ones from the brake arms and put the new ones on. Never replace just one brake block, and be careful to align it with the rim, so that the whole surface of the block is in contact with the rim when the brake lever is pulled. Brake levers are low maintenance, and do not need

to be stripped and cleaned often. You should also check your cables. Brake cables stretch, with a marked effect on performance. When you notice braking is less efficient than before, loosen the cable where it passes through the brake arms, then pull it through so it is tight again. The brake arms are exposed to all the dirt and grit that flies up off the

wheel, so keep them clean. Don't clean your disc brakes too often, as tiny bits of brake pad embedded in the disc surface improve performance, but it is important to keep the disc and callipers aligned – just loosen the callipers, line them up, and tighten again. Do not allow oil to get on to the surface of disc brakes – this will affect their performance.

Brake care		
Task	**Frequency**	**Time taken**
Check brake blocks	Once a week	30 seconds
Replace brake blocks	When they are worn	5 minutes
Tighten brake cables on calliper brakes	Once a week	5 minutes
Clean calliper brake arms	Once a week	1 minute
Check alignment of disc brakes	After every ride	30 seconds
Realign disc brakes	When they are out of true	5 minutes

Bike Maintenance

You have a choice when it comes to looking after your bike. You can invest small, convenient amounts of time on a regular basis, or you can pay for inaction with large amounts of time every few months, by which time your bike is dirty, worn and inefficient.

Although you do not need to clean your bike after every ride, it will save you trouble in the long term if you clean it after riding off-road, in muddy conditions or in rain. If you leave mud or grit on your bike, the parts are liable to rust or wear more quickly. In the winter, salt from roads can affect the smooth working of the bike and lead to rust.

Keeping your bike clean

The tools you will need are a bucket of warm water with detergent, a cloth and a brush. As a general rule, try to clean your bike once a week, and less in the summer months. To hold the bike firmly, attach it to a stand. Using a brush or a cloth, wash the frame, forks, wheels, including the spokes, hub and rims, the cranks, seatpin, handlebars and stem (where they are not covered by handlebar tape), brake levers, brakes and cable housings. Rinse the parts with clean water then polish with a clean dry cloth.

Replacing handlebar tape

If your handlebar tape becomes very worn and dirty from use, or if you scuff it in a crash, it is time to replace it. This is a fairly easy task, requiring only some sharp scissors or a knife and a roll of new handlebar tape.

Take the bar end plugs off; you may need to use a screwdriver or other tool to loosen them. Fold the edges of your brake lever hoods forward so they are out of the way and expose the old bar tape. Unwrap the old bar tape, cutting off pieces here and there and discarding them. Remove any leftover glue.

Replacement bar tape usually comes with two short lengths of tape – these are for covering the brake lever clamps. Stick these two lengths on first. Then start winding tape from the bottom of the handlebars, making sure that there is enough tape at the start to tuck into the handlebar ends.

Above: Use a soft, clean cloth and detergent to wipe your frame, paying particular attention to corners where dirt can accumulate.

Keep winding round, overlapping up to half the width of the tape each time round. Pull on the tape as you are wrapping, to maintain the tension and avoid slackness, which will quickly come unstuck as you are riding.

When you get to the brake levers, work around them, making sure not to leave any part of the bars uncovered, then continue to wrap the tape around and around all the way to the tops of the handlebars.

Cut off any excess tape, and use black electrical tape to secure the end of the tape at the centre of your handlebars and tuck the other ends into the hollow end of the handlebars. Replace the bar end plugs, ensuring that the end of tape is tucked inside, and you are ready to go.

It's important to make sure the bar end plugs are firmly pushed in. Riding without these can be dangerous if you crash, and hit the bars with your leg.

Above: Brush off any grit or mud before rubbing the frame with a damp cloth, then polishing with a clean cloth.

Above: When the handlebar tape becomes worn and uncomfortable to hold, it can be easily replaced.

Replacing a tyre and tube

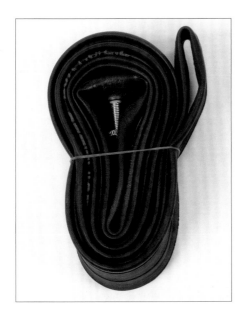

Tube: *Keep spare inner tubes in case you have a puncture that you cannot repair.*

1: *To remove tyre, insert a tyre lever. Keep it wedged there and insert the next. Then, lever along the rim to get the rest out.*

2: *Once you have got one side of the tyre away from the rim, use your fingers to remove it completely.*

3: *Put one side of the new tyre inside the rim, then be ready to insert inner tube.*

4: *Put the valve through the hole in the rim, put the inner tube inside the tyre.*

5: *Continue working the inner tube inside the tyre, around the wheel.*

6: *Press the other side of the tyre inside rim. Take care not to puncture the tube.*

7: *When the tube is inside the tyre and the tyre is inside the rim, pump it up.*

Basic maintenance equipment

Surgical latex gloves
Full set of Allen keys
Pliers and adjustable spanner (wrench)
Tyre levers
Track pump (upright with pressure gauge)
Screwdrivers and chain breaker
Degreaser
Chain lubricant
Freewheel remover with chain whip
Spanners (wrenches)
Bike stand
Cable cutter
Repair kit

Preventing Problems

Bike maintenance can be broken down into a few basic tasks, which, if done on a regular basis, will keep your bike running smoothly. Rather than waiting for problems to develop, it is a good idea to pre-empt these by regular, careful maintenance.

Sticking to a few golden rules will help you to keep your bike in good order. Just by getting into the habit of regularly cleaning your bike, you will familiarize yourself with all its parts and will be alert for anything that is out of order.

Drivetrain maintenance

The drivetrain (chainwheels, chain and sprockets) is the part of your bike that is most vulnerable to dirt build-up and damage. Over time, dirt from the road or bike path will stick to the chain lubricant to form a thick black coating. If this is not cleaned off, the moving parts can be damaged by the grit being ground in. Every week, if you ride your bike regularly, it's a good idea to use a chain bath to clean the chain. This is an

Disassembly, cleaning and maintenance

1 Break the chain using a chain breaker. These push a rivet through so that the links can be pulled apart (never push a rivet all the way through, as you will not be able to get it back in). Some chains, called powerlink chains, have a single link that can be unhooked manually.

2 Take the back wheel off. Using a chain whip and freewheel remover, take the sprockets off the back wheel.

3 Undo your chainrings with Allen keys.

4 Scrub all sprockets, chain rings and chain using a degreaser. If very dirty, leave them to sit in a tub of degreaser.

5 Loosen cables and remove front and rear mechanism. Scrub with detergent. Use

degreaser for a large build-up of dirt.

6 Replace cables if they are stretched by running them through from the handlebars down to the mechs.

7 Reattach front and rear mech. Pull cables through so they are taut. Tighten.

8 Put freewheel back on wheel. Replace wheel. Run chain through front and rear mechs, and reattach chain using chain tool.

9 Use a rag to apply a light but even layer of lubricant to the chain.

10 Double-check that indexing of gears is accurate (such that a single gear change moves the chain one sprocket). Adjust using the barrel adjuster on the rear mechanism.

Cleaning bike parts

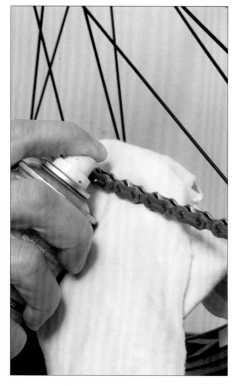

Chainwheel: *Use warm water with detergent to clean your chainwheels regularly and prevent dirt building up.*

Chainset: *Examine the alignment of your chainset regularly to ensure that the chainwheel has not been damaged.*

Lubricate: *Clean your chain regularly by spraying it with a chain cleaner and lubricant, then wiping with a cloth.*

Maintaining your bike

Toolkit: *Always carry a toolkit that contains basic equipment.*

Chain cleaner: *Run your chain through a special bath, filled with cleaner.*

Brake blocks: *Replace brake blocks when worn, as they can be hazardous.*

attachment which fits around the chain, and contains brushes and a bath which can be filled with degreaser or cleaner. Simply run the chain through a few times, and the dirt will be scrubbed off.

You should also pay attention to the chainwheels, by scrubbing with detergent and water, and also the sprockets, by removing the rear wheel and scrubbing with degreaser or detergent. Then use a rag to apply a small but consistent layer of lubricant to the chain.

Golden rules

If you keep your bike clean, and lubricate the moving parts on a regular basis, it will work more efficiently, and last much longer without breaking down. This will save you money in the long term, and also ensure that your bike remains safe to ride. Worn brakes are hazardous. Always replace worn parts before they become dangerous. A poorly maintained chain can snap, with dangerous repercussions. A well-maintained bike is a safe bike.

Adjust your brakes

1 When brake blocks are worn, remove them and put new ones in, checking they are aligned with the rim.
2 If cables are stretched, replace them. Pull the cable through to the brake arms.
3 Tighten the cable. Check that the brake arms are centred. Adjust using the adjustment screw on the calliper.
4 Check that brakes are tight. If not, hold the brake blocks almost to the wheel rim, pull the cable through and tighten the bolt holding the cable.

Clean your drivetrain

1 Attach a chain bath containing degreaser to your bike, and run the chain through until the dirt has come off.
2 Remove the back wheel from your bike. Using a brush and degreaser, scrub the freewheel clean of dirt.
3 Scrub the chainwheels with detergent and water for light dirt. Use degreaser if necessary.
4 Put the back wheel in, and use a rag to apply a small but consistent layer of lubricant to the chain.

Above: In wet and muddy conditions, your bike builds up a lot of dirt and grease that can damage small parts.

FAST RIDING

Riding bikes is practical and fun, and that is reason enough to ride. Regular riders will notice that cycling makes positive changes in their body. The more, and harder, they ride, the fitter they become. They start to challenge themselves with longer rides and a regular training schedule designed to move on to greater levels of fitness. There are many opportunities to challenge bike riders: sportives, endurance races and trail rides. Because of all the benefits, cycling is rapidly growing in popularity.

Left: Greater fitness levels make serious riding fun.

SPORTIVES

Sportive rides are the perfect compromise between leisure riding and all-out racing. Sportives have elements of both, and the best thing about them is that you can choose how seriously, or not, to take the event. Sportives are billed as personal challenge rides. They usually take place over long, but not impossible distances, sometimes taking in famous climbs, or arduous terrain – they are challenge rides, after all. Many also offer shorter distance rides to complement the main event, which means they are more inclusive.

Above: A group of riders take part in a sportive ride.
Left: Sportive rides often take place in mountainous areas.

The Sportive Bicycle

A sportive bike can provide a similar performance to a racing bike. It is so similar, in fact, that most people who participate in both road races and sportives find that they can use the same bike without noticing any particular disadvantage.

Sportive bikes need to be reliable, light, fast, efficient and comfortable. They look very similar to racing bikes, with narrow slick tyres and drop handlebars. The only difference with a real high-end racing bike will be more relaxed geometry in the frame, which will make for a more comfortable ride over a long distance. A racing frame will be extremely rigid, so that little power is wasted in frame flex, while a sportive bike needn't be so rigid. However, in their speed and weight, they have far more in common with a racing bike than with a touring bike, for which comfort is everything.

Events
Sportives tend to range from 25km (15.5 miles) for a short distance event complementing another ride, to between 170 and 200km (105–125 miles) for the longest events. They often take a big loop into isolated terrain. It is important

Below: Sportive bikes need a good range of gears, and the compact chainset has become a popular choice because it offers the required flexibility.

Above: A typical sportive bike is lightweight so that riding up steep hills becomes easier, but it is also comfortable for riding long distances.

that the bike is well-maintained so it won't let you down at a critical time.

Although there are sportives in all regions, from flat to mountainous, many take place in the Alps and northern Italy, where the routes take in large climbs. Popular British sportives are also very hilly, so a lightweight bike could help to make the difference between a gold and silver award.

Go for comfort
The length of most sportive events means that comfort is important. While a stiff, lightweight racing bike is the fastest option, don't sacrifice comfort for speed. If you do, you will ride the first two hours faster, then slow down for the second half of the event, as the discomfort increases. All except specialized racing bikes are suitable for sportive events.

The debate about frame materials continues, and there is no simple answer. The best material for one person may not be the most suitable for another. If you can afford a carbon fibre or aluminium frame, these will get you round the course the fastest. These frames are unlikely to last for a lifetime, however, while a good quality steel frame will last forever, well maintained.

After choosing which frame to use, the next most important decision involves gearing.

Racing bikes are designed for high speed events, and come with 52–42 or 52–39 chainrings, and 12–21 or 12–23 blocks on the back. For flatter sportive events, these might be sufficient but it is worth considering getting a compact chainset, with 50–34 rings, for riding in the hills. For self-sufficiency, make sure you can carry two water bottles, a pump, and a saddlebag or panniers containing spare tubes and tools.

Right: Fit a saddlebag with spare inner tubes and tyre levers.

Anatomy of a sportive bike

❶ Wheels: Size 700 x 23C with 28 or 32 spokes to save weight, narrow-section rims for aerodynamics, slick tyres for lower rolling resistance.

❷ Frame: Can be steel, or more modern lightweight materials such as carbon fibre or aluminium. Geometry is less relaxed than a touring bike, and similar to that of a racing bike, for a faster, more responsive ride.

❸ Brakes: Lightweight good quality calliper brakes. Models such as the Campagnolo Chorus and Shimano

Ultegra are popular, with very good performance.

❹ Chainrings: Compact chainsets, with a smaller inner ring, are becoming very popular with sportive riders. Fifty teeth on the bigger ring and 34 on the smaller is a good combination. Or possibly a racing set, with 52–42 toothed rings. Some people put a triple chainring on their sportive bikes, especially in mountainous events.

❺ Sprockets: Ten-speed freewheel, with a 12–25 block. For very steep

and long hills, depending on the chainring size, it might be advisable to fit a 27-tooth sprocket.

❻ Gear changers: Combined with the brake levers to save weight and for accessibility while riding.

❼ Saddle: Comfortable but narrow.

❽ Handlebars: Drop handlebars offer a range of positions. Riders can be aerodynamic on descents, and sit up for ease of breathing on the climbs.

❾ Pedals: Lightweight clipless pedals for shoes to attach to directly.

Clothing for Sportives

Sportive riding is a summer sport, so clothing needs to be lightweight, breathable, comfortable and aerodynamic. Modern fabrics are perfect in that they keep the body cool if necessary and also can act as insulation in cold weather.

One of the most important items of clothing for summer riding is a pair of Lycra racing shorts with a synthetic padded insert. For long rides on a fairly hard and narrow saddle, comfort is paramount. Ordinary cycling shorts are fine, but many racers wear bib shorts, which have straps stretched over the shoulders. Bib shorts fit snugly, and can be a more comfortable option over long distances.

Cold conditions

On chilly days, it is also worth covering the knees to protect them from the cold – longer shorts are available, but a better solution is to get some detachable knee warmers that extend from the thigh, inside your shorts, down to below the knee. If it warms up, you have the advantage that you can take them off.

A base layer is a good idea, even on hot days. Base layer garments wick sweat away from your body. In mountainous events, it can get quite chilly when descending, especially at altitude, and if you are covered in sweat this can be a problem. The lightest base layers have plenty of ventilation – some are string-vest style, which help keep you cool on hot days.

Wear an ordinary cycling top over your base layer. This should not be too baggy, otherwise it will catch the wind and slow you down. On the other hand, don't squeeze into a top that is a size too small either – find a comfortable snug-fitting breathable cycling top.

Like knees, arms can get chilly on cool days or on long descents. If it looks like being a cold day in the saddle, wear some detachable arm warmers. These will add a crucial layer of insulation, and

Right: For a sportive, lightweight, breathable clothing will make the event more comfortable.

Above: Cycling tops should be fairly tight-fitting and snug, but should still feel comfortable.

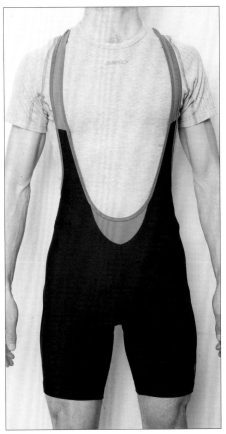

Above: Padded bib shorts over an insulating base layer are comfortable and aerodynamic.

Above: In cooler conditions, a gilet and arm warmers add an extra layer.

pack down compactly if the day warms up. On cool days, also consider a gilet, which is a sleeveless zip-up top to insulate the body.

Footwear

Shoes should be stiff-soled, with attachments for shoeplates, which clip into the pedals. The stiff soles ensure that your feet do not bend around the pedals and so stop you wasting energy, and stop the feet becoming sore. Your shoeplates should use the same system as your pedals. Most shoes can accommodate all the main industry standard systems. When choosing shoes for size, be aware that your feet expand in the heat, so if they are tight when you buy them, they will be tighter when you are some distance into an event. You don't need to buy excessively loose shoes, but do buy for comfort. Shoes with Velcro fastenings are the most popular: they are easy to put on and take off, and can be loosened temporarily if your feet get uncomfortable.

Headgear

Most sportive organizers insist that you wear a helmet. It should pass all the safety standards (as should all helmets sold). The helmet should fit snugly and not move when the head is shaken about, and should also be well ventilated. Replace your helmet every two years, and at once if it suffers an impact (even if no damage is visible).

Sportive wear

Cycling shoes: Stiff-soled for efficiency
Cycling socks: Insulated
Cycling bib shorts: Padded
Knee warmers: Optional, for cooler days
Base layer: To wick away sweat
Cycling top: Lightweight and breathable
Arm warmers: Optional, for cooler days
Gilet: Optional, for cooler days

Above: Road cycling shoes are stiff-soled for better power transmission, and fastened with Velcro.

Above: If you are going to wear a helmet for a few hours in hot weather, comfort and coolness are important.

Setting Goals

Before entering a long-distance sportive, it is sensible to attempt to achieve the necessary level of fitness first. If you are an experienced participant in other sports, your fitness should transfer easily to cycling.

Your sportive riding experience will be more positive if you use it as a long-term goal, with a sensible build-up and a commitment to do your best.

Before entering an event, you need to assess two things – current ability and potential ability. You can then set your long-term goal and, with that in mind, decide how much training you are going to need to do to fulfil your potential.

If you are starting from zero, with little exercise in the last few years, the first thing you need to do is go to see a doctor for a medical check. Once you have the all-clear to begin your exercise regime, build up slowly and get used to riding the bike and accustom yourself to the physical exertion. It is realistic to set a goal of entering a shorter sportive within a few months, but try to think in terms of using shorter events and the time between them as stepping stones to a longer event a year down the line.

Commit yourself

You will get the most out of yourself and the sport if you work on the principle of building up to a certain level, consolidating your fitness, then using that as a foundation upon which to build your step-up to the next level. In other words, make the bike into a lifestyle choice, and commit to

Above: Running provides good base fitness and lower-body workouts that are beneficial for cyclists.

improving yourself continuously. You will be amazed at how far you can make yourself go in this way. Over a few years, you could be riding 50km events in your first season, 100km events in your second, and full-length 170km sportives in your third. Along the way you will reduce body fat levels, become more toned, massively increase your energy levels, and achieve some incredible goals. If you are new to cycling, but are fit and have kept up an interest in other sports, it is realistic to set higher goals, but you must still be aware that it will take time for your body to adapt to the new stresses you are placing on it. With an adaptation period, and a sensible build-up, it is realistic to envisage riding a 100km event within three to six months of starting out, while

---

What should your goals be?

Cyclist

Achievements attainable for a racing cyclist:

In 3 months: full-length sportive, silver standard

In 6 months: full-length sportive, silver standard

In 1 year: full-length sportive, gold standard

Long-term goal: Finish in top 20 of a big sportive

Commuting leisure cyclist

In 3 months: 50km sportive

In 6 months: 100km sportive

In 1 year: full-length sportive

Long-term goal: silver standard in a long sportive

Non-cyclist

Achievements attainable for a regular sports player:

In 3 months: 100km sportive

In 6 months: full-length sportive

In 1 year: full-length sportive, silver standard

Long-term goal: gold standard in a full-length sportive

Sedentary individuals

In 3 months: 50km sportive

In 6 months: 50km sportive, at a faster pace

In 1 year: 100km sportive

Long-term goal: full-length sportive

Above: After an organized training build-up, you are ready to enter your first sportive.

keeping an eye on setting a longer term goal of a full-length sportive within a year.

If you have ridden your bike regularly as a commuter or leisure cyclist, the adaptation should be straightforward, since your body is used to spending time in the saddle. The challenging part will be twofold – you need to get used to riding long distances, and you also need to get used to riding a little faster. The

easiest adaptation comes from racing cyclists who want a less time-intensive and stressful goal than road racing. Most amateur racing events are under 100km, so it takes a little extra time to get used to the longer distances. If the body is already used to cycling training, just alter the workouts a little.

Of course, most people fall somewhere in between all these categories. They also react differently to training – some become fitter very quickly, others take time to adapt. Some enter a marathon event such as the Tour de France's Etape du Tour,

Above: Mountain bike enduro events are a good target for riders who are aiming to increase their fitness.

which is a 180km ride through some of the most challenging mountain roads in cycling, with only a few months to train. The important thing is to always be aware of the signals your body is sending out.

Below left: Swimming helps to achieve stamina, strength and suppleness.
Below: Athletes who play sports such as tennis will build fitness quickly.

What to Expect in a Sportive

There are hundreds, if not thousands, of sportive events organized around the world, and each one is different. Some are very flat, while others include multiple climbs of 30km (18 miles). Some start with 5,000 riders or more; others attract 100 competitors.

Although a good foundation of base fitness in cycling will help you to get round any sportive fairly easily, training needs to be geared to the specific event you have entered. Before entering, try to find out as much information about the route as you can. Most events have internet sites, with downloadable maps and profiles of all the routes.

The profile is the most important part. It will show all the climbs and descents. Sometimes the scale can be misleading, so check the altitude scale on the left-hand side of the profile. Most sportive events have one, two or three signature climbs, which will be the main challenges of the day, and your success will depend largely on how well you pace yourself on these climbs.

The ups and downs of racing

If an event includes a long climb, your training and preparation need to take this into account. A 15km (9 mile) climb places severe stresses on the body, and if your training rides all took place on flat roads, your body will be less able to deal with the challenge. Make sure that your training includes climbing. If you live in a flat area, consider going on a training camp in a hilly or mountainous area. If you have a good level of base fitness, a week spent in the mountains will allow your body to adapt to the rhythm and

techniques of long climbs. Not all events take place in the high mountains; there may be many shorter climbs, of between 3 and 7km (2 and 4 miles) in length. None are very hard in themselves, but the repetition makes each subsequent climb harder than the last. These are easier to train for – just try and replicate the number and length of climbs in your long training rides.

The downhill and flat sections are just as important – look at the profile to see where they are. A long descent is a

Above: Hilly sportives will test your fitness to its limits – success in these events depends on your long-term training technique.

good time to recuperate, so it might be worth trying a little harder on the climb in the knowledge that you have plenty of time to recover from the effort. Alternatively, some climbs lead you on to a plateau, or to the base of another climb – you'll need to be aware of the shorter recuperation time involved.

Steep terrain

Profiles can be misleading. Organizers concentrate on including the major climbs, but they may just draw a flat line between them. In reality, these flat sections may be a series of rolling climbs, with steep sections that sap your strength. Be prepared for this eventuality.

Left: The Etape du Tour follows the same route as a mountainous stage of the Tour de France and attracts thousands of entrants.

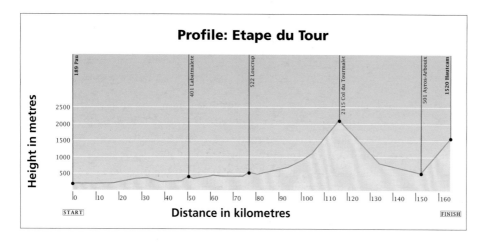

Profile: Etape du Tour

Height in metres

2500
2000
1500
1000
500

189 Pau
401 Labatmalete
522 Loucrup
2115 Col du Tourmalet
501 Ayros-Arbouix
1520 Hautcam

|0 |10 |20 |30 |40 |50 |60 |70 |80 |90 |100 |110 |120 |130 |140 |150 |160

START **Distance in kilometres** FINISH

On the day

Most events start in the morning, so, depending on how far you live from the ride, it might be better to arrive the day before.

When you arrive, set up your bike so it is ready for the event. Pump up the tyres, make sure the components are clean and working well, double-check that the saddle and handlebars are in the correct position, and test the gears and brakes.

If you have had a long drive, your legs will be a little stiff, so it's a good idea to test the bike out on a short and easy ride. This is not the time for training – just a 30-minute easy ride to get your bike and body ready for the next day. Bring a spare set of kit for this ride, so you don't get your event clothes dirty or sweaty. Sometimes it is possible to sign on the day before, and you should do this if possible, so you can get your race number on the bike and avoid queues on the morning of the event.

The evening before, wrap your food and pack it into your pockets, prepare your drinks, eat a large dinner and get a good night's sleep. On the morning of the event, get up in plenty of time to eat a reasonable breakfast and get to the start. In larger events you will be directed to a pen according to race number, but in all cases, the earlier you arrive, the closer to the front you will be. If you want to win the event and you start at the back, you'll have several hundreds or thousands of riders to pass. Help yourself by getting there in good time. You are now ready to go.

Above: Riding consistently well in a hilly sportive depends on fitness and determination – but the effort will be worth it.
Below: The Gran Fondo Pinarello is one of the biggest and most famous sportive events in Italy – its mountainous profile makes it a serious physical challenge.

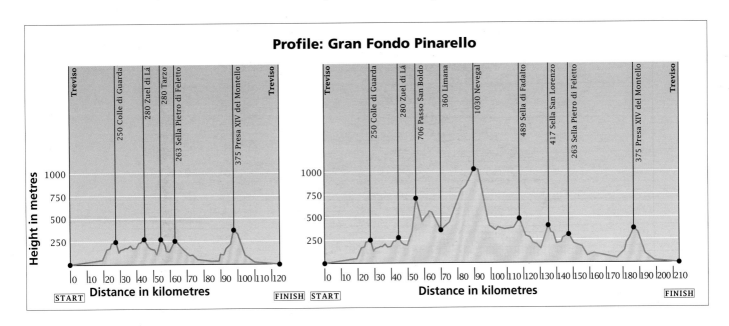

Profile: Gran Fondo Pinarello

Pacing and Gearing in a Sportive

Riding a sportive is not about pedalling like fury as soon as the gun goes off. Strategy and tactics and a thorough awareness of your own capabilities are more likely to get you to the finishing line with the chance of a good result.

A sportive is a race, so you naturally want to get around the course as fast as you can. But this does not involve putting your head down and riding hard from the gun. By riding intelligently, spreading out your effort and concentrating on riding as efficiently as you are able, you will achieve the best possible result.

Pacing

To succeed at pacing, you must look at the profile, have an awareness of your own ability and knowledge of the conditions on the day and be flexible in case of surprises. Preparation helps here – set your bike up correctly, with the right gears, and train for the challenges of your specific event. The best way to maintain a pace you know you can handle is by using a pulse monitor during training and the event. The effort you are making when cycling is reflected in a higher pulse as your heart works harder to transport blood to the muscles. Training with a heart monitor is covered on page 155, but the main point to remember is that you can only sprint for a limited period, whereas a steady, controlled effort can be sustained for longer.

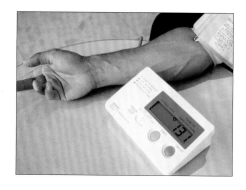

Above: A digital machine measures the pulse and blood pressure.
Below: Riding steadily over long distances will get you to the finish faster.

This is not a foolproof way of looking at it, since other factors, such as refuelling, previous efforts and even general tiredness also have a big effect on fatigue levels. However, by using a pulse monitor as a guide, you can maintain a sustainable level of effort. The more experience you gain in training and riding sportives, the more you will understand the way your body in particular reacts to the effort.

When no other factors are taken into consideration, it is theoretically ideal to maintain the same pulse rate and level of effort all the way through an event, but it is more realistic to anticipate changes of pace according to circumstances and the way you feel.

The golden rule, especially for inexperienced riders, is not to go too hard at any time. Accumulated fatigue can mount very badly if you go too hard early on. One good way of avoiding fatigue is to train yourself to spin the pedals faster in a lower gear. Different riders' bodies work efficiently at different pedalling rates, but according to sports doctors, pedalling a large gear slowly places greater stress on the muscles, which tire quickly, and pedalling a small gear fast places greater stress on the cardiovascular system while saving the muscles. Train yourself to turn the pedals at 90 revolutions per minute, and your body will become more efficient at handling the effort.

Gearing
For a mountainous sportive, it is a good idea to be conservative in your choice of gears. Fatigue builds up insidiously on long climbs, and if you are feeling weary, and already in your bottom gear, you can lose a lot of time.

Racing bikes tend to use 52 and 42 rings on the front, and 12–21 or 12–23 at the back. This is good for the fast and intense pace of a short race. However, for a sportive and for riders who are less fit, there is little point in trying to ride the same gears as a racer.

To provide lower gears, you can either fit larger sprockets to the rear wheel, or smaller chainrings at the front. If you change the block at the back to a 12–27, the difference between gears is

large, so that it is very difficult to find the right gear on a climb. You may be over- or under-geared, with no chance of finding the right rhythm.

The alternative is to fit a compact chainset. These have become popular with sportive riders in the last few years. These typically have 50- and 34-tooth rings, and combined with a 12–25 block at the rear, should bail you out of all but the very worst situations. More importantly, they also allow you to spin a lower gear and save energy.

Right: A compact chainset gives flexible gearing in most situations and is invaluable for sportives with long climbs.

Above: On the steepest hills, it doesn't matter how strong you are – you'll need to fit a low gear in order to be able to pedal up.

Maintaining energy levels
As sportives are long events, refuelling should be a vital part of your strategy. Start by eating a large meal with plenty of carbohydrates the evening before, followed by a substantial breakfast on the morning of the event. Carry some snacks that you can eat during the ride: try bananas, energy bars, dried fruit, sandwiches and anything that you find palatable during exercise. Drink plenty of water and energy drinks during the ride, especially on a hot day.

Left: Eating carbohydrates, such as pasta, produces more energy before a sportive event.

Climbing in a Sportive

Many sportive events include significant climbing. Organizers love climbs because they split the field up into manageable proportions, and riders love them for the challenge. With careful planning beforehand, you can turn the hills to your advantage.

Climbing hills on a bike is so difficult and energy intensive that by focusing your training and planning on going uphill as fast and as efficiently as possible, you can make a big difference to the success of your ride. That does not mean you can ignore other aspects of your cycling, but it is on the climbs that the most time can be lost – and gained.

Hill profiles

As part of the preparation for your sportive goal, check the profile to see how many significant climbs there are, and how difficult each one is. Some organizers even provide a detailed breakdown of the climbs, with average gradients for each kilometre ridden. This knowledge is a powerful weapon in your sportive-riding armoury – if you know that a 10km (6 mile) climb has 6 steady kilometres followed by 4 steep kilometres, you know not to overdo it in the early part of the climb and can

Below: Planning ahead and conserving energy when necessary is the best way to climb hills in a sportive event.

Above: When climbing in a group, follow your own pace to the top.

therefore save some energy for the difficult part. If the steep part comes at the bottom, it is a good idea to pace yourself carefully until the climb levels out a little, then go harder with the knowledge that it is not going to get any steeper.

Pace yourself

The frequency and positioning of the climbs will also make a big difference in your planning. The Auvergnate sportive, in France, has four significant climbs, crucially, two of them come right at the beginning. This is too early for heroics, so careful riders will pace themselves well on these two climbs.

Going hard right at the start of a sportive, especially uphill, might lead to an energy crash later. The Auvergnate's two hardest climbs come much later on – it is important to save energy for these two challenges.

Once you are on a climb, and you have an idea of the gradients, your fitness and your physical state, you can get on with tackling it as efficiently as possible.

Apart from physical strength and fitness, climbing well involves being able to focus and concentrate while relaxing. Relaxing sounds like the last thing you should do during such hard work, but while the legs turn, and the body provides an anchor for them to do so, the arms should be nice and relaxed, holding but not gripping the bars.

The right rhythm

Climbing is physically demanding: it hurts, and it can drain your resources incredibly quickly, but if you are able to remain focused and relaxed you can get into a good rhythm, which is what climbing is all about. This is easiest to establish on a steady climb, but it is still also possible on climbs that change in pitch every few hundred metres. Basically, the right rhythm is the one that

Above: On the steepest grades, reduce your speed accordingly – a constant effort up a hill is more efficient than a constant speed.

gets you to the top as fast as possible without going into the red zone (going too hard, then becoming very tired very quickly). The only way to really learn this is through experience. Use a pulse monitor if necessary, but it is better to learn to listen to the way your body feels so that your experience can tell you if you need to back off or go harder. This takes time but can be achieved.

Above: When making a long climb, pay constant attention to what your body is telling you and try to keep to your ideal rhythm.

Once you have established what feels like the right rhythm, sometimes it will take you all the way to the top. However, you must be focused enough to realize if you are going too fast or too slow, even if it is by a microscopically small degree. In this case, just try to alter your effort level a little, slightly up or down, and settle into the new rhythm.

On a climb that is constantly changing in pitch, you have to be able to maintain the same rhythm. This can be achieved by using the gears. Aim for the same pedal cadence and pulse rate by changing down on steeper sections, and changing up on shallower gradients.

Below: The profile of the climb at Mont Ventoux, in gradient percentages. The road to the summit has an average gradient of 7.6 per cent and is one of the most difficult and notorious climbs in the Tour de France.

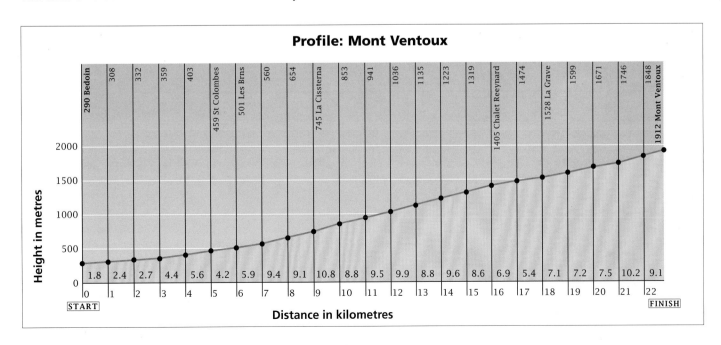

Profile: Mont Ventoux

Riding a Sportive in a Group

On the start line of a sportive, you are sharing the road with up to several thousand other cyclists. It is unlikely that the group will ride round the entire course in one block, but by learning to ride in a smaller group, you can save a great deal of energy and time.

Cyclists riding in a group are faster than individuals riding on their own. The reason for this is that one of the biggest obstacles moving a bike forward is wind resistance. In a headwind, this resistance is made even worse, but it will have significantly less effect if someone is in front of you.

Efficient riding

By cycling behind another rider, it is estimated that you can save as much as 30 per cent of the effort he or she is making for the same speed.

What this means is that a group can work together efficiently and maintain a very high speed with less expenditure of energy. If a group of 12 riders spreads into a line and each takes a turn at the front before moving to the back of the group, they will only spend a twelfth of the time riding into the wind, which is the hardest part. The rest of the time they are moving to the back of the group, which takes less energy, or sitting in the line sheltered behind another rider. In an hour, if everybody is sharing the workload equally, an individual will only have to spend five minutes on the front. That is a lot easier than riding into the wind on your own for an hour. The

Right: Riding on your own is less energy-efficient than riding in a group.
Below: When you are riding a sportive in a group, share the work by taking turns at the front, where the air resistance is greatest.

Above: Pace yourself and ride with others of similar ability, especially in a long sportive. Riders in a group who work out a formation will find that they can cut down their finishing time as well as increase their speed.

Tactical sportive riding

In the last few pages, we have emphasized that riding to your own pace is the best way of ensuring maximum performance and that going into the red zone can have a detrimental effect on energy levels later in the ride. (Going into the red zone is the equivalent of starting to sprint when out jogging.)

There are some occasions when other factors come into play. Imagine a situation where you are about 50m (165ft) from the back of a group near the top of a long hill, and riding at a rhythm which you know through experience is the right one to get to the top efficiently. You are better off riding at your own pace than trying to catch up faster riders. However, if they are only just ahead of you, it's worth chasing them down if there is a flat section after the descent.

By riding in a group, you will save energy in the long term and it will be worth the initial effort to catch them up for the effort you will save by sharing the workload.

If you are in the opposite situation, 100m (328ft) ahead of a small group of riders, it may be best to slow down and wait for them. If you are about to ride a long flat section, there is no point riding hard to hold them off – they will be riding far more efficiently than you, because they are sharing the workload. Instead, grab a bite to eat, sit up a little, stretch and wait for them. You will save a great deal of energy this way.

The guiding principle for sportives is: you are on your own on the climbs and descents, but co-operation with others on flat sections can make the difference between gold and silver awards.

technique of sharing the workload in the group is known as through-and-off, or drafting. It is not a simple case of riding in a straight line. Wind direction makes a difference, as do the relative abilities of the riders in the group. The wind is rarely a zero degree headwind blowing right into your face. More often, with changes in road direction, it is a crosswind and comes from one side or another. The technique for riding in a crosswind still involves riding in a line, but riders also spread out laterally, with the first rider in the group on the side from which the wind is coming. The second rider sits behind him or her, and also to one side, with the following rider taking a similar position and so on down the line. The front rider does his or her turn at the front, then goes back down the line to the back. And so on. This is an efficient way of riding, no matter how strong the wind, and if you join a strong group during a sportive, especially during the flat sections, it will make a difference to your finishing time.

Above: When there is a crosswind, riders form a lateral formation for energy-efficient riding.

Above: When a group rides into a headwind, one rider takes the front position and others spread out behind.

Above: In a smaller group, riders take it in turns to lead, while the others shelter behind the leader.

Descending in a Sportive

Some sportive organizers add to the cyclist's agony by finishing their events at the top of a hill. For all other events, what goes up must come down – for every mountain climbed, there is a descent waiting on the other side.

A lot of time can be lost on a descent. Nervousness about high speed and cornering can cause riders to overuse their brakes. They may also tense up, which makes it harder to flow through corners following the correct line.

Of course, the consequences of going out of control on a descent are far greater than on the flat or riding uphill. Speeds are much higher, so crashes are potentially far more dangerous.

By gaining confidence and relaxing, the descending involved in a sportive should be one of the most fun parts of the ride – and it hurts less than climbing.

Before you even start descending, the most important thing is to have trust in your bike. If it is well maintained, with sharp brakes, and correctly inflated, unworn tyres, you are reducing the chances of something going wrong. If your bike starts to rattle while you are going at 60kph (37mph) down a hill

because it has not been maintained, it is a problem. Second, you must have confidence in yourself and your ability to relax, focus and choose a line.

The shortest line

On a descent where the corners are not that sharp and you can see all the way through, just follow the shortest line down possible (without straying to the other side of the road). Allow your speed to rise to a point where you are totally confident of being able to handle it. If you find yourself starting to go faster than is comfortable, just feather the back brake to check, but not substantially reduce, your speed.

Your bike needs hardly any steering to get round these kinds of corners – shift your weight in the saddle, using your body to turn the bike, and just apply a little pressure to the handlebars to ease the bike through the turn. As

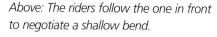

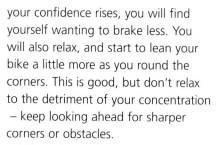

Above: The riders follow the one in front to negotiate a shallow bend.

your confidence rises, you will find yourself wanting to brake less. You will also relax, and start to lean your bike a little more as you round the corners. This is good, but don't relax to the detriment of your concentration – keep looking ahead for sharper corners or obstacles.

When descending, be aware of other competitors and road users and what is going on around you, and try to anticipate what others in front of you will do. If you are unhappy descending, drift to the back of your group so you can follow the other riders' lines through the bends. If somebody in front of you is going too slow, hang back until the right moment to go past them.

Left: When taking part in sportives in mountain areas, safe descent is vital.

Rounding a hairpin bend

1: *Enter a bend from the wide angle.*

2: *Lean over and cut into the corner.*

3: *Hit the apex with outer leg straight.*

4: *Swing out again after the apex.*

5: *Accelerate out of the bend.*

Hairpin bends

Descending becomes more complicated when the corners are sharper, as often happens in mountain regions. Engineers build roads with many hairpin bends, and getting around one of these losing as little speed as possible involves sound technique and steady nerves. As you approach a hairpin, you will probably be travelling quite fast. Keeping the same speed as you round the corner will result in a crash, so you have to check your speed. It is important to start and finish your braking before you start turning, or you risk your wheels locking and throwing you off the bike. The quickest way round is to enter wide, then lean your bike over and turn so that you pass close to the apex of the corner, then exit wide. Using the whole road is the way to maintain maximum speed, but if you cannot see through the corner, do not cross to the other side of the road as there may be oncoming traffic. If the way is clear, use a little more of the road, but safety should be your first concern.

As you turn, keep your inside leg up, point the knee towards the corner and put your weight on your outside leg, but don't be tempted to lean your whole body too far over. By keeping your head erect, you will hold your body upright enough to avoid toppling over. As you start to exit the curve, you can bring your inside knee back in, and you are ready to exit the corner.

By cornering on a hairpin bend, you have lost speed, and if you want to get to the bottom as quickly as possible, it will be necessary to accelerate hard once you are riding in a straight line again. With the gradient helping you, it won't be long before you are back up to full speed and ready to start braking for the next bend.

Applying Your Skills in a Sportive

Never go into an event without thoroughly researching the route. By doing your homework and analysing the distance and profile you can work out the best way for you to ride the race, and thus plan your training accordingly.

Riding a sportive successfully should be part of a long-term, goal-orientated strategy. The sense of satisfaction achieved by planning the build-up to an event, carrying out your training plan and riding the event successfully, is immense. If you surpass your expectations the sense of achievement is all the greater, and even if you are faced with unexpected challenges, dealing with them without panicking can also add satisfaction. Check out events well in advance in cycling magazines and websites.

Using the example of the Marmotte sportive in France, which takes in several Alpine climbs, a plan can be devised for the build-up, training and riding of the event to illustrate how these long-term goals can be achieved.

Research the profile and distance

Before starting the training and thinking about how to ride, you need to research the distance and profile of the event. In the case of the Marmotte, it is 174km

La Marmotte
Start Bourg d'Oisans, France.
Finish L'Alpe d'Huez.
Distance 174km/108 miles.
Number of significant climbs Four.
Total length of climbs 71km/44 miles.
Vertical height gain 5,000m/16,400ft.

(108 miles) long, which is above average. Your long training rides will have to be lengthened to prepare your body for the extra time in the saddle.

The profile of this event is intimidating. There are a few flat opening kilometres, followed by the long ascent of the Col de la Croix de Fer. The climb looks difficult – it is 27km (17 miles) long, averages a 5 per cent

Left: Train regularly in the months leading up to your target event. It will pay dividends during the competition.

Above: Ride your target event at your own speed. Don't be pressured by anyone coming up behind you.

gradient, and tops out at 2,068m (8,550ft) altitude. There is also a downhill section halfway up the climb, followed by a very steep upward incline. When riding, it will be important to pace yourself on the lower section to save some energy for later. Then you can rest on the descent before you reach the second section.

The descent of the Croix de Fer is nice and long – plenty of time to relax and save a bit of energy. It is followed by quite a long flat section to the foot of the next climb. During this part of the ride it is important to get into a group to save energy, and worth waiting for a group if there is none ahead of you.

The Col de la Télégraphe is the next climb – 12km (7.5 miles) long and less steep than the Croix de Fer, with less variation in gradient. It is important to establish a rhythm early on this climb, and make minor adjustments if you start to get tired or feel you are going too slow. The steepest part is at the top, so you might have to reduce speed in order to make the same effort for the final section of the race.

The descent of the Col de la Télégraphe is only a few kilometres long – not enough time to recover significantly, and with the 18km (11 miles) of the Col du Galibier approaching, it makes it all the more important to pace yourself sensibly on the Télégraphe.

The Galibier starts steadily, but gets steeper at the top. Pace yourself at the bottom, even if it feels like you are holding back. Then you will have more energy for the top half.

From the top of the Galibier, there are more than 40km (25 miles) of descent, which is an excellent opportunity to recuperate. This stretch takes you all the way to the foot of the final climb to L'Alpe d'Huez. There are 14km (8.5 miles) uphill to go, with the steepest section at the bottom. Pace yourself sensibly there, then establish a steady rhythm once the climb gets less steep.

Do the training
The training you need depends on whether your goal is to win the event, to achieve gold standard or silver

standard, or just to finish the event. You also need to tailor your training according to your experience and ability if you are to achieve your goal.

Whichever category you fit into, the training for the Marmotte needs to be extensive and regular.

Over a period of several months, you'll need to do at least one long ride each week, building up so that you can comfortably handle the distance. To prepare for the climbing, it will be necessary to practise riding uphill as much as possible. A great way of getting yourself into shape for a sportive is to ride another sportive. Why not find one about a month before the Marmotte to test your fitness and practise your pre-ride routine?

Ride the event
The Marmotte is long and hard, but with suitable preparation and training it should not hold any surprises for you.

The main thing to remember is to moderate your pace at the beginning of the route, especially during the first flat kilometres, where it is easy to get carried away and ride too hard.

Try to stay in a group for the flat sections, pace yourself carefully on the climbs and stay relaxed and focused for the descents.

Below: The profile of the Marmotte shows that there are some very steep and difficult inclines to climb.

Above: Train hard over a few months before your chosen event. Practise on similar terrain, especially riding uphill.

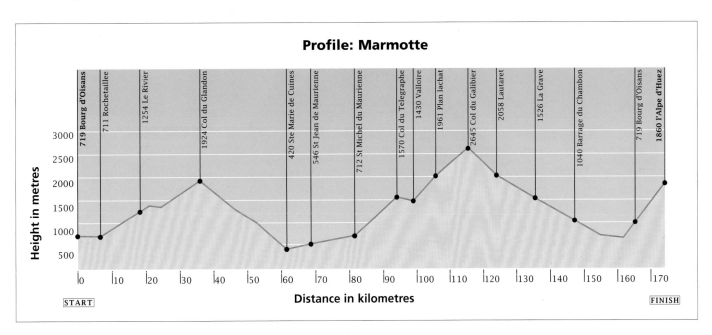

Profile: Marmotte

Great Sportives of the World: The Etape du Tour

The Etape du Tour is one of the most popular sportive events in the world. Each year, thousands of competitors ride a single stage of the Tour de France, during which they cross some of the most difficult mountains of the race.

The Tour de France is most renowned for its mountain stages. The fastest and fittest cyclists in the world compete with each other on the slopes of climbs such as the Col du Galibier, L'Alpe d'Huez and Mont Ventoux.

Since 1993, amateur cyclists and sportive riders have also been given the opportunity to compete on a Tour de France mountain stage in the Etape du Tour. Over the years, it has become a globally important sportive event, with 8,000 cyclists taking part.

More than 2,000 of these riders come from outside France. Most are from the United Kingdom and the United States, but some of the cyclists come from as far afield as Japan or New Zealand. The organizers of the Etape du Tour, who also organize the Tour de France, want

to make their event as spectacular as possible, and they often select one of the hardest stages of the actual race for the Etape route. With few exceptions, they favour stages from the Alps or the Pyrenees, involving the celebrated climbs of the race.

Because there are so many participants, the riders start in waves, counting around a thousand. Entry criteria are stringent, and there are cut-off points along the route – if you ride too slowly, you will be prevented from finishing the event. But while the rules are strict, the satisfaction to be gained from completing the Etape is immense, with the added bonus that you can compare your time with the professionals, who will ride the same course only days later.

A mark of how fit the actual Tour riders are is that the fastest Etape rider is often still an hour or so slower than the last-placed professional.

Tactics for the Etape

Unlike the Marmotte sportive, or the events in the following pages, the Etape follows a different route every year, which means that the preparation and tactics alter from event to event. The 2008 edition from Pau to Hautacam included a long, flat opening section, followed by two difficult climbs (the Col du Tourmalet and Hautacam), while the 2004 edition had a whole series of smaller climbs over the course of a long distance.

Meanwhile, the 2006 edition was one of the hardest in the history of the event, with three of the hardest climbs of the Tour de France – the Col d'Izoard, the Col du Lautaret and L'Alpe d'Huez – on the route.

On a route like that of the 2008 Etape, the biggest temptation would be to start too fast on the fast flat roads in the first half of the event. Pacing is even more important than usual when the end is harder than the start. The route also includes two smaller climbs early on – it's important to take obstacles like this easily, to prevent the build-up of fatigue. On the other hand, the first major climb, the Col du Tourmalet, is harder than the final climb. This means that it might be possible to make a bigger effort on this ascent, knowing that the final climb won't be as bad. However, the tactics for the 2007 event would

Left: The Etape du Tour is one of the most famous sportives in the world – it follows the same route as a Tour de France stage.

have been very similar to those of the Marmotte. With three major climbs en route, including an uphill finish, pacing needs to be steady and conservative.

In spite of its difficulty, or perhaps because of it, entries to the Etape are oversubscribed. Participants from outside France must enter through designated organizing companies, and provide a medical certificate. But if you are fit, and keen to emulate your heroes in the Tour de France, the Etape is one of the most rewarding sportives in the world.

Above: The huge popularity of the Etape du Tour is evident from this picture taken in 2004. The numbers have grown year on year, and as many as 8,000 riders from all over the world now take part. The route varies each year but it is always a difficult one.

Year	Mountain range	Start	Finish	Distance	Climbs
2008	Pyrenees	Pau	Hautacam	156km/97 miles	Col du Tourmalet, Hautacam
2007	Pyrenees	Foix	Loudenvielle	199km/124 miles	Col de Port, Col du Portet d'Aspet, Col de Mente, Col du Port de Balès, Col de Peyresourde
2006	Alps	Gap	L'Alpe d'Huez	193km120/ miles	Col d'Izoard, Col du Lautaret, L'Alpe d'Huez
2005	Pyrenees	Mourenx	Pau	179km/111 miles	Col d'Ichère, Col de Marie-Blanque, Col d'Aubisque
2004	Massif Central	Limoges	St Flour	239km/149 miles	Col de Néronne, Col du Pas de Peyrol, Col d'Entremont, Plomb du Cantal

The Etape du Tour in recent years

Great Sportives of the World: Flanders and the Ventoux

The Tour of Flanders is one of the most famous professional bike races in the world. The climb of Mont Ventoux is among the best-known ascents in the Tour de France. It's possible to tackle both in the form of a sportive.

The Tour of Flanders and the Mont Ventoux sportives are a good challenge for ambitious amateur cyclists. Both cover the routes of well-known bike races, although they are very different in their challenge and character.

The Ventoux sportive is similar to the majority of this kind of event – it covers large climbs and is extremely arduous. The Tour of Flanders is different – because it takes place in Belgium, it therefore cannot include

Above: The Tour of Flanders attracts many amateur riders who want to follow in the tracks of their professional cycling heroes.

high mountain passes. But it still remains an extremely challenging and tough event.

The Tour of Flanders
Unlike the Tour de France, which is a stage race taking place over three weeks, the Tour of Flanders is a single-

day event. Flanders, in Belgium, is probably the most cycling-obsessed region in the world, and thousands of fans turn out to watch the race, which happens on the first Sunday of April.

While the Tour de France has its mountains, Flanders has its bergs – these are small but very steep climbs that range between 300m (984ft) and 3km (4 miles) in length, and often have a cobbled surface which makes riding them extremely difficult. Although the route alters slightly most years, there are always between 15 and 20 bergs, which are packed with fans on race day.

The day before the professional event, there is an amateur event over the same roads. The professional race is 270km (168 miles) long, which is an extremely tough proposition, even for fit amateurs, so the organizers also run a 140-km (87-mile) sportive.

Weather conditions are often difficult in Belgium in early April – the Tour of Flanders is traditionally run over flat roads which are extremely exposed to crosswinds. Rain and cold also make it a challenge. Tactically, to do well in the Tour of Flanders sportive, you must be skilled at riding in a group, to minimize the effect of the wind. If the wind is coming from ahead, ride directly behind the rider in front. But if the wind is coming from either side, move to one side of them, so that you are protected.

The climbs also take a special technique, especially in wet conditions. The cobbles are bumpy and slippery, and the steepness of the hills means that traction is easily lost. Usually on a steep hill, standing up on the pedals is the most efficient way to the top, but on slippery cobbles, stay seated, keeping your weight over the back wheel to stop wheelspins from happening. And ride in a low gear, to prevent stalling – the steepest of the climbs are around 25 per cent (one-in-four) gradient.

The Ventoux

The 'Giant of Provence', as Mont Ventoux is known, is one of the most arduous climbs regularly used in the Tour de France. It rises 1,912m (6,273ft) above sea level in Provence, and is all the more impressive for its isolation – it towers above the surrounding hills. Mont Ventoux gained infamy in the Tour de France when British cyclist Tom Simpson died of heatstroke, exacerbated by performance-enhancing drugs, on its slopes during the 1967 race. Ventoux is also famous for being one of the few mountain stages in the Tour de France that seven-times winner Lance Armstrong never managed to conquer.

Above: The Tour of Flanders in 2007 attracted many spectators to watch the professionals ride by.

The Ventoux is a hard, steep climb, with a summit very exposed to wind and sun. There are three roads to the top. The Ventoux sportive is an annual event which takes place in the early summer. It starts and finishes in Beaumes-de-Venise, and is unusual in that the route crosses the climb twice – once from the hardest side, which starts in the town of Bedoin, and once from the easiest side, which starts to the east in Sault. The route includes hilly sections between the two main ascents, and a final 30km (18½ miles) with two significant climbs. The route is 170km (106 miles) long, so it is hard even for the fittest cyclists. This means that tactics for the Ventoux need to be carefully planned. The first 30km (18½ miles) are flat and fast – it is easy to go too hard here, so instead, find shelter in a group of riders and take it easy to the bottom of the first ascent of the Ventoux, which is the hardest part of the course. The climb from Bedoin to the summit of the Ventoux is consistently steep, and 23km (14 miles) long, which means that it takes most amateur cyclists at least an hour and a half to climb it. Too hard an effort here will result in fatigue later.

Right : The mountainous route of Mont Ventoux is so steep and long that even professional cyclists find it difficult.

The final 7km (4 miles) take riders above the treeline, where they are exposed to the hot sun on clear days, and often strong winds. The descent of the Ventoux is one of the fastest in any sportive in the world, but following it, there are 50km (31 miles) of rolling roads where it is easy to go too hard. On both the initial climb and this section, save a bit of energy for the final climb of the Ventoux, up from Sault. This climb is less steep than the approach from Bedoin, but fatigue makes it as hard, or harder than the first climb. And you still need to save energy for the final 30km (18½-mile) stretch to the finish.

If you wish to enter the Ventoux sportive, go to the event's website, at www.sportcommunication.com.

Great Sportives of the World: Cape Argus and Gran Fondo Gimondi

Two of the most popular sportive events in the world are the Cape Argus Cycle Tour and Gran Fondo Felice Gimondi. One takes place in South Africa, the other in Italy, and both are renowned for their dramatic scenery.

Sportives are not just a physical challenge. One of their main attractions is that they take place in spectacular locations, in the mountains, in often beautiful settings. Many events, including the two described here, are a perfect combination of leisure, enjoyment and challenge.

Cape Argus Cycle Tour

This event happens in March, and it is the biggest sportive in the world. Unusually, it takes place outside Europe, in South Africa, with a route that skirts the Cape Peninsula in Cape Town. The event, which started in 1978 with 525 cyclists, has now grown to attract 35,000 entrants who include elite international athletes at the front, covering the 100km (62-mile) route in under 2½ hours, through serious amateurs, to leisure cyclists looking for a personal challenge.

The biggest attraction of the Cape Argus Cycle Tour, aside from the privilege of sharing the road with the biggest group of cyclists in the world, is the breathtaking scenery along the South African coast. The press photographs of

Below: Cyclists climb Suikerbossie Hill in the annual Cape Argus Cycle Tour.

Above: The Cape Argus Cycle Tour is the world's largest individually timed race.

thousands of riders snaking along the coastal road of the peninsula, which is closed to traffic for the day, are so impressive that they attract great public interest in the sport of cycling.

The Cape Argus differs most from the traditional European sportives in the difficulty of the route. It's hilly, but by no means mountainous – the highest point of the event is under 200m (640ft) above sea level. This means that it is more

accessible to leisure cyclists. And at 100km (62 miles), it can be achieved by anyone who has done a little training.

There are five main hills, and many smaller rises along the route, which are steep, but are mainly under 4km (2½ miles) long. Entrants can thus ride in a different way than in the big mountain sportives of Europe. Along the flat roads of the coast, riding in a group will help enormously, by providing shelter from wind resistance. It's also possible to ride at a much more even speed, which makes judging overall pace much easier. Don't start too hard, but the route is not so difficult that you need to save yourself specially during the early stages.

Gran Fondo Felice Gimondi

While the Marmotte and Etape are very hard, events like the Gran Fondo Felice Gimondi are the perfect balance of physical challenge, and rideable terrain.

Climbs of the Gran Fondo Felice Gimondi

Climb	Length	Altitude	Height gain	Average gradient
Colle dei Pasta	3.8km/2 miles	406m/1,340ft	140m/1,340ft	3.7%
Colle Gallo	7.5km/5 miles	763m/2,518ft	426m/1,405ft	5.7%
Selvino	11km/7 miles	960m/3,168ft	653m/2,155ft	5.6%
Forcella di Bura	20.4km/13 miles	766m/2,528ft	613m/2,023ft	4.5%
Forcella di Berbenno	4.5km/3 miles	663m/2,188ft	273m/901ft	5.3%
Costa Valle Imagna	9.5km/6 miles	1,014m/3,346ft	715m/2,360ft	6.6%

The Gimondi, which starts and finishes in the cycling-crazy town of Bergamo in Italy, has six significant climbs, the highest of which is about 1,000m (3,200ft) in altitude. Rather than the steep 25km (15½-mile) slogs of the Alps, these are much smaller climbs, which offer a reasonable challenge without being too tough. At 163km (101 miles), the distance is about average for a big international sportive.

The Gimondi is an interesting study in how to ride a sportive. The climbs vary in difficulty. The Forcella di Bura, which is the fourth climb of the day, is over 20km (12 miles) long, but only has an average gradient of 4.5 per cent, whereas the Costa Valle Imagna, the final climb of the day, is less than half the distance at 9.5km (6 miles), but is much steeper at 6.6 per cent. Each climb demands a different effort, and it is important in this event not to ride too fast on the early climbs. The Colle dei Pasta, which is the first climb, is more of a warm-up for the later climbs, but the second and third hills, the Colle Gallo and Selvino, are increasingly longer.

The final climb is the hardest, which means that pacing is very important – there are five chances to go too hard earlier in the ride, and it is usually better to resist the temptation and reserve plenty of energy for the end.

Right: Two riders cycle home after taking part in a sportive event.
Below: The Gran Fondo Felice Gimondi is a major sportive event, named in honour of Felice Gimondi, a notable professional racing cyclist in the 1960s. He won three Grand Tours, one of only four cyclists to do so.

Great Rides of the World: The Great Races

You don't have to enter a sportive event to experience the great races of the world. Sometimes, it is enough to go and just ride them as a one-day event. All you need is a map, a bike and no small amount of energy and enthusiasm.

At the Etape du Tour, you can ride a stage of the Tour de France. The Marmotte, Gran Fondo Felice Gimondi and Ventoux sportives all offer the chance to compete against thousands of other cyclists on some famous cycling routes. But it's also possible to just go and ride the routes of some of the great races without having to enter a sportive. Road racing takes place on roads which are open to the public for the other 364 days of the year, and it's possible to ride any of them.

Milan–San Remo

Known as the 'Sprinters–Classic', the route of Milan–San Remo is mainly flat, along the northern Mediterranean coast of Italy. As a result, sprinters, who are generally big, strong, heavy riders who are less good at climbing hills, dominate the race history. The best part to ride is the final 100km

Below: The champion, Eddy Merckx, won the prestigious Milan–San Remo seven times.

(60 miles) of the race, or more if you are fit enough. The route is a pleasant ride, with only a few hills to deal with. The most difficult are the 6km (4-mile) Cipressa and 4km (2.5-mile) Poggio, in the final 30km (18.5 miles) before the finish, but they are well-surfaced and steady.

> **Milan–San Remo**
> **Where to stay** San Remo.
> **The ride** Savona–San Remo (110km/68 miles).
> **Climbs** Capo Mele, Capo Berta, Cipressa, Poggio (max altitude 240m/780ft).
> **Other rides in the area** Head inland from the coast to explore the quiet hills.

Paris–Roubaix

Most cycling events get their difficulty from hills. However, Paris–Roubaix is one of the flattest races in the professional cycling calendar. It gets its toughness from several sections of cobbled farm track, which have bumpy and unpredictable surfaces and are extremely

> **Paris–Roubaix**
> **Where to stay** Valenciennes.
> **The ride** Valenciennes–Roubaix (110km/68 miles).
> **Climbs** No significant ones.
> **Other rides in the area** Cross over the Belgian border to explore the Chimay.

difficult to ride on. The best preparation for riding on the cobbles is to modify your bike so it will absorb as much of the shock as possible. You will need thicker tyres, and stronger wheels if possible. Professional cyclists put two layers of bar tape on, to make gripping the handlebars easier.

When riding the cobbles, maintaining speed is very difficult, but crucial if you are to avoid getting knocked off your line. Stay relaxed and vigilant and try to look a few metres ahead at all times,

Below: The roads of the Paris–Roubaix race are as challenging and difficult as any mountain pass.

Above: The cobbled track in the Paris–Roubaix event is very hard to ride on.

Above: Italy's Paolo Bettini is a former winner of the Tour of Lombardy.

Tour of Lombardy

The climbs of the Tour of Lombardy, in Italy, are in some of the most beautiful cycling country in the world. They are long, moderately steep, and offer a good physical challenge. The route circles Lake Como, and covers 260km (162 miles). Even missing the first part of the race and riding from Como involves 220km (137 miles) of hilly riding – it's probably best to divide it into two halves, and stop over in Parlasco, on the west side of the lake.

so you can spot any large cobbles that jut upwards. This kind of surface takes a lot of getting used to.

Liège–Bastogne–Liège

A more traditional cycling challenge is Liège–Bastogne–Liège – its difficulty comes from a succession of long and steep climbs winding through the forests of the Ardennes in Belgium. The race starts from Liège, and heads down to the turning point at Bastogne. It's a good idea to pick it up from here – the hills are almost exclusively in the second half of the race. None of the climbs are

> **Liège–Bastogne–Liège**
> **Where to stay** Bastogne.
> **The ride** Bastogne–Ans (150km/93 miles).
> **Climbs** Many, including the Côte de Stockeu, Haute-Levée, Redoute and Sprimont.
> **Other rides in the area** Head west to Huy to ride the famous Mur climb, which features in the Flèche Wallonne race.

longer than a few kilometres. But their steepness and repetitive nature sap the energy from the legs. One good idea is to fit a compact chainset, so that you have a wide selection of low gears.

Approach these climbs like mountain roads – it's important to establish an early and good rhythm, because if you go too hard too soon, you will suffer in the final kilometres. The most famous climb of the Tour of Lombardy is the Madonna del Ghisallo, with a chapel at the top, filled with cycling memorabilia.

Left: The peloton starts in Liège for the Liège–Bastogne–Liège challenge ride.

> **Tour of Lombardy**
> **Where to stay** Como.
> **The ride** Como–Como (220km/136 miles).
> **Climbs** Parlasco, Colle di Balisio, Madonna del Ghisallo, Civiglio, San Fermo di Battaglia.
> **Other rides in the area** The hills around Lake Como are some of the best for cycling in the world.

MOUNTAIN BIKING

Mountain biking is one of the most beneficial
and fun exercise regimes you can follow. While
road riders have to share the road with traffic, on a
mountain bike you are generally in splendid isolation, in
beautiful surroundings, on challenging terrain.
It doesn't even matter if it rains. While bad weather
can be demoralizing for other forms of cycling, wet
weather is all part of the fun of mud-plugging (off-road
riding). There are many different disciplines to try out
on a mountain bike, from trail riding and downhill
riding to freeriding.

Above: Riding off-road is one of the pleasures of mountain biking.
Left: Mountain biking through a forest on a rocky road will help to improve your fitness,
while being extremely enjoyable.

Choosing a Mountain Bike

With such a wide range of off-road bikes available, it can be hard to choose what type to buy, let alone a specific model. When buying a bike your needs, budget and ambitions all have to be taken into consideration.

Before taking the plunge to buy a bike, you have to decide whether you want a specific bike for a specific task, or a more versatile model to allow you to explore more than one branch of off-road cycling.

Specific bikes are easy to decide on. If you want to ride trials, only a trials bike will do – the specification is so exact and developed that a normal mountain bike will be unable to meet performance needs. You really need a downhill bike for cycling down hills properly. It is possible to ride down some courses on a hardtail bike with suspension forks, but

Right: For trials riding, you'll need a specialized bike.
Below: A full-suspension mountain bike is suitable for heavy-duty off-road riding.

you will have to keep your speed so low to cope with the bumping and shock that it will detract from the fun.

If you decide that you are going to ride off-road, then you need a more general bike, and this is where the massive choice starts to get confusing. You might be more specific, and decide that you want to race cross-country, but then you have to choose between hardtail and full suspension, V-brakes or disc brakes, even between eight- and nine-speed freewheels.

For those who just want to enjoy the occasional bit of trail riding, a hardtail bike with V-brakes and suspension forks will probably return the maximum benefit. A bike like this is versatile enough to be ridden on the trails and make it a rewarding experience, but it is

Above: A downhill bike is designed for one purpose only – it's too heavy to ride back up a steep slope.

not so specialized that it can be used only for this purpose. There is also the advantage that it can be used as a runaround urban bike and fulfil that function perfectly well.

If you are going to take the sport more seriously and hit the trails on a regular basis, perhaps embarking on longer challenge rides, your equipment needs to be a bit more specialized.

There is no easy answer to the hardtail versus full suspension debate – the topic has been debated for years. All you can do is make your own decision, based on what you think you will get out of each type of bike.

If you are light and good at climbing, you might consider going for the full suspension – the extra weight will slow you down on the hills, but as you climb fast, you can afford to slow yourself down marginally. On the other hand, when it comes to bowling down the other side of the hill, the full suspension will allow you to maximize your speed and efficiency. Likewise, an occasional

rider who prefers a bit of light trail riding on a warm day might not need to install disc brakes, when V-brakes will do just as well. If you are planning to go out in all weathers throughout the year, disc brakes are probably the right option. The most important thing is to

Above: Hardtail mountain bikes are good for off-road riding, and are more efficient for all-purpose riding.

work out which bike will give you the most enjoyment and let you cycle effectively.

The Hardtail Bike

Hardtail mountain bikes are light and fast and handle precisely, and they are excellent for speed and efficient climbing. The front suspension provides comfort and control of the bike and the fat tyres allow smooth riding on roads.

A basic mountain bike, either with suspension or regular forks and a normal aluminium frame, is known as a hardtail. Although full-suspension bikes are currently popular for their greater shock absorbency in bumpy conditions, a traditional hardtail can still be the best bike for basic cross-country and trail

riding. They are lighter than full-suspension models. They also have the advantage that, combined with slick tyres, they make a far better road bike. When buying a mountain bike, it is easy

Right: Gear shifters are located on the handlebars for quick changing.

Anatomy of a hardtail bike

① Frame: Aluminium frame, compact, but with plenty of clearance for fat tyres. Skinny seatstays absorb much more impact.
② Fork: Suspension fork for shock absorption and a more comfortable ride on rough and bumpy surfaces. Most forks can be adjusted for shock absorbency, depending on the type of terrain.

③ Wheels: 32-spoked wheels, with 26in rims, which are smaller than those on a road bike. Width can be 1.5–3in.
④ Tyres: Thick and knobbly for extra grip on loose surfaces.
⑤ Chainrings: Triple chainrings offer more possible gears.
⑥ Sprockets: Eight or nine, depending on preference and model.

Much wider spread, to give very low gear options for steep hills.
⑦ Brakes: V-Brakes for greater stopping capacity than regular callipers. Disc brakes are becoming more popular for their efficiency in all weathers.
⑧ Gear shifters: Integrated into brake system for ease of access.
⑨ Saddle: Comfortable, supportive saddle, good for rough terrain.

Trials bike

Trials bikes are an offshoot of mountain bikes used for jumps and riding over obstacles, either artificial or natural. Riders keep their feet up, and ride, hop and jump from obstacle to obstacle, balancing on the super-fat tyres even when the bike is not moving.

A trials bike has a very short seat tube, which enables the body to move over the bike and perform a jump called a sidehop, in which the bike jumps both up and laterally. The frame is very stiff and responsive, with no need for energy-absorbing suspension. Riders gain control from a wider set of flat handlebars, which give more leverage.

Wheels are usually 26in, with fat tyres at low pressure to grip surfaces. A single small chainring, usually fitted with a guard to protect it from damage when it hits an obstacle, is combined with a seven-, eight- or nine-speed freewheel. Brakes need to be very strong – many riders choose hydraulic systems, which lose less power than a traditional cable. Some riders don't even use a saddle on their trials bike – the jumps are all executed standing up.

to be impressed by the sophisticated technology of full-suspension designs, but depending on your needs, hardtail mountain bikes are resilient and reliable. Hardtails are more sensitive to accelerations, giving a more responsive ride, which purists and traditionalists prefer. For general fitness riding and enjoying getting out on the trails, a basic hardtail model with eight-speed freewheel and V-brakes is a good choice.

Frames and components

The majority of hardtail frames are aluminium, and they are compact and low. A long seatpin, small frame and 26in wheels, which are smaller than road wheels, keep the rider's weight low to the ground. This makes the bike more controllable at low speeds, either going up steep hills, or dealing with highly technical sections. Riders often have to jump off their bikes, and a low top tube makes this easier.

The triple chainset, with chainrings with 42, 32 and 22 teeth, plus an eight-speed freewheel is a good combination for riding your mountain bike over a

Above: Disc brakes are powerful enough to check speed even on loose surfaces and down steep hills.

variety of terrains. On very steep hills, which you can often encounter on a trail ride, the inner chainring should be able to deal with the gradient.

Brakes can be either disc or the traditional V-brakes, depending on what you want to get from your riding. Disc brakes perform better in bad

Above left: Suspension forks and disc brakes help control your bike.
Above: Chunky tyres are necessary for off-road riding, to aid grip.

conditions, and overall, offer more stopping power. V-brakes are simpler and lighter.

Full-suspension Cross-country and Downhill Bikes

In recent years, the technology of full-suspension frames has improved significantly. For trail riding, the full-suspension bike gives a much more comfortable ride, which is especially important when riding long distances.

Bumps and shocks tire and bruise the body – riding a full-suspension bike can reduce these shocks and make the experience of trail riding positive and even more enjoyable.

Full-suspension bike
There is no doubt that riding a full-suspension bike down hills is easier than on a hardtail, on which all the bumps you ride over are transmitted straight to your saddle area. The suspension irons out the lumps and bumps, giving a faster, more comfortable ride.

The payoff for the extra comfort, however, is reduced speed and extra weight. Full suspension adds a few kilograms to the weight of your bike, because of the extra tubing and machinery involved in the suspension system. Every time you ride up a hill, you will be carrying more weight than a

Below: Full-suspension frames make for a less harsh ride over bumpy ground.

Above: Keep your mountain bike clean and well maintained – riding off-road in poor conditions can wear down components very quickly.

traditional hardtail, and the efforts quickly mount up and can tire you out. However, the more technical the terrain, the more the full-suspension bike comes into its own. So over the course of a long ride, including uphills, downhills and technical sections, the full suspension will probably have a net benefit effect on the speed of your ride.

Downhill mountain bike
With most other types of mountain bike, riders always have to compromise between speed and comfort. The downhill mountain bike is designed purely to absorb bumps and shocks. Downhill mountain biking has its roots right back in the origins of the sport. The first mountain bikers were the Californians who rode general-purpose

bikes down Repack Hill in the 1970s, and the tradition has continued to the present day, when the downhill is a major event in the World Cup series, attracting huge crowds with spectacular races. Downhill cycling is a time trial from the top of a hill to the bottom, with bends, jumps and steep straights on which riders can reach massive speeds, sometimes over 95kph (60mph). The downhill bike, more than any other, relies on strong suspension with a great deal of travel (amount of give in a suspension system) to absorb the shocks at speed. It also needs to be manoeuvrable – courses often include sharp bermed (high-sided) corners and narrow sections that demand great control, even at speed.

Frames are full suspension, with lots of travel and large springs to absorb the impact of bumps that are hit at 80kph (50mph). The fork suspension travel is enormous, since it is the front wheel that takes the brunt of the hits. Controlling speed effectively means that disc brakes are the only real option, as they have a larger braking surface than regular mountain bike V-brakes. The chain is kept in place with a retainer, and the chainring is protected.

The riding position on a downhill bike is not over-streamlined, in spite of the fact that aerodynamics are important. The saddle is kept low, to keep the rider's weight close to the ground and the bike stable.

Above: The travel on full-suspension bikes can be altered depending on the terrain you expect to encounter.

Anatomy of a full-suspension cross-country bike

❶ Full-suspension frame: Provides greater shock absorbency, and greater control and traction in rough terrain.
❷ Suspension fork: Takes all the impact where the bike feels it most – at the front wheel.
❸ Brakes: Disc brakes are essential for better stopping power at speed and

for cycling in poor conditions such as mud and water, bumpy surfaces and rocky roads.
❹ Wheels: Rims are 26in with 32 spokes for lightness and strength. Width is 1.9 or 2.1in, for the right balance between grip and rolling resistance.

❺ Tyres: Thick knobbly tyres grip the ground in rough terrain.
❻ Gears: Nine-speed freewheel, combined with a triple chainring with 22, 32 and 42 teeth.
❼ Pedals: Reversible clipless pedals so that the shoe can clip into either side of the pedal.

Clothing and Equipment

The varied conditions experienced when out mountain biking mean it is a sensible idea to wear specialized clothing that will minimize discomfort. Comfort is a priority as well as protection from the cold and wet.

In the summer, clothing is simple. A pair of shorts, plus a base layer for your top, and a loose cycling jersey are the most comfortable option. Some mountain bikers wear skin-tight Lycra road-racing shorts, while others prefer the look of baggy shorts, but be careful of catching them on your saddle as you stand up on the pedals. Jerseys do not need to be as tight fitting as those of road riders, since speeds are lower and aerodynamics less important. A loose-fitting jersey will help keep you cool.

Gloves are essential. No one is immune from crashing, and you will need to protect your hands and fingers if you stack your bike. Full-fingered gloves are advisable for off-roading.

Helmets, too, are just as important for off-road riding as they are on the road. If you come off, you could be seriously injured if your head hits a rock or tree roots.

If you are not planning on having to put your feet down, you can use stiffer-soled shoes similar to those of road cyclists. However, most mountain bikers will want the kind of shoe that clips into your pedals, but is also comfortable and

Above: Extreme conditions make it necessary to wrap up warm.

flexible for walking. For steep sections of trail you may need to dismount and walk, and it helps to have some grip.

In winter it is important to dress well because of the wet conditions. Depending on how mild or cold it is, you may need a windproof and waterproof jacket. Even if it is not raining, water can still spray up off your companions' wheels. Long leggings will keep your legs warm and shoe covers will protect your feet from the elements. A warmer pair of gloves and a hat are also useful. Even when the sun is not shining, it is a sensible precaution to wear goggles to protect your eyes.

Left: A lightweight waterproof jacket will protect you from the rain.
Right: Keeping feet warm is important.

Mountain bike tyres pick up mud and stones and sometimes they can be flicked up into the face of the rider behind.

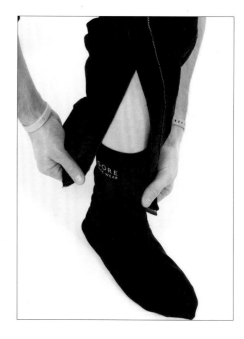

Above: Baggy winter clothing is warm and practical for off-road riding.

Above: If speed is important to you, Lycra leggings are more aerodynamic.

Above: In summer, shorts and a long-sleeved top will protect you from scratches.

Full-face helmet

Shoulder pad

Shoulder pad

Padded jacket

Elbow pad

Flexible padded gloves

Knee pads

Padded shorts

Shin pads

Downhill body armour

Downhill racers need serious protection for their bodies, in case of a crash.

On your head, you need a full-face helmet. It is not enough just to wear an ordinary hard shell helmet – these do not protect the face. A comfortable and effective full-face helmet will protect the whole of your head, as well as the back of your neck. Cover your eyes with goggles that fit inside the opening of the helmet.

Body armour will protect your arms, legs and body. Parts of your anatomy tend to hit the ground more than others and these parts have extra-hard shell protection. The knees and shins have a hard shell, as do the shoulders, elbows, wrists and chest. Downhill crashes tend to cause injuries from skidding along the ground, Full body armour, however is specifically designed to minimize this damage.

Padded downhill gloves are flexible, to allow you to control the brakes and steering without loss of sensitivity, while for your feet, protective shoes with thick soles help when you put your feet down in the corners.

Trail Riding Skills: What to Expect

Riding a mountain bike along a trail is exhilarating and fun, but it also requires concentration and a good skills base. By practising your technique, you can make your off-road riding a much more rewarding experience.

The very best mountain bikers rarely bounce along bumpy trails, they glide and flow. This is the riding style you should aim for – relaxed, efficient and comfortable. By shifting your weight around subtly, finding the right line and letting the bike do some of the hard work, you can start to ride with more economy.

Each different kind of surface demands a slightly different approach, but there are some general rules and techniques to apply to your riding that can help you improve. These involve keeping momentum, absorbing shocks and keeping your weight back.

On rough surfaces, it can seem as if the bike is fighting you and trying its best to stop. These surfaces can cause inexperienced riders to lose speed, and the slower you go over or through an obstacle, the harder it becomes to deal with. So try to maintain momentum into, through and out of especially

rough patches. Try not to hit obstacles at maximum speed, but keep a positive pedalling action and pick your way through trying to lose as little speed as possible. Losing speed means using more energy to keep going.

Shocks

Absorbing shocks is an important part of maintaining momentum. When you hit a loose surface or technical section, sometimes the reaction is to try too hard to control the bike, which makes your body tense and stiff. Relaxed arms and legs are natural shock absorbers, and if

Left: On extreme descents, keep your weight back as far as possible.

Above: When descending, keep your weight over the rear wheel for traction and balance, while at the same time lightly braking.

you can absorb the bumps, your progress will be smoother.

Lastly, your bike will react better to the terrain if more of your weight is over the back wheel. If you hold your weight too far forward, steering is compromised on rough terrain. Putting your weight over the back wheel increases traction while pedalling and will give you more control over your speed. Your front wheel should be free to manoeuvre, but should not be so loosely held that it bounces around.

Muddy conditions

The more sticky the mud is, the lower the gear you will need. Sit well back and maintain traction. Pick your line and try to stick to it, keeping your weight off the front wheel so that if it starts to get stuck you can easily pull it out before it sinks and pitches you off. You should be able to ride over the rocks, but hitting them at a bad angle knocks the front wheel out of alignment, affecting momentum and steering, so plan ahead

to follow a line that avoids bigger stones. The ride is bumpy, so stand up and bend your arms; the arms and legs act as shock absorbers. In most off-road situations, spinning a low gear is better than pushing a large gear, but in rocky terrain, a larger gear is better to try to maintain speed and momentum. If you are deflected into a new line by bigger rocks, follow that new line. When you steer, use your body and hips to help to change line.

Riding over roots

Roots are present on many off-road trails. In wet weather they usually become slick, and if you hit them at the wrong angle, you can take your bike out from under you, even if you have fitted rugged tyres. The way to tackle roots is to hop the front wheel over them, avoiding wet roots if possible, then use the back wheel to generate speed to pass over them in a straight line, at a right angle to the root.

Dealing with mud and rocks

Mud: *Put the bike into low gear. Pick a line and try to stick to it.*

Rocks 1: *Follow a line and plan ahead to avoid large stones.*

Rocks 2: *Stand up in the saddle so that the legs and arms absorb the shock.*

Dealing with roots

1: *Approach the roots and plan a path through them.*

2: *Hop the front wheel over the roots. Beware of wet, slippery roots.*

3: *Pass over the roots at a right angle to the direction of growth.*

Trail Riding Skills: Choosing a Line

Riding in a straight line is easy but the challenge of mountain biking involves the unpredictable nature of the trails. Being able to pick your line, anticipate problems and corner fast and safely are important skills.

When riding, it is natural to look just ahead of the front wheel, so that you can deal with problems as they arise. But looking farther ahead is far more efficient – that way, you can avoid problems before they happen, rather than have to deal with them.

Look ahead

Pick your line well in advance. When you can see a rough patch approaching, look for a suitable entrance point, a good line through, and a possible exit. That way, you have already ridden the section in your mind before you actually get to it on the bike and will be prepared for each stage. Sometimes you may have to change your tactics if your original line turns out to have a hidden obstacle, but that is all part of the fun and challenge of mountain biking.

Looking ahead can help with gear selection, too. If you get caught out by a sudden steep rise it is easy to stall, but if you have changed down already in preparation for a climb, you will be ready to ride all the way up.

Right: Even when pedalling uphill out of the saddle, it's still important to concentrate on controlled steering to get you safely up.
Below: Allow your bike to steer for you by following the natural line of the trail.

Above: Be prepared to take action if you come to a sudden corner on a single track.

Above: Use your upper body to help steer your bike, leaning into the turns to aid traction.

straight line – you'll be constantly turning and changing your line during the course of a ride.

Cornering involves three phases – the approach, the turn and the exit.

In the approach, use your brakes to moderate your speed. The aim is to enter the corner as fast as possible without the risk of overshooting. As you enter the corner, lean your body over to counteract the centrifugal force, and stay seated. This allows you to push down on your outside leg while bending your inside leg away from the bike for extra balance. Keep your weight centred over the bike, spreading it equally between the front and back wheel to maintain grip.

Once you are past the apex, your aim is to accelerate out of the corner. As soon as you have rounded the bend and can see your exit point, start to pedal.

On a smooth corner with a banked surface, your speed can be high all the way through. Be prepared to slow down more for gravelly surfaces, adverse cambers and other obstacles.

Singletrack

Riding singletrack is one of the most rewarding off-road cycling experiences you can have – it tests your reflexes, fitness and bike handling.

Singletrack is just that – a one-lane mountain bike trail wide enough for one bike at a time. It twists and turns unpredictably, and has all the variety of surfaces that off-road riding has to offer. Often they come unexpectedly –

you may dive out of a sharp corner only to discover a large rock under your front wheel or find yourself up to your hub in mud. Riding singletrack is a matter of ducking and diving around the corners and being able to deal with obstacles that come when you least expect them. Singletrack demands a much more erratic speed than larger trails. You will very often have to brake sharply for corners, then accelerate out of them. The aim is still to maintain flow, but within the bounds the singletrack imposes on you.

To control speed in twisting sections, use the back brake, and manoeuvre the bike using both body weight and turning the handlebars. Use the front brake for sharper stopping. You'll need to change gear often as the speed alters. Because of the need to accelerate, it is better to spin a lower gear and anticipate changes down so that you are ready to speed up again.

Cornering

An important skill in mountain biking is cornering quickly and safely. There are very few trails that travel in a totally

Left: Always try to anticipate what is coming up when riding at speed.

Above: Accelerate out of tricky situations to prevent getting stuck in a rut.

Trail Riding Skills: Descending

Descending is theoretically the easiest thing about trail riding on a mountain bike. Gravity pulls you downward, and all you do is control the bike by keeping your weight back. Then just relax, steer, brake a little and enjoy the ride. But it takes skill, too.

Your main priority when descending is safety. On shallow descents this is straightforward – keep a laid-back position, and use the brakes when you need to. Look well ahead and plan your line. If the surface gets bumpy and you have a hardtail bike, stand up on the pedals to let your legs act as shock absorbers.

Steep descents involve a little more care. You need to be aware of your centre of gravity, and be more focused on the movement of the bike underneath you. Your line should be the shortest one, surface permitting, so cut corners tightly.

Keep your weight back when descending – too much weight above the front wheel can move your centre of gravity far enough forward that you become unstable. The steeper the descent, the farther back you need to sit. Once it becomes really steep, you can hang off the back of the saddle with

Right: Keep weight back when descending to prevent tipping over forwards.
Below: When descending, use your arms and legs to support your body weight.

Right: Keeping your weight above your back wheel helps maintain traction and allows you to react to obstacles.

your bottom above the rear wheel. In this position, your centre of gravity is still low enough to keep you stable, but pay attention to your steering.

Finding a way down

Steering on the descents is easier if you shift your weight and lean rather than turn the handlebars. This is all part of being relaxed and letting the bike do the work of finding its own way down.

On a slippery or loose surface, descending becomes more complicated. Overusing the brakes can result in a crash, so the best technique is to moderate your speed before you hit the gravel. Unless there is particular difficulty ahead, don't brake on a loose surface, but if you have to, keep your weight well back, your centre of gravity low, and feather the brakes so that you regain control.

Drop-offs

On some off-road descents, mountain bikers can encounter drop-offs, which are vertical drops in the path or trail. Some are so small that you might not even notice them, but others are quite dramatic and take a lot of practice before you can deal with them confidently. To ride a drop-off, you don't need to be riding fast, but it helps if you are riding positively and confidently. Do not use your brakes once you are committed to the move.

On the approach, move the bike into a straight line and put your weight slightly over the rear wheel. As the front wheel goes over the edge, pull your handlebars up, bending your arms, and stay back over the rear wheel. Your rear wheel should hit the edge, and your momentum should cause both wheels to land together at the bottom of the drop-off. Your bent arms will take some of the shock of landing.

During the final approach, look at where you intend to land and plan your exit strategy so that you don't lose momentum.

Drop-offs

1: *Put your weight over the rear wheel and pull up the handlebars.*

2: *Look ahead and decide where you are going to land.*

Trail Riding Skills: Climbing

Climbing is an unavoidable, and difficult, part of trail riding. It is part of the huge variety of terrain you can come across, even on just a single ride, and being able to do it effectively will make your ride a more positive experience.

The steepness of a hill dictates how you tackle it on a mountain bike. On a shallow incline, it is just a case of sitting comfortably, with your body stretched out as you ride to the top. On steep climbs, or climbs with loose surfaces, technique plays a significant part in getting up.

Relaxation is also important. Instead of bunching up your entire body and holding the handlebars in a death-grip, concentrate on breathing evenly, open out your chest a bit, and hold the bars firmly, towards the outside. If you have bar-end attachments, use those to stretch yourself out a bit.

Maintain traction

When the surface of the climb is loose, keeping traction is the biggest challenge. A wheelspin can slow your progress almost to a halt, so to ensure it

Above: When climbing steady gradients off-road, stay in the saddle and sit back, spinning a low gear.

doesn't happen, sit back and keep your weight over the back wheel. At the same time, to keep your centre of gravity low and increase traction in both wheels, stretch out so that your body is almost parallel to the top tube.

Loose surfaces can also affect your bike when you are standing up and pedalling up a hill. If you sway your bike from side to side, as sometimes feels natural, you run the risk of it slipping out from underneath you. Try instead to move your body from side to side, keeping the bike upright beneath you.

On a very steep climb, with your weight back, it is possible for the front wheel to come off the ground and cause you to lose momentum. On a steeper climb, move your weight forward a little, consciously maintaining traction in the rear wheel.

Golden rules of climbing

1 Stay in the saddle

Climbing is all about establishing a rhythm, and the easiest way to do this is to relax and focus, and stay in the saddle. Grip the bars firmly but not tightly, settle your weight where it feels comfortable and effective, and climb with good rhythm. Save standing up for where you have to accelerate, or stretch out your legs.

2 Bend forward, stretch yourself out, keep your weight back

When climbing, rear-wheel traction is everything. Keep your weight back over the rear wheel to prevent it slipping, but stretch forward with your upper body to get a lower centre of gravity. This will also help traction.

3 Use a low gear

It is less tiring to your muscles to spin a low gear fast than try to turn a big gear over. By staying in a low gear you will have more energy later on. Also, changes in gradient can slow you down – if you are already pedalling slowly you run the risk of stalling.

4 Change the numbers

You can climb faster without even having to go out riding. Climbing effectively is all about power-to-weight ratios. So spend some time and effort, and money if necessary, on losing weight, both you and your bike. Then do some specific hill-climbing training to boost your power. Your climbing will improve out of all recognition.

5 Take the easiest line

The easiest line is not necessarily the shortest one. Corners are often much steeper on the inside than on the outside. The extra distance on a shallow gradient can be less tiring than the short distance up the inside with a steep gradient.

Climbing

Sit down: *Most of your climbing should be done sitting down, with the weight over the back wheel for traction.*

Weight back: *If necessary, stand on the pedals on steeper gradients, but keep the weight back.*

Side to side: *When climbing, move from side to side. Keep the bike straight, to prevent it slipping out beneath you.*

Stand up: *Standing up on the pedals stretches the legs, helps combat tiredness and gives a little extra acceleration.*

Weight forward: *On the steepest climbs, move your weight forward a little for traction with the rear wheel.*

Keep going: *Maintain your speed and effort to the top of the climb to prevent stalling.*

Downhill Racing

Taking part in a downhill race is not as easy as just sitting back and freewheeling while the bike does all the work. It is a serious athletic challenge, and all mountain bikers should have a go at it – it is fast, exhilarating and fun.

On the face of it, downhill riding looks like the easy option for mountain bikers. Dressed from head to toe in protective body armour, riders plummet down steep paths on bikes that look more like motorbikes. If they want to go down again, they catch the ski-lift back up to the top. This isn't simply laziness; downhill mountain bikes are so engineered that they weigh a great deal more than normal bikes, and riding back up would be very difficult.

Downhill riding takes a cool head, nerve, co-ordination and skill. It also takes physical strength – on well-designed courses riders rarely freewheel. Instead, shallower gradients and sharp corners require fast riding and acceleration to maintain velocity.

Your first few downhill runs should be more about gaining confidence and getting used to the way a downhill bike handles. Get used to the brakes and acceleration, and then ride a bit harder. Preparation on a downhill run is essential, and it's worth walking the course to inspect it before you ride. By getting a mental picture of the right line to take, and where to brake, when it

Above: Riders can reach incredible speeds on the steepest gradients in downhill events.

does happen it will be more natural. Actually riding the correct line is a matter of experience and anticipation. By looking well ahead of your front wheel, you will be in a position to choose the right line.

Corners and jumps

The start of a downhill ride is an important part of the whole descent. The margins of victory in competitive downhilling are often very small, and the difference can be made in the initial acceleration. A powerful sprint out of

Left: Full protective body armour is absolutely essential for anyone taking part in downhill racing.

the starting blocks will give your ride physical momentum. It is also a statement of intent – by starting as fast as you mean to go on you can give yourself a psychological boost. Once you are into the ride, you can deal with the sections as they come.

Most corners have berms, which help you to maintain your line through them. When you approach a bermed corner, brake before you start to turn, then hit the berm on the top half. Lean over and shift your body weight on to your outside pedal, which should be down,

and following the line should be straightforward. Follow these steps and your cornering will be a lot faster and better controlled.

Some corners don't have berms, and the best technique is to use your lower leg in the corner for balance. Riders come round some corners so fast that their bike is almost horizontal, with their leg skidding around on the floor to keep them upright, and to help the bike around the corner before getting it upright again. Use longer, straight

Above: At the start of a downhill race, acceleration is all-important, and riders sprint out of the gate.

sections to build up speed, but be careful of your exit – if you fly too fast into a technical section, you can crash. Some sections will be quite flat, and it's important to try and sprint through these, in order to maintain your speed.

At certain sections, there are small jumps. Hit these jumps with your wheels straight, lift the front wheel up, closely

Above: Hitting a ramp at speed means riders can jump. It's vitally important that the bike is straight for landing.

followed by the back wheel, and be careful to land straight. Look ahead while you are making the jump, so that the exit from your landing is as safe and speedy as possible.

The most important and useful skill to develop, along with your confidence, is your ability to let yourself and the bike flow down the hill. Your reactions to the course have to be fast and fully committed.

Left: Cornering at speed on a berm.
Below: During flat sections, the rider holds speed by pedalling hard and maintaining an aerodynamic tuck.

Freeriding

A recent development in mountain biking is freeriding, which is perhaps the ultimate expression of the sport. It is an improvisatory way of combining cross-country riding, downhill riding, trails and trick riding.

The inspiration for freeriding initially came from snowboarders. Freeriding in snowboarding takes place off-piste, away from the beaten track; mountain bike freeriders do the same. Sometimes freeriding involves building jumps and narrow wooden walkways to ride on. Often it is a case of finding your own trail and using logs and rocks.

The definition of freeriding by the sport's originators in British Columbia is that there is no definition.

There is an element of downhill riding, but freeriding also involves riding through more technical terrain. While downhill riding involves getting from A to B as quickly as possible, freeriding means getting from A to B in as stylish and innovative a way as possible.

Freeriding has provided cycling with some of its most photogenic moments since its development at the turn of the century. Freeriders have sought out steeper drops to ride off, and they build ever larger jumps. The original freeride trails incorporated narrow walkways 3m (10ft) in the air. These days the walkways are 12m (40ft) off the ground.

A freeriding bike is very like a downhill bike. The frame is heavy duty with full suspension, although as it often

Right: Freeriders build their own obstacles, putting narrow walkways up to 12m (40ft) off the ground.
Below: Huge jumps are an integral part of freeriding, with the best riders finding ever larger drops to ride.

Above: Freeriding bikes have full suspension, with enough travel in the front forks to absorb impact off jumps.

has to be ridden up hills and for longer distances, it is not as bulky. Its wheelbase is shorter and the head tube is steeper, which gives more control when performing jumps.

Special bike features

The long travel suspension forks have been retained from downhill bikes – freeriding involves dropping off obstacles and jumps, and the shock of

landing needs to be taken in the forks. Disc brakes with a large braking surface also survived from downhill bikes – landing off a 3m (10ft) cliff involves a fair amount of acceleration, and speed might need to be checked very quickly.

Unlike a downhill bike, however, the freeride bike has a triple chainset and therefore a larger range of gears. The

Left: Freeriding courses often incorporate narrow log beams, which test the riders' balance to the limits.

Above: There is no limit to the complexity of freeriding courses.

greater variety of terrain expected to be encountered by a freerider also requires the gears to deal with it.

Freeriding involves elements from many mountain bike disciplines: the trick-riding abilities of the trials rider, the reflexes and nerve of the downhill rider, the physical strength and urge to explore shared by all trail riders, and the competitive instincts of the racer.

Mountain Biking: Branching Out

Mountain biking isn't just about trail riding and cross-country. There are a multitude of other racing and riding disciplines that are challenging and fun, including bicycle four-cross, slalom, trials and dirt-jump riding.

Mountain biking is primarily about having fun, and there are a variety of disciplines outside cross-country riding. Four-cross and slalom are action-filled races over short distances including jumps, berms and downhills. Trials riding is more technical – it's all about hops, jumps and tackling obstacles. Dirt-jump riding is an underground scene with the emphasis on style and expression.

Four-cross

At a bicycle four-cross event, four riders start at the same time, and race to the bottom. Bikes are full suspension, with short seat tubes and low saddles like a trials bike, and crashes are common. Riders need nerves of steel and great technical ability to ride down a steep section of hill with jumps and corners, elbow-to-elbow with other riders. Speed alone might not be enough – races are often decided by the jumps, and course designers keep the suspense alive to the finishing line by incorporating as many unpredictable elements as possible.

Above: Bicycle four-cross is a fast and furious race on specially designed courses, with four riders going elbow-to-elbow in a downhill dash to the line.

Slalom

A type of racing that involves two riders going head-to-head on two near-identical but separate courses down a hill is 'slalom'. Originally, it was simply erecting the poles in a field and letting the riders go, but it evolved into an organized part of the sport. The course became more technical, with jumps and berms between the slalom poles. With the development of the 'dual' slalom, in which riders start separately, until their lanes merge, there was more conflict. Once you have established a lead in an event like the slalom, it is easy to keep it, so a typical race sees aggressive fighting to reach the merged lanes in first place.

Trials

Another form of mountain biking, trials, entails performing tricks and jumps over a series of obstacles. In trial biking

Left: In a slalom race the bikes ride down separate but identical courses.

Trials riding: jump

1: *A rider starts to jump off the top of an obstacle.*

2: *In mid-air, the rider positions his bike to effect a good landing.*

3: *The rider is not allowed to put his feet on the ground.*

competitions, riders have to negotiate a set course without putting their feet down, or allowing any part of their bike apart from the tyres to touch the obstacle. If they do, they are penalized. There is also a time limit, and when riders exceed it, they gain a penalty point for every 15 seconds taken over the limit.

Below: Four-cross courses can incorporate jumps taken at great speed to try to gain an advantage over rivals.

Trials riding takes great skill and balance – riders can use their strong brakes and soft, grippy tyres to balance on their rear wheel and hop on to obstacles up to 1.5m (5ft) in the air.

Dirt-jump

One of the more underground areas in the sport is dirt-jump mountain biking. While other riders go off in search of obstacles, part of the process of dirt-jumping is building your own. This has

led to clashes between dirt-jumpers and landowners who have recently discovered that there is an unapproved dirt-jumping track on their land. Like freeriders, dirt-jumpers insist that their sport is not about competition but free expression. The aim is not to be the fastest, or the highest, or even to be able to perform the best tricks, but simply to execute a jump in a way that feels natural and expressive to the individual rider.

Great Mountain Bike Rides in Canada: North Shore and Whistler

North Shore, in British Columbia, is one of the world's major centres for mountain biking. Initially it was a well-kept local secret, based around Mount Seymour, Mount Fromme and Cypress Mountain. Whistler has hundreds of mountain bike trails.

The North Shore is endowed with challenging trails for singletrack riding, while Whistler has trails for every ability.

North Shore
Now regarded as the home of freeriding, North Shore, with its jumps, ramps and elevated trails offers some of

Below: British Columbia is a major area for cross-country mountain bikers.

British Columbia Bike Race

Stage	Start	Finish	Distance
One	Victoria	Cowichan Lake District	112km/70 miles
Two	Cowichan Lake District	Port Alberni	115km/72 miles
Three	Port Alberni	Comox Valley	83km/52 miles
Four	Comox Valley	Sechelt	60km/37 miles
Five	Sechelt	Gibsons	55km/34miles
Six	Squamish	Whistler	75km/47 miles
Seven	Whistler	Whistler	25km/16 miles

Above: Although there are well-marked trails, many riders choose their own.
Left: The North Shore area was where freeriding developed.

the best and most varied mountain biking in the world and it is legendary in the sport. There are many watercourses and forests with huge trees, and because there are creeks and fallen timber, narrow, high bridges have been built that are often used as launch ramps. The trails at Mount Fromme are easy to explore, although riders are expected to stick to a few rules regarding the trails, other users and the environment. Exploration is in keeping with local traditions – just arrive and see what happens.

Whistler
One of the biggest cross-country trail locations in the world, Whistler has hundreds of kilometres of trails, based at three locations in the area. One of the most famous rides in Canada is the seven-day British Columbia Bike Race, from Victoria to Whistler. Each day involves around 4 to 8 hours riding and a daily distance of 50–100km (31–62 miles). There are seven stages of the ride and the climbing can be exacting. Mud can make the route hazardous. If you have prepared and are in fair shape, you will have a good riding experience.

Right: The cross-country riding in British Columbia is challenging, but the views make the effort worth it.

Great Mountain Bike Rides in the USA: Moab, Utah

Moab, in the south-eastern corner of Utah, is one of the best places for mountain biking in the world, with mile upon mile of trail of every description. Every mountain biker should go there at least once.

The most famous trail in Moab is Slick Rock, a 15.5km (9.6-mile) loop of sandstone rock. While it gains its name from the difficulty of riding horses on the hard stone, for mountain bikers there are few better surfaces to ride on. The sandstone offers unbelievable traction. The original trail is marked out with white paint. The terrain is steep and hard, and set in a Moon-like landscape. While it is short compared to many off-road loops, the demanding technical nature of the course is such that it can take hours to complete.

What makes Slick Rock such a natural place for mountain bikers is that it couldn't have been better designed as a technical mountain bike course. The trail incorporates natural bowls, some with steep sides, which are ideal places to experiment with tricks, jumps, drop-offs and more extreme riding. There are none of the restrictions that define most trails – on a singletrack course you have no choice but to follow the path. On Slick Rock, going off-piste and improvising your own way down is part of the experience.

The other main off-road trail in Moab is the Porcupine Rim Trail, which is less famous than Slick Rock, but has a better reputation among Utah's mountain bike aficionados. It is a 33km (20.5-mile) trail that finishes in Moab and consists of extended stretches of broken rocky singletrack. It is known for the 915m (3,000ft), 18km (11-mile) descent from the top of the first climb all the way

Below: The arid sandstone area of Moab, Utah, is one of the biggest mountain biking challenges in the world.

down to the Colorado River. In Moab there are also dozens of short trails, long trails, hard trails and beginners' trails. One trail, farther from Moab, the White Rim, is based on a 160km (100-mile) loop in the Canyonlands National Park. This ride takes two or three days, and you need camping equipment.

Above left: Although this looks as if it would be extremely difficult, Moab sandstone has superb traction, making technical manoeuvres like this possible. Above: The trails in Moab are highly demanding and technical – riders often have to improvise their way out of difficult situations.

Below left: The desert around Moab is wide open, with plenty of opportunities for easier, less technical riding. Below: With the changing scenery and riding like this, it is no surprise that Moab is now considered to be one of the top worldwide mountain biking destinations.

Great Mountain Bike Rides in Europe

The mountain ranges of Europe are natural playgrounds for the off-road enthusiast. For cross-country and downhill riders, the French Alps and Pyrenees are among the most desirable destinations in the world for off-road riding.

Mountain biking has become a major summer sport in the Alps. Those in the tourism industry have realized that ski resorts can be used by mountain bikers during the summer, and in some areas have made great efforts to design attractive destinations for off-road riding.

Rides in France

In the French Alps, Morzine has become a Mecca for downhill riders with four of the best downhill tracks in the world within a few kilometres of the town. The Les Gets course is used for the World Cup event, while the Super Morzine is one of the longest downhill tracks in Europe. There are many trails for riders of all abilities, ranging from steep and difficult

Above: Morzine offers a huge variety of trails, ranging from easy to extremely challenging. The downhill tracks are among the best in the world.
Above right: The Alps in summer have become a major destination for cross-country mountain biking.

downhills at the top of mountains to easy cross-country trips.

Morzine is also a centre for cross-country riding, with popular local routes into the mountains. The Col de Cou is a steep climb which rises 400m (1,312ft) from bottom to top with a 1,000m

(3,280ft) descent to reward the effort of making the top. Morzine has more than 400km (250 miles) of bike-specific tracks for mountain bikers, but the most interesting proposition for experts is the 110km (68-mile) Portes de Soleil route.

Many of the cross-country rides can also incorporate chairlifts to take out some extended uphill grinds, although for some this is all part of the fun. And whether you pick an easy trail or a serious downhill run, there is fantastic scenery to enjoy.

As well as Morzine, Chamonix, in the shadow of Mont Blanc, has developed many mountain bike trails.

Rides in Spain

Spain has an advantage for mountain bikers, especially in the south, in its good all-year-round weather. The Sierra Nevada mountain range has some of the highest mountain biking in Europe, while the Alpujarras in Andalucía has been described as a cross-country paradise for aficionados.

The Pyrenees are following close behind the Alps as a destination for mountain bikers. The Valle de Tena is located in the western Pyrenees, right on the French border, with a good network of trails, and no restrictions on routing. The Val d'Aran has abundant cross-country trails, and you can create longer routes by including road links.

The Picos de Europa, which is based around Potes, is one of the world's best mountain bike destinations, with challenging trail rides and many long descents.

Top right: The terrain makes mountain biking in Spain a challenging experience. Right: Many European mountain biking centres have extensive singletrack trails. Below: Mountain biking in Europe benefits from clement weather all year.

Great Mountain Bike Rides in the UK

There are many fantastic rides in the UK; among the most notable are the trails in the South Downs, Wales and the innovative 7stanes in Scotland, which links seven mountain bike centres in the south of Scotland by a variety of trails.

Although spectacular mountain bike rides in the UK are numerous, a handful stand out. For a long ride, the South Downs Way is unbeatable. Wales is crisscrossed with trails and there are mountain bike centres to help along the route. Scotland, however, is acknowledged as having the most diverse and difficult rides.

South Downs Way

The first national trail in the UK to be designated a long-distance bridleway, the South Downs Way has become a challenge for mountain bikers. It starts in Winchester and follows the South Downs all the way to the coast at Eastbourne. The total length, from end to end, is 160km (100 miles), with 4,150m (13,600ft) of ascent and

descent. The highest point is Ditchling Beacon, at 248m (814ft) altitude. The ride is seen as a serious challenge not for the toughness of its terrain, but its distance. It has become a challenge to ride the entire length in a day, although most people tend to split it into two days.

Rides in Wales

Established as the main area for British mountain biking, Wales has hundreds of miles of purpose-built singletrack and trails shared between the biggest centres at Coed y Brenin forest and the Afan

Right: Empty moorland in Derbyshire is ideal for cross-country mountain biking. Below: This route on the South Downs Way can be tackled in one or two days.

Forest Park. Purpose-built mountain bike centres are a good way of enjoying the sport without the risk of cycling on private land or getting lost. Afan Forest has a network of trails, including the original 22km (13.6-mile) Penhydd trail, which is a suitable distance for ambitious novices and intermediate riders. For more experienced riders, trails such as the Skyline Trail, at 46km (28.5 miles) in length and with 2,000m (6,500ft) of vertical gain, are a substantial challenge.

Rides in Scotland

Mountain bikers in the UK find that Scotland has the most varied and challenging terrain. The low population and mountainous landscape are perfect for long rides and expeditions. Biking centres have sprung up over the last few years, such as the 7stanes network. Trails range from 400m (1,310ft) in length to the 58km (36-mile) Glentrool ride. Fort William has become popular since hosting the World Cup mountain biking events.

Above left: Even in a densely populated country like Britain, there are still some wide-open spaces to explore.
Left: The UK has some of the best and most extensive singletrack riding.

Above: Riders tackle a challenging cross-country mountain biking trail in Afan Forest in Wales.

Great Mountain Bike Rides: Multi-day Events Around the World

For the ultimate mountain biking challenge, many riders are signing up to multi-day events in the great mountain ranges. The TransAlp, TransRockies and Cape Epic Challenges give riders a chance to test themselves against the toughest terrain in the world.

For more experienced riders, multi-day events are increasingly popular. The TransAlp, the TransRockies and the Cape Epic, all with great climbs, are three of the most demanding.

The TransAlp Challenge

An eight-day challenge ride across the Alps, the TransAlp climbs a series of high passes in daily stages ranging between 50 and 100km (30–60 miles). It has run every year since 1998, starting in Mittenwald in Germany and finishing in Riva del Garda in Italy. The routes are a combination of off-road tracks, gravel paths and asphalted surfaces. Some days involve a height gain of over 3,000m (9,842ft). It is an extremely arduous race, one of the most difficult mountain bike events in the world. Riders have to be fit and follow an advanced training schedule to prepare. Such is the popularity of the TransAlp that more than 500 teams take part every year.

2008 Route TransAlp Challenge Ride				
Stage	Start	Finish	Distance	Altitude gain
1	Füssen	Imst	80km/50 miles	1,962m/6,437ft
2	Imst	Ischgl	76km/47 miles	3,171m/10,403ft
3	Ischgl	Scoul	75km/47 miles	2,547m/8,356ft
4	Scoul	Livigno	77km/48 miles	2,621m/8,599ft
5	Livigno	Naturns	122km/76 miles	2,909m/9,544ft
6	Naturns	Kaltern	97km/60 miles	3,930m/12,894ft
7	Kaltern	Andalo	74km/46 miles	3,071m/10,075ft
8	Andalo	Riv	miles	1,480m/4,856ft

2008 Route TransRockies Challenge Ride				
Stage	Start	Finish	Distance	Altitude gain
1	Panorama	K2 Ranch	52km/32 miles	2,478m/8,177ft
2	K2 Ranch	Nipika Resort	74km/46 miles	3,813m/12,582ft
3	Nipika Resort	Nipika Resort	44km/27 miles	1,514m/4,996ft
4	Nipika Resort	Whiteswan Lake	110km/68 miles	2,567m/8,471ft
5	Whiteswan Lake	Elkford	89km/55 miles	2,147m/7,085ft
6	Elkford	Crowsnest Pass	102km/63 miles	2,998m/9,893ft
7	Crowsnest Pass	Fernie	79km/49 miles	2,101m/6,933ft

The TransRockies Challenge

The success of the TransAlp Challenge led to its format being copied around the world, with the Canadian TransRockies Challenge starting up in 2002. The route is still developing, but it can be extremely punishing, and the weather can be variable. Like the TransAlp, the TransRockies is split into daily stages, covering 600km (372 miles) in seven days and climbing a total of 12,000m (39,000ft), a little below the TransAlp, but still a very hard challenge.

The short history of the TransRockies gives a perfect illustration of the unpredictable nature of this kind of event – in 2003 forest fires forced the

Left: Riders negotiate the TransAlp, one of the most difficult bike events.

Above: Mountain bikers tackle a scree trail in the Rocky Mountains.
Above right: The route of the Cape Epic is entirely off-road and goes along rugged tracks, through the beautiful scenery around the Cape.

organizers into a swift re-routing exercise at very short notice, while the 2004 event was hampered by heavy rain.

The Cape Epic Challenge
The first event in the South African Cape Epic Challenge, in 2004, attracted more than 500 riders for the 800km (500-mile) route, and within two years it had doubled in size to 1,000 riders and increased its length to 921km (572 miles). Every year it starts in Knysna Waterfront and finishes in Lourensford Wine Estate. The total climb for the eight-day 2007 event was 15,045m (49,360ft), comparable to the TransAlp.

Preparation
Taking part in multi-day events like the TransAlp, TransRockies and Cape Epic is not to be undertaken lightly, because 100km (62 miles) is a long way to ride off-road on a single day, let alone on

2008 Route Cape Epic Challenge Ride				
Stage	**Start**	**Finish**	**Distance**	**Altitude gain**
Prologue	Pezula	Pezula	17km/11 miles	310m/1,020ft
1	Knysna	Saarsveld	123km/76 miles	3,091m/10,141ft
2	Saarsveld	Calitzdorp	137km/85 miles	2,518m/8,261ft
3	Calitzdorp	Riversdale	133km/83 miles	2,340m/7,677ft
4	Riversdale	Swellendam	121km/75 miles	2,620m/8,596ft
5	Swellendam	Bredaarsdorp	146km/91 miles	1,819m/5,968ft
6	Bredaarsdorp	Hermanus	130km/81 miles	2,095m/6,873ft
7	Hermanus	Grabouw	91km/57 miles	1,985m/6,512ft
8	Grabouw	Lourensford	68km/42 miles	1,760m/5,774ft

several days. To get the most out of the experience, it is necessary to be honest and realistic about your own capacities, and to train hard over a long period to prepare for the event. Try following or adapting some of the training programmes in this book to prepare yourself, and take part in some shorter events to make sure that your body can take the longer distances and repeated efforts of a multi-day event.

Right: Many challenging mountain bike races go through spectacular, mountainous terrain, such as this one at Mount Hood, Oregon.

GETTING FIT

To get the most out of your cycling you need to put in some hard work. Entering a cyclo-sportive on the road or an enduro event off-road is easy to do. But getting yourself into the best possible condition, in order to do yourself justice in the event, takes planning and training. You need to train hard, but you also need to train smart, focusing on strengths and skills. A series of training schedules are suggested for you to adapt to your own needs. All the workouts can be done on or off-road – whatever's most convenient for you.

Above: Establishing a regular training routine is the key to getting fit.
Left: With a little hard work you will be fitter, more energetic, and have more fun.

Fuelling for Cyclists

In order to train effectively, and recover from the efforts you make in training, you need to eat correctly. Training hard takes energy, and before riding you need to ensure that you have consumed enough fuel to get you through.

What you want to avoid is a hunger crash – known in common cycling slang as the 'bonk'. Great name, terrible feeling. Make sure you eat enough before a ride, during it if necessary, and afterwards to allow your body to repair itself and to restore energy levels. However, there are some things that you should resist.

If you aim to lose weight, change your mindset and decide to reduce body fat. By cycling, you are building muscle, which is heavier than fat. Don't use the bathroom scales to assess how healthy you are – instead, monitor your body-fat levels and energy levels. You can buy body-fat monitors that will help you chart your progress. Energy levels are easier to monitor – simply judge whether you feel better or worse.

To lose body fat you need to expend more calories than you consume. But don't be tempted to speed up the process by skipping meals before or after riding. Aim for a more gradual loss of fat, so you can maintain your energy levels, continue cycling and get fitter and stronger.

Below: Drink regularly on training rides to avoid dehydration. You may want energy drinks, but you need water, too.

Quality nutrition
It is important to eat good quality food made from fresh ingredients. A natural diet is worth the effort – your energy levels will be higher, your immune system stronger, and your health will receive a boost. Ready meals, fast food and sugary drinks are loaded with fat, salt and refined sugar. Instead of these, eat plenty of fresh fruit and vegetables, lean meat, pulses, nuts, grains and dairy products. When training, it's important that your diet includes the right balance of the major food groups: carbohydrates (simple and complex), protein, 'healthy' fats, and vitamins and minerals.

Above: Refuelling on the go is an essential part of cycling training. Bananas are easy to carry and pack a lot of energy so are ideal for cyclists.

Carbohydrates
The bulk of your energy should be provided by carbohydrates. They break down into glycogen, which is stored in your muscles and liver before being converted to glucose to provide energy for your muscles. Your body stores enough glycogen for about one and a half hours, so if your training ride is longer, take high-carbohydrate food with you to maintain energy levels.

Far left: Carbohydrates such as bread and grains are needed for energy.
Left: Eating meat and fish regularly will provide protein to help your body recover from the effort of training.
Below far left: Dairy products also provide daily protein.
Below left: Eat as many fresh vegetables as possible to get essential vitamins.

There are two kinds of carbohydrates – simple and complex. Simple carbohydrates are found in foods such as fruit and refined sugar, and are quicker and easier for the body to absorb. However, they often give a 'rush' of energy that can be followed by an energy crash.

Complex carbohydrates are slower to be absorbed, and provide a steadier release of energy. They can be found in rice, pasta, potatoes and other starchy foods. If you are training hard and regularly, it is essential to eat plenty of carbohydrates.

Protein
Some energy is provided by protein, which is also really useful for cyclists in repairing damaged muscle fibres.

Proteins contain amino acids, which rebuild body tissue and help keep your immune system strong. Proteins are found in all meat, poultry, fish, eggs, cheese, nuts and pulses, and to a lesser extent in grains. It is essential for endurance athletes to consume a healthy level of protein, to help the muscles grow stronger over the course of a training programme. Chicken and fish are generally better than red meat in providing the necessary protein in your diet. Red meat has plenty of protein, but also has high levels of fat. Once in a while is fine; every day is not.

Fat
Although eating too much fat is unhealthy, you still need to include some in your diet. For long rides it is the main source of energy. There is also evidence that it may help in boosting your immune system. Be aware, however, that there are 'bad' fats and 'good' fats. Saturated fat and trans-fatty acids that occur in animal fats are 'bad' fats and should be avoided. Unsaturated fat is 'good' fat, and can be found in products such as olive and sunflower oil.

Vitamins and minerals
To run effectively, the body needs the help of vitamins and minerals. They are found mainly in fruit and vegetables. When you are exercising regularly, your body needs a good supply of vitamins and minerals, especially vitamins C (in citrus fruits and vegetables) and E (in cereals, seeds and nuts), which reduce damage done to your body and help it to recover. It is also important to keep iron levels up, as iron (in liver, watercress and red meat) enables the blood to carry oxygen efficiently. A balanced diet, with plenty of fresh fruit and vegetables, should provide enough in the way of vitamins and minerals. Getting these through food is the best way. During periods of intense exercise, or when you are tired, a multivitamin supplement can help boost your levels.

Water
Dehydration can occur after training sessions. Drink water through the day, especially during and after exercise.

Typical eating plan

Breakfast
Bowl of homemade muesli with dried apricots, a sliced banana and milk.
Toast with honey, jam or Marmite.
Freshly squeezed orange or grapefruit juice.
Coffee or tea.

Lunch
Salad of fresh vegetables and pulses – lettuce, tomatoes, bell peppers, cucumber, chickpeas, red cabbage, beansprouts.
Add lean meat or cheese.
Bread roll.

Dinner
Grilled chicken with lemon, garlic and olive oil.
Boiled potatoes or rice.
Steamed broccoli or other green vegetable.

Through the day
Drink plenty of water.
Take a vitamin supplement if you think your energy levels are low.
Snack on fruit or breakfast cereal.

Basic Training 1: Endurance

The biggest part of your cycling training will be working on your endurance potential. The more this is improved, the longer you will be able to keep going without getting tired. It needs dedication, but the results make it worthwhile.

Good endurance allows your body to adapt better when you start working on more specific fitness. If you think of your fitness for cycling as a pyramid, the bottom layers are all endurance. The bigger the base of the pyramid, the taller it can be built.

At a basic level, building endurance is simple. By riding your bike regularly, and increasing the distance and time of your rides, you will increase your endurance.

Endurance training workouts

Long steady distance training (LSD) is one of the most enjoyable parts of a cycling exercise programme. It does exactly what it says – an LSD ride involves riding for long periods at a pace you can maintain. How long, how

steady and how far an LSD ride needs to be depend on your own fitness and abilities, and what your aims are. If your long-term goal is to ride a 50km (31-mile) sportive event, it is not essential to train to ride a 100km (62-mile) event, but if you have the time and energy it won't do any harm, and you might be able to set a higher goal. Training rides of 50km will not build enough endurance if your goal is a 100km event.

As for terrain, you can choose hilly routes, flat routes or somewhere in between for your LSD rides.

Right: Regular training boosts fitness. Below: You will perform better in a sportive if your training was specifically targeted for that event.

Just maintain a constant intensity of effort, using between 70 and 75 per cent of your maximum heart rate. If your MHR is 200, riding with your heart rate at 140 to 150 beats per minute is the right level. If you are just starting out cycling, these rides should start at 30 minutes, but you can quickly build up to two hours. Experienced and fit cyclists can maintain this pace for several hours.

Recovery rides

These are similar to LSD rides, but shorter and less intense. After a hard day of training, your body needs to rest and recover and attempt to adapt to the stresses you have placed upon it.

Above: Endurance training should take place at a pace that you can hold for long distances.

A recovery ride will speed up your body's recovery from hard training and flush out waste products from your muscles. If you go out for an easy ride, at low intensity, and over a short distance, your body will be less stressed and will not start breaking down. It will boost your system and raise your metabolism without making you tired.

It's important not to be tempted to go too hard on a recovery ride, even if you feel that you can. Save yourself for when you are rested. Likewise, there's no need to go out for hours – an hour or less turning the pedals at a high but easy cadence in a low gear is the perfect recovery effort. Your pulse should be between 50 and 70 per cent of your MHR, depending on how tired you are. Err on the side of caution for these rides.

As your cycling training and fitness develops, you will learn to listen to what your body wants and decide whether to ride or not. Avoid too much climbing for your recovery rides – it is better to stay within a comfortable level of exertion. If

Left: During some training rides, shorter, more intense efforts will improve your fitness levels.

Working with your heart rate

Your heart rate is one of the most reliable and accessible ways of judging how much effort you are making. By using a pulse monitor, working out your maximum heart rate (MHR), and looking at what physical effort you can maintain at different percentages, you can make your training much more effective.

The traditional way of guessing one's MHR was to subtract one's age from 220, so a 30-year-old man should have an MHR of 190. However, the population varies so this rule is fairly inaccurate. By far the best way of finding out your MHR is to push yourself so hard that you cannot go any faster, then check the readout on a pulse monitor. You may be one or two beats out, but for all except elite athletes, this is an acceptable margin of error. The best way to find your MHR is to go out on a ride, find a hill, and sprint up it at a rate that is unsustainable. Sooner or later, the agony will force you to stop – when this happens, try to squeeze out 5 more seconds of energy. Then push a tiny bit more, and just as you feel like getting off your bike and lying where you fall, look at your pulse rate monitor. It should be showing your MHR.

Above: A heart-rate monitor measures the pulse in beats per minute during exercise.

you go hard enough to get tired, you will be too fatigued for your next workout to be effective.

If you have a recovery ride scheduled but are feeling very fatigued, it may be a better idea to take the day off. Put your feet up so your body can repair itself.

Basic Training 2: Speed

It is fun to be able to ride long distances at a steady pace. It's even more fun to be able to ride fast and vary the pace of your training rides. Riding fast, either sprinting or maintaining an above-average pace for a few kilometres, is what defines cycling as sport.

It is an amazing feeling to be able to accelerate under your own power, especially at the end of a ride. The fitness required to do this demands training and energy, but training like this gains momentum that carries on into your next workout. When you are training hard, and getting fitter and faster, the feeling of improving is a major motivator.

Being able to ride fast as well as steady will add a new dimension to your cycling. It will improve your energy levels and fitness. In a sportive event you will be able to chase a group so as to benefit from their shelter. It could make the difference between winning a gold award and a silver award.

You should embark on speed training once you have established a good base of cycling fitness through endurance rides. Experienced riders have the base fitness to start this type of training after a couple of months of endurance riding. If you are new to cycling, give it a little longer. Remember that fitness is like a pyramid. The bigger your base endurance the higher the peak. When embarking on these training sessions, always warm up thoroughly, and allow enough time for recovery at the end.

Sprints

During a normal LSD ride, put in two or more sprinting efforts. Look ahead for a street sign or tree on a flat road.

Right: Between efforts, pedal easily to recuperate and prepare for your next try. Below: Speed training will enable you to ride harder and longer, which helps in sportive events and racing.

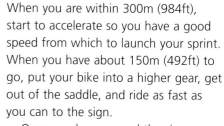

When you are within 300m (984ft), start to accelerate so you have a good speed from which to launch your sprint. When you have about 150m (492ft) to go, put your bike into a higher gear, get out of the saddle, and ride as fast as you can to the sign.

Once you have passed the sign, you can change down gears and settle back into your LSD pace, or a little below if you are having trouble recovering. You don't need to look at a pulse monitor for this exercise – your aim is to go as hard as possible for a short distance, to build speed and strength. Recover for as long as you need to feel relaxed and normal again – at least 10 minutes – then go for another sprint and repeat the procedure. Following this sprint, assess how you are feeling now. If you are tired, carry on at LSD pace for the rest of your ride. If you feel good, do another one, two or even three sprints in exactly the same way.

Left: The fitter you are, the better your performance in a sportive will be.
Above: Professional riders hone their fitness with plenty of speed sessions.
Left: Speed efforts should be at an intensity that is close to your maximum.

Spinning drills

Cycling takes strength, but it also helps if your legs are supple and flexible. The faster you can spin the pedals, the more supple your legs will become.

Once a week, go for a ride and aim to spin the pedals at 100 revolutions per minute or more throughout.

This is difficult to get used to, especially if you are new to cycling, but turning the pedals fast eases the pressure on your muscles.

Tempo riding

Riding faster for long periods of time is called 'tempo riding'. This is an essential part of building fitness for riding enduros as well as competing in sportive events.

Tempo sessions involve riding at a steady pace that will eventually tire you out. At the end of an LSD session, it is good to feel that you could go on farther, but a tempo session should be designed to push you harder.

For your first session, warm up for 30 minutes, then ride for 15 minutes at 75 to 80 per cent of your MHR. This is fast enough to induce discomfort, but at a level that you can hold for the length of the set – in this case for about 15 minutes.

Steadily increase the time you spend at tempo pace in subsequent workouts until you can ride like this for an hour.

Jumps

These are similar to sprint workouts. The efforts are shorter, but involve more repetitions. During an LSD ride, on a slight incline or along the flat, change up into a big gear, accelerate and ride 15 pedal revolutions as hard as you can. Recover for 2 minutes, then go again, four more times. Continue, at a steady pace, for 10 minutes, then repeat the above, with five repetitions. If you feel good after this, do one more set of five jumps.

Fartlek training

Speedplay, or fartlek in Swedish, is a less structured way of adding sprints, jumps and varying tempos to your training.

During a fartlek ride, simply ride hard, steady, all-out or slowly according to the way you feel, and on a variety of terrain. When you reach a hill, sprint over the top. On a long flat section, look for a sign and sprint for it. Then ease off for 5 minutes before riding the next 3km (1.8 miles) at a fast pace. Or do whatever you feel like doing.

Fartlek is good training for the unpredictable way sportives and enduro events can evolve. By incorporating fartlek sessions into your training routine you can get used to changes in pace. If you have been following a strict plan for a few weeks, a varied fartlek session can be motivational.

Basic Training 3: Climbing

Riding fast uphill on a bike is a very specialized kind of physical exertion. It is probably the most painful aspect of cycling for sport, but if you do the appropriate training, it correspondingly offers the greatest sense of achievement.

There is really only one way of improving in the hills: you have to ride a lot of hills. Training for hill riding is hard work, but will have a big effect on your ability to tackle them in an event. Not many people enjoy hill training, but if you can motivate yourself to work hard on your climbing, you will be at a comparative advantage. You will also benefit the rest of your cycling – strenuous training in the hills strengthens your legs and body, and works your cardiovascular system hard. A cyclist who regularly trains hard in the hills is a cyclist whose fitness will increase dramatically.

After you have done a few weeks of the speed workouts, you will be ready to start working on your climbing training. You need to have worked on endurance building to get benefit from these sessions.

Right: When going uphill, climb out of the saddle now and then to stretch you legs and alter your position.

Hilly tempo ride

Design your training route to take in as many hills as possible – repeating some climbs if necessary. Try to avoid long flat sections. Variety of hills is a good thing – if possible, incorporate some short, steep ascents, long steady climbs, and

Above: It is the hills that can test your fitness to the limits.

everything in between. This workout is unstructured along the same lines as a fartlek speed session – just go hard when you reach a climb. Try to spend

most of your time sitting in the saddle and riding in a controlled way. Don't burn yourself out by going too hard, especially at the bottom of the climbs, but ride at 80 per cent of your MHR when you ride uphill. Once you have completed two or three sessions you can start to incorporate short bursts of faster climbing halfway up a hill, or really sprinting for the top. These efforts will take you over 80 per cent of your MHR, but you will start to develop the ability to recover from these efforts and settle back into your tempo pace. Above all, this workout should be fun and free. You can reward yourself for the efforts you put in on the climbs with descending practice on the other side.

Above: Practise climbing with riders of a similar ability so that you do not overreach yourself.

Above: There is no substitute for hard effort in the hills during training to boost fitness and strength.

Above: Keep a steady effort over the course of a hill, rather than sprinting.

Short steep hill repetitions

Find a hill that has a gradient of about 8 per cent. Warm up, then ride up at a fast pace, about 80–85 per cent of your MHR, for three minutes. Ride in the saddle until you start to feel fatigued, then stand up on the pedals to maintain your pace. When the time is up, stop and turn around, or continue at a very slow pace so you recover completely before the next climb. Repeat this effort. If you are very tired, warm down and ride home. Otherwise, you can do up to four repetitions.

Long steady climbs

Find a climb that is up to 3km (1.8 miles) in length and is no steeper than 6 per cent. Once you have warmed up, ride at 80 per cent of your MHR, staying in a seated position, for 6 minutes. Practise breathing steadily, relaxing the shoulders and arms, and focus on turning your legs at 80–90 revolutions per minute. Recover completely, then do three or four repetitions depending on how tired you feel.

Hill sprints

Find a short, steep climb that takes a minute to get up at speed. Build up momentum into the climb, then try and maintain your speed all the way to the top. The final 100m (330ft) will be very hard, but sprint out of the saddle until you have crested the climb. Recover completely and repeat two more times.

Mountain climbs

If you live in a mountainous area, find a long climb – 5km (3.1 miles) or more, with a 5 to 7 per cent gradient. Spin up in a low gear, staying seated, at 75–80 per cent of your MHR. The aim is to build resistance to fatigue and practise riding the types of climb you will encounter in a hard sportive event.

Below: Climbing the steepest hills is tough, but with determination you will be able to make it to the top.

Weight Training for Cyclists

Cycling is the best training for cycling. If you are planning on entering an enduro, a sportive or a race, there is no substitute for miles on your bike. However, it is a good idea to complement your cycling with other forms of training if you have the time for it.

Weight training is a good method to give yourself all-round body strength, but cyclists should not do too much of this kind of exercise. The more bulk you build through weight training, the heavier you will become, which means more body weight to carry up hills. Don't overdo it.

For the best results in terms of strength, you should focus on three different sets of exercises when you are weight training to improve your performance as a cyclist. These are: leg exercises, which will enable you to ride more strongly; upper body exercises, because the arms have to work quite hard to support the body on the bike; and core exercises, to strengthen the abdominal

muscles and the back and which will provide a strong 'anchor' for the legs to work against.

When weight training, always start out under the guidance of a qualified instructor and take his or her advice to devise a programme of training. Start off with three sets of 12 repetitions of each exercise, using a weight that is half of the maximum you can manage. Increase weights gradually, and move up to three sets of 15 repetitions.

Always warm up thoroughly. Either cycle to the gym or try cycling on a stationary bike for at least 15 minutes. After a weight training session, do a series of stretches, and warm down, either on a stationary bike, or by cycling home.

Leg strength exercises

Strengthens: Hamstrings

Hamstring curl
Put your feet between the pads. Pull up, bend the leg until the calf muscle almost touches the back of the thigh. Release.

Leg extension

Strengthens: Quadriceps

Prepare by hooking your feet under the machine, holding on to the handles and bracing against the back. With toes pointing slightly outward, extend your lower leg until your leg is straight, then let the weight down again.

Squat

Strengthens: Quadriceps

Face forward with feet 15cm (6in) apart. Squat until your thighs are parallel with the ground. Keep your back straight. Stand up slowly, keeping your back straight. Don't lock out the knees and don't let the knees bend outward.

Leg press

Strengthens: Quadriceps

Sit with your feet 15cm (6in) apart on the plate. Push up until your legs are straight. Let the weight down until your knees are bent at about 90 degrees. Push up again. Keep the knees working in a straight line parallel with your feet.

Heel raise

Strengthens: Calf muscles

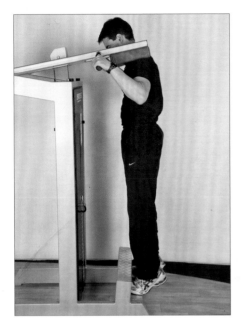

Stand with your toes on a step, with a weight across your shoulders, feet 15cm (6in) apart. Rise up until you are on tiptoes, then lower yourself down.

Crunch

Strengthens: Abdominal muscles

Lie flat on the ground with knees bent at 90 degrees. With your hands behind your head, slowly lift your shoulders off the floor. Lower the head back to the floor.

Back extension

Strengthens: Lower back

Lie on your front with the upper body hanging down. Brace feet against the supports. Slowly raise the upper body until almost straight. Lower back down.

Lat pulldown

Strengthens: Latissimus dorsi

Brace your legs under the support, reach up with straight arms and hold the bar with hands shoulder-width apart. Pull the bar down until it touches your chest. Let it back up slowly. Keep a straight back for the exercise.

Bench press

Strengthens: Pectorals, shoulders

Hold the weight and raise it with your hands above your shoulders, then push up until your arms are straightened, but don't lock them out completely. Carefully lower the weight until the bar just touches your chest.

Seated row

Strengthens: Shoulders, upper arms

Sit on a mat on the floor, with a straight back, feet braced against the footrests with knees slightly bent. Pull the bar toward the lower chest with the upper body still, until your hands touch your chest. Release slowly.

Stretches for Cyclists 1

Stretching helps loosen muscles and prevents the risk of sudden injury from working them too hard too quickly. To avoid injury and to gain the most from your workouts, you need to warm up and warm down properly.

Tight muscles can reduce power, co-ordination and endurance, all qualities that are necessary for cyclists.

To compensate for this, it is necessary to follow a regular routine of stretching, which will increase flexibility. Being more flexible will aid your recovery from workouts, and give you good posture and confidence to go with your increased energy levels and fitness.

With stretching, little and often is better than a long session once a week. By spending just 15 minutes after each training session stretching your muscles, you can make a big difference in your body's flexibility.

When performing the stretches on the next few pages, stretch until you feel the muscle tightening, relax your breathing, and hold the position for 15 seconds. Then release slowly. Don't bounce, or move too fast. Instead, gradually employ your muscles' full range of movement, and stay relaxed. Don't tense up any other muscles and don't hold your breath.

You should also be aware that stretching is not always a good idea. Never stretch when your muscles are 'cold', and listen to your body's reaction to stretching. If you feel sudden pain, stop the stretch and ensure that you have not injured yourself. Cyclists need to pay particular attention to the hamstrings and lower back. Tightness in one of these areas can lead to tightness or injury in the other. The hamstrings are not fully extended when cycling, and the repetitive nature of the cycling motion will eventually lead to your hamstrings becoming much less supple.

Stretch after your rides, but also after weight-training sessions, and any other exercises. For a little time and effort, you can gain flexibility, and prevent injury. Proper preparation is vital for anyone wanting to get fit. Going straight into

a hard workout without warming up puts you at risk of injury and you will not be able to perform so well during your training session. If you finish your workout without warming down, your legs will be stiffer afterward and probably also the next day – if you have a workout planned for that day, it will not be as effective, because your muscles will be too tired to work properly.

A typical training session	
Minutes	**Activity**
15	Warm up on the bike
50	LSD ride including 30-minute tempo riding session
15	Warm down on the bike
10	Stretch
Total:	90 minutes

Warming up

To warm up, simply ride slowly, steadily increasing your workload until you can feel yourself breathing a bit more heavily. Once you get to this level, which should take about 5 minutes, maintain the same effort for another 10 minutes. Concentrate, focus and relax, especially if you have a difficult workout coming up. While your body warms itself up, your mind should be preparing itself for the workout. Warming up gets the metabolism fired up and ready to deal with the bigger effort that is going to follow. Your body temperature will rise, your heart will start to send more blood around your body and this will prepare your system for your training session.

Winding down

Once you have finished your workout, you need to put the same principle into reverse. Simply wind down by riding the last 15 minutes of your ride in a low gear, spinning your legs out at an easy

speed. This allows your body to flush out some of the waste products that build up in your muscles during hard exercise. A short warm-down after every ride will reduce any leg stiffness you may have.

The advantage of cycling is that you can do your warming up and warming down on the bike – just build in about 15 minutes' worth of riding distance on to the front and back end of your ride, and the job is done.

Stretch after exercise

The best time to stretch is while your body is still warm after your workout. If this is impractical, stretch in the evening, after taking a warm shower or bath. Do as many of the stretches illustrated here as possible, paying particular attention to your legs and the lower back. If you feel you are especially inflexible or want to develop your stretching routine, speak to a physiotherapist, who will be able to advise you on specific exercises for parts of the body.

Above: Weight training and stretching will help to improve your performance on the bike by making you stronger and more flexible.

Head stretch

Stretches: Neck

Tilt head sideways to the left then the right then forward to stretch the back of the neck. Hold 5 seconds. Then tilt the head backward. Hold for 5 seconds.

Quad pull-up

Stretches: Quadriceps

Stand on one leg, and bend the other leg up behind you. Grasp the foot and pull up until you can feel the quadriceps stretching. Stretch out the other arm for balance. To increase the stretch, pull the foot up higher. Repeat with the other leg.

Gluteal stretch

Stretches: Gluteus maximus

Stand on one leg, bend it slightly, then rest your other ankle on the thigh. Bend forward until you feel the stretch in the buttock of the leg you are standing on.

Side lunge

Stretches: Inner thigh

Place feet wide apart, bend one knee so your weight goes down on it. Lower your bottom as far as you can toward the floor with your arms out straight and hands clasped for balance. Keep other leg straight. Repeat on other side.

Lateral leg stretch

Stretches: Long adductors, inner thigh

Place the feet wide apart and lean forward so your body weight rests on your hands. Widen your stance. Rotate hips inward to stretch each leg in turn.

Touching toes

Stretches: Hamstrings

With feet slightly apart and legs straight, raise arms above your head, stretch so the back lengthens, then bend down as far as you can toward your toes. Don't bend the knees. Hold for 15 seconds, breathing steadily, then stand upright.

Stretches for Cyclists 2

Specific stretches will help to improve your flexibility when you are cycling. Because the range of movement on a bike is limited – your legs don't fully extend through the pedal stroke – the muscles become stronger but tighter. These lunges and stretches aim to stretch all of the body.

Forward lunges

Stretches: Hip flexor

Put one leg in front, the other behind, and bend your front knee, keeping your back straight. Lower yourself until the knee of your back leg touches the floor.

Follow the exercise on the left: one leg in front with knee bent, and touching the floor with the other knee. For extra stretch, raise your hands as far as you can above your head.

Abdominal stretch

Stretches: Abdominal muscles

Lie on a mat on the floor, on your front with your knees, toes and chest touching the floor, and hands beside your chin.

Push up with your arms and bend the back, stretching the abdominal muscles. Keep your head level, facing forward.

Ankle rotation

Stretches: Calf muscles, shins

Place hands on the hips for balance. Lift left foot off the ground. Keep the other leg straight and still and rotate the left foot widely around the ankle. Change to the other side and repeat the exercise.

Shoulder stretch

Stretches: Posterior shoulder

Bring one arm across your chest, just below the horizontal level. Hook the other arm around so your straight arm rests in the crook of the elbow. Use your bent arm to pull the other arm towards the body. Repeat on the other side.

Calf stretch

Stretches: Calf muscles

Lean with your hands against a wall with one leg stretched out behind you and the other supporting you. Push down with the heel of your straight leg, and use your arms to get closer to the wall.

Bicep stretch

Stretches: Biceps

Stretch your arm out as straight as you can behind you at shoulder height. Place your hand on a wall. Rotate your hand anticlockwise. You will feel a stretch in your biceps. Repeat the exercise using the other arm and hand.

Lat stretch

Stretches: Latissimus dorsi

With hands shoulder width apart, hold a horizontal bar above your head. Let your weight suspend from the arms, to stretch the upper back and shoulders. Rest and repeat but don't overdo it.

Wrist stretch

Stretches: Forearms

Have arms straight in front of you, the palms facing outwards and the backs of the hands facing each other. Put the right hand over the left, so the palms meet, and clasp fingers. Pull hands under and towards you. Swap hands.

Cross-training for Cyclists

For racing cyclists, training on the bike and following a regime of weight training leave little time for other sports. However, taking part in other sports can help improve your overall fitness, flexibility and co-ordination.

For the keen leisure cyclist, sportive and enduro rider, playing other sports can help to improve cycling fitness and all-round fitness. Some sports can even be linked with cycling. Triathlons, which combine swimming, cycling and running, and duathlons, which involve both running and cycling, are currently enjoying a boom.

Both swimming and running are endurance sports, which means that training in these two sports will increase non-specific cardiovascular fitness, with possible benefits for cycling. These two activities also use muscle groups that cycling under-uses, which leads to greater all-round fitness and helps prevent injury.

Other sports are also good for cycling. Any team sport that involves running will boost fitness and all-round flexibility. Ball games are good for hand–eye co-ordination and balance, which will contribute to developing better bike-handling skills.

Above: Running regularly boosts endurance and offers an alternative to bike training when riding is impractical. Left: Racket sports like badminton and tennis help co-ordination and flexibility.

Swimming and running

If you have been cycling for a long time, the first thing you need to be aware of is that years of not doing any running-based sports will leave you susceptible to muscle strains, injuries and stiff legs. Before embarking on other sports, start increasing the amount of time you spend stretching.

The easiest sports for cyclists to relate to are swimming and running, which involve similar training regimes. Running uses a different set of muscles from cycling, so the important thing is to build up slowly. Buy a good pair of training shoes for running in, and for your first run, go out for a 20-minute session. Spend the first 5 minutes walking fast, then jog slowly for 10 minutes. Finally, walk for the last 5 minutes. Remember to stretch, emphasizing the legs.

The next day, go for an easy bike ride, at LSD tempo at the most. This will help your legs to recover. You may experience stiffness, especially if you ran too fast, so spin the stiffness out with some familiar cycling movement. Stretch.

Build up your running until you reach a point where you can go for a 45-minute run with no after-effects. Then you can include a couple of runs a week in your cycling training. The advantage of running is that it is much more labour-intensive than cycling – you can get the same amount of exercise in a 30-minute run as you can in 1 hour of cycling. If you are busy, running is a good way to maintain fitness for cycling.

Sports for cyclists				
Sport	Endurance	Flexibility	Co-ordination	Agility
Badminton	-	X	X	X
Cricket	-	-	X	-
Football	-	-	X	X
Martial arts	-	X	X	X
Mountaineering	X	-	-	-
Rock climbing	-	X	X	X
Rugby	-	-	X	-
Running	X	-	-	X
Swimming	X	X	-	-
Taiko drumming	-	X	X	-
Tennis	-	-	X	X
Triathlon	X	X	-	-
Ultimate Frisbee	-	X	X	X

Swimming is initially difficult for cyclists because it makes much more use of the upper body, whereas cycling emphasizes the legs. Swimming workouts also strengthen the core muscles, which will contribute to a stronger cycling style. Training for swimming also trains the mind to be more conscious of exercise economy. The more economical a cyclist is, and the more efficient his or her style, the faster they will go for the same effort. With swimming, brute strength and high fitness levels count for much less than

technique and skill. By working on the correct technique, a swimmer uses his or her fitness to maximum advantage. By applying lessons like this to cycling, you can improve cycling efficiency.

Other sports

Ball sports such as football and racket sports like tennis are also good for cyclists, offering a full physical workout. Co-ordination and agility from catching or aiming at a fast-moving object results in better reflexes and balance, and helps with bike handling and manoeuvring.

Top: Rock climbing improves balance, co-ordination and overall body strength. Above: Swimming helps to increase upper body strength and endurance.

The most important aspect of cross-training may not be the physical benefits of extra co-ordination, flexibility and endurance, but mental benefits. The training for cycling can be very serious, especially for difficult workouts. Cross-training lets cyclists enjoy sport without the pressure of performing. This can have a positive effect on mental attitude.

Keeping a Training Diary

It is important for cyclists to have long-term goals. Riding week-in, week-out can be lots of fun, but building up towards a goal is a way of getting more satisfaction and a sense of achievement out of the sport.

If you decide what you want to achieve and build up to, it is a good idea to keep a training diary. This allows you to record your progress, and to plan your workouts around your goal.

If your goal is to finish a 170km (105-mile) mountainous sportive in four months' time, and you can currently ride 100km (62 miles) before fatigue sets in, plan to increase your longest ride distance on a weekly basis until the final run-up to your event. Write your plan into your training diary, and then, as each day passes, you can write in the actual workout you did on each day. You will have a record of whether or not you are on track.

Below: Once you have a goal in mind, you can plan your training accordingly, never losing sight of the end point.

Above: All serious racing cyclists keep a training diary, to plan workouts, and to get to know their reaction to training schedules.

What to put in your training diary
Use the sample training diary opposite as a schedule for a week's training. Fill in the gaps each day. If you wish, add your own supplementary pages and end up with a record of your training activities.

At the front of the diary, insert a printout of the current year, with months across the top and days down the side. Next, write in your main goal or goals for the year. This will give you an idea of how long you have until you need to be at peak fitness, and also a good idea of how your training is going. As you cross off the days, you can compare how you are progressing with how long you have to go.

Next, print out sheets of paper similar to the diary pictured here. Each page covers one week, with space for scheduled workouts, actual workouts and all other information that you need. At the start of each week list your aims, either short- or long-term, for that week. They could include at least one long ride, two hill sessions, a fartlek session, or whatever you have planned. Your initial goal could be to ride in a build-up event for your main goal.

Take your pulse

Each day, on waking, check and write in your weight and resting pulse rate. These are good indications of your condition. A high pulse rate could indicate that you are fatigued or feeling stressed. Significant weight loss could mean that you have been training hard and need to back off for a couple of days. Once you have been up for an hour or so, give yourself a mark out of 10 for your energy level. Are you raring to go and bouncing around the house, or are you feeling flat and listless?

This score is a subjective mark, but seeing how you react physically to your training is important for gauging how hard you need to make it for further sessions. If you have two very hard weeks of training, and then take two days off, an easy day the next day and then feel 10 out of 10 on the fourth, that's a good indicator that your training has paid off. It also shows that after a hard series of workouts you feel recovered and strong by the fourth day – this information might help with peaking for your goal.

Plan ahead

For each day, write in your scheduled workout – this can be done well in advance, but it is best to leave it until you have at least started that week, so your planning can be as accurate as possible. Then, as each day passes, enter what you actually achieved. Perhaps you planned a 2-hour workout, but had to stay late at the office and only had time for an hour. Don't berate yourself for missing the training, just keep a record of what happened and see if you can compensate another day.

Lastly, at the end of the week fill in a summary of the total number of hours' training, the distance covered, your weight (including any gain or loss) and body fat percentage, if you have the means to measure it.

Over the long-term, by keeping a record of your training, you can chart your progress, and work out what training strategy will work best for you. The information gained also helps you to plan your training into the future.

Sample training diary

Date:

Aims for the week:

1 One long ride
2 Four rides total
3 Stretch every day

Thursday
Weight:
Resting pulse:
Energy level:
Scheduled workout:
Actual workout:
Distance:
Time:
Intensity:

Monday
Weight:
Resting pulse:
Energy level:
Scheduled workout:
Actual workout:
Distance:
Time:
Intensity:

Friday
Weight:
Resting pulse:
Energy level:
Scheduled workout:
Actual workout:
Distance:
Time:
Intensity:

Tuesday
Weight:
Resting pulse:
Energy level:
Scheduled workout:
Actual workout:
Distance:
Time:
Intensity:

Saturday
Weight:
Resting pulse:
Energy level:
Scheduled workout:
Actual workout:
Distance:
Time:
Intensity:

Wednesday
Weight:
Resting pulse:
Energy level:
Scheduled workout:
Actual workout:
Distance:
Time:

Sunday
Weight:
Resting pulse:
Energy level:
Scheduled workout:
Actual workout:
Distance:
Time:
Intensity:

Summary
Hours trained:
Kilometres ridden:
Weight:
Body fat percentage:

Left: It is easier to assess your fitness day by day and month by month when you fill in a training diary.

Four-week Training Schedule

All improvement through training comes from long-term planning and increasing the intensity and length of exercise. Otherwise, it is easy to just follow the same schedule week-in, week-out, which will lead to stagnation.

Racing cyclists follow the principle described earlier that fitness is like a pyramid. There is a long period of base building. Then more intense work is added before building up to a high peak of fitness. This system is known as periodization. Once your base training is done, by adding more difficult workouts, there will be a constant improvement as time goes on.

Here is a sample four-week training programme for a cyclist who has been riding for a while, but without doing specific workouts. There is a saying that you need to be fit enough to start training. It is assumed that you have been riding your bike regularly

for four to six months. If you have not, spend a little more time just working on base fitness and riding hours. Once your training schedule is about to start, write in your planned workouts in the first week of your training diary.

Week one
This first week is based entirely around long steady distance riding. The aim is to build base fitness, so week one is centred entirely around long steady distance riding (LSD). By trying too hard to go fast when you are sprinting or fast hill riding, one of two things can happen. Either you will tire yourself out and end up missing sessions, or your

Above: A recovery ride in pleasant scenery makes a change from training. Below: Long steady distance (LSD) riding is the foundation for most cycling training schedules. Long rides improve fitness and endurance.

Week one
MONDAY Rest following long ride on Sunday
TUESDAY LSD ride 1:30
WEDNESDAY Recovery ride 0:30
THURSDAY LSD ride 1:00
FRIDAY LSD ride 1:00
SATURDAY Recovery ride
SUNDAY LSD ride 2:00
TOTAL HOURS: 6:00

Week two
MONDAY Rest
TUESDAY LSD ride 1:30, including 30 minutes of spinning drills
WEDNESDAY Recovery ride 0:30
THURSDAY LSD ride 1:00
FRIDAY LSD ride 1:00, including one set of jumps
SATURDAY Rest or recovery ride
SUNDAY LSD ride 2:30
TOTAL HOURS: 6:30

Week three
MONDAY Rest
TUESDAY LSD ride 1:30, including 30 minutes of spinning drills
WEDNESDAY Recovery ride 0:30
THURSDAY LSD ride 1:30, including two sets of jumps
FRIDAY LSD ride 1:00
SATURDAY Recovery ride 0:30
SUNDAY LSD ride 2:30
TOTAL HOURS: 7:30

Week four
MONDAY Rest
TUESDAY LSD ride 1:00, including 30 minutes of spinning
WEDNESDAY Recovery ride 0:30
THURSDAY LSD ride 1:00
FRIDAY Recovery ride 0:30
SATURDAY Recovery ride 0:30
SUNDAY LSD ride 2:30
TOTAL HOURS: 6:00

fitness will initially improve, only to gradually stagnate owing to lack of a decent base.

Monday is a rest day – it usually comes after the hardest session of the week on Sunday. It is a good time to recuperate and get used to the fact the week has started. If you really feel like it, a 30-minute recovery spin would be a good opportunity to get some relaxing riding in. On Tuesday, go for an LSD ride of 1½ hours. You will be nice and fresh having taken Monday off. Wednesday is a recovery ride, then you have two days in a row of LSD training. If you wake up feeling tired on Friday, cut the session back to a recovery ride. If you are feeling great, feel free to add on 30 minutes. All through your training week you should be flexible and listen to your body. Saturday is a recovery ride, then on Sunday, the longest ride of the week – 2 hours of long steady distance.

Week two
Depending on how you reacted to week one, week two adds half an hour and incorporates some basic speed sessions, as much for the variety as for the fitness benefits. If you are tired after week one, repeat it for another one or two weeks – you need to build a solid base and progress at a realistic pace.

Monday is a rest after Sunday's long ride. On Tuesday, go for a ride of 1½ hours, and spend 30 minutes of it spinning a low gear very fast. This will build fitness and suppleness.

Wednesday is a recovery ride, and Thursday is a LSD ride. On Friday, go out for 1 hour, but test your legs out with a set of jumps. Saturday is a rest day or a recovery ride, while Sunday's distance is increased by 30 minutes.

Week three
Monday is a rest day following Sunday's long ride. Tuesday is the same as last week – a ride of 1½ hours, with 30 minutes of spinning. On Wednesday, go for a short recovery ride, followed on Thursday by a steady ride incorporating more jumps. The legs should be starting to get used to the extra effort. On Friday, if you are still feeling OK, you can do 1 hour, although you should cut this short if you are feeling tired. Saturday is a recovery ride, and then the longest ride on Sunday – 2½ hours.

Week four
During a training schedule, try to plan three weeks of improvement, then use the fourth as a consolidation week. The workouts are a bit easier, but they allow your body to rest and rebuild itself much stronger, in preparation for a new cycle

to begin the following week. Week four is similar to the other weeks in terms of ride length, though it will be beneficial to keep the spinning drills in on Tuesday. On Sunday, you'll be raring to go, so put in another long ride.

Above: Riding for around 1½ hours will build suppleness and fitness.

Eight-week Training Schedule: Intermediate

If you have successfully completed the four-week schedule you may feel ready to move on to the next stage of training. The important thing is not to move on unless you are absolutely certain you can cope and you will begin to make progress.

Once you have finished a basic four-week training schedule, assess how you feel. If you are very tired, repeat the schedule. Your body needs time to build a base, and it is more important to do that than to rush on ahead and risk overtraining. Even experienced cyclists may want to err on the side of caution and make sure that their groundwork is solid. If you feel you have improved and are ready for the next step, move on to this intermediate schedule. The emphasis will still be on a firm foundation, but with more variety, to start building upward.

Week one
Monday is a rest day following Sunday's long ride. On Tuesday start working on suppleness, but with a longer period of

Above: Professional cyclists generally follow a well-tried training schedule that has been worked out over years of experimentation and experience.

spinning. On Wednesday, ride for 1 hour at a steady pace. On Thursday, the ride is 1 hour, with three or four full-on sprints. Assess how you are feeling: if you are very tired after the third sprint, don't do a fourth. Friday's ride is a recovery ride, followed by a 1-hour steady ride on Saturday, then 3 hours at a steady pace on Sunday.

Week two
It's quite a big jump this week, with the introduction of the first fartlek session, although the total hours are similar to week one. Monday is a rest after Sunday's long ride. On Tuesday, ride a

Left: When you start the eight-week training schedule, the three-hour ride on Sunday can be very hard.

1-hour fartlek session, sprinting for signs, increasing the pace when you feel good and backing off when you are tired. Don't get carried away – some of the ride should be hard, but some of it should be at a steadier pace. On Wednesday and Thursday, steady rides will continue to build a solid foundation, with more sprints on Thursday. Friday is a recovery ride; Saturday and Sunday are steady rides, a longer one on Sunday.

Week three
The schedule is similar to week two, with a longer ride on Saturday.

Week four
After three weeks of improvement and hard work, ease off and use the fourth week to consolidate your gains. Monday

Week one
MONDAY Rest
TUESDAY LSD ride 1:00, including 30-45 minutes of spinning drills
WEDNESDAY LSD ride 1:00
THURSDAY LSD ride 1:00, including sprints
FRIDAY Recovery ride 0:30
SATURDAY LSD ride 1:00
SUNDAY LSD ride 3:00
TOTAL HOURS: 7:30

Week two
MONDAY Rest
TUESDAY Fartlek ride 1:00
WEDNESDAY LSD ride 1:00
THURSDAY LSD ride 1:00, including sprints
FRIDAY Recovery ride 0:30
SATURDAY LSD ride 1:00
SUNDAY LSD ride 3:00
TOTAL HOURS: 7:30

Week three
MONDAY Rest
TUESDAY Fartlek ride 1:00
WEDNESDAY LSD ride 1:00
THURSDAY LSD ride 1:00, including sprints
FRIDAY Recovery ride 0:30
SATURDAY LSD ride 1:30
SUNDAY LSD ride 3:00
TOTAL HOURS: 8:00

Week four
MONDAY Rest
TUESDAY LSD ride 1:00, including spinning drills
WEDNESDAY LSD ride 1:00
THURSDAY Rest
FRIDAY LSD ride 1:00
SATURDAY Recovery ride 0:30
SUNDAY LSD ride 3:00
TOTAL HOURS: 6:30

Week five
MONDAY Rest
TUESDAY Fartlek ride 1:00
WEDNESDAY LSD ride 1:30
THURSDAY LSD ride 1:00, including sprints
FRIDAY LSD ride 1:00, including 20 minutes tempo
SATURDAY Recovery ride 0:30
SUNDAY LSD ride 3:00
TOTAL HOURS: 8:00

Week six
MONDAY Rest
TUESDAY Fartlek ride 1:00
WEDNESDAY LSD ride 1:30
THURSDAY LSD ride 1:00, including sprints
FRIDAY LSD ride 1:30, including 30 minutes tempo
SATURDAY Recovery ride 0:30
SUNDAY LSD ride 3:00
TOTAL HOURS: 8:30

Week seven
MONDAY Rest
TUESDAY Fartlek ride 1:00
WEDNESDAY LSD ride 1:30
THURSDAY LSD ride 1:00, including sprints
FRIDAY LSD ride 1:30, including 30 minutes of tempo
SATURDAY Recovery ride 0:30
SUNDAY LSD ride 3:30+
TOTAL HOURS: 9:00

Week eight
MONDAY Rest
TUESDAY LSD ride 1:00, including spinning drills
WEDNESDAY LSD ride 1:00
THURSDAY Rest
FRIDAY LSD ride 1:00, including spinning drills
SATURDAY Recovery ride 0:30
SUNDAY LSD ride 3:00
TOTAL HOURS: 6:30

is a rest day, then you have two short, steady days, one with spinning drills, but no extra efforts. Thursday is a day off, then there's another steady day on Friday. After another recovery ride on Saturday, you can go for a nice long ride on Sunday, by which time you'll be ready to start working even harder.

Week five
The main improvement this week will come from the incorporation of tempo riding during Friday's ride. Sunday is a long ride, at 3 hours.

Week six
Similar to last week, but Friday's tempo session rises to 30 minutes.

Week seven
The hardest week yet, with another tempo session on Friday. Ride for longer than 3½ hours on Sunday if you feel like it.

Week eight
This is a nice easy week to round off three very hard weeks of training.

Managing your training
If your fatigue builds past manageable levels, cut back. You might have to do another four-week base-building block, or repeat a week, to get used to the extra effort without adding distance and intensity. If you get through the training, you should be in good shape.

Eight-week Training Schedule: Advanced

Now that you have done one or two, or even three weeks of base-building, followed by an eight-week intermediate schedule, you should be ready to start on an eight-week advanced schedule. The training sessions here are very tiring.

Once you embark on the advanced eight-week training schedule, you will need to remain in peak physical condition. It is, therefore, vital that you pay more attention than ever to correct nutrition, resting when you are tired, sleeping well and staying mentally fresh.

The distances covered during this eight-week period should enable you to aim for an off-road enduro ride of around 4 hours, or a road sportive of a similar duration. If your long-term goal is for a longer ride, you might want to focus less on sprinting and speed work, and concentrate more on endurance and stamina.

Conversely, if you're aiming for a shorter, fast ride, you could spend extra time on sprinting and speed work, but you shouldn't neglect regular LSD riding – endurance is always important.

Above: Advanced training schedules are tough on the body, but by training and resting correctly, you will reap the benefits.

Left: At this stage you will be in good physical condition and should be able to enjoy the longer rides in the advanced training schedule.

Week one
The intensity of your training schedule will rise again, with the introduction of a hilly tempo ride on Tuesday after Monday's rest day.

Thursday will see a 30-minute tempo ride on the flat, with steady riding either side. Friday's session is a fartlek ride – instead of structured sprints once a week, this session will cover the speed work. Sunday's long ride is 3½ hours. During this period you should be

listening carefully to your body, and making sure that fatigue is not building up. Training sessions are more or less a waste of time if you are not feeling fresh – it's more important to do two sessions properly than four with accumulating tiredness reducing your ability to work hard.

Week two
This week has a similar schedule to last week's, with an extra 30 minutes tacked on to Wednesday's ride.

Week three
Identical to last week, except that Sunday's ride is longer, and the tempo session on Thursday now lasts a little longer. Being able to hold a steady tempo while avoiding the build-up of fatigue is one of the key skills in endurance cycling.

Week one
MONDAY Rest
TUESDAY Hilly tempo ride 1:00
WEDNESDAY LSD ride 1:00
THURSDAY LSD ride 1:30, including 30 minutes of flat tempo
FRIDAY Fartlek ride 1:30
SATURDAY Recovery ride 0:30
SUNDAY LSD ride 3:30
TOTAL HOURS: 9:00

Week two
MONDAY Rest
TUESDAY Hilly tempo ride 1:00
WEDNESDAY LSD ride 1:30
THURSDAY LSD ride 1:30, including 40 minutes of tempo
FRIDAY Fartlek ride 1:30
SATURDAY Recovery ride 0:30
SUNDAY LSD ride 3:30
TOTAL HOURS: 9:30

Week three
MONDAY Rest
TUESDAY Hilly tempo ride 1:00
WEDNESDAY LSD ride 1:30
THURSDAY LSD ride 1:30, including 45 minutes of tempo
FRIDAY Fartlek ride 1:30
SATURDAY Recovery ride 0:30
SUNDAY LSD ride 4:00
TOTAL HOURS: 10:00

Week four
MONDAY Rest
TUESDAY LSD ride 1:00, including spinning drills
WEDNESDAY LSD ride 1:00
THURSDAY Rest
FRIDAY LSD ride 1:00
SATURDAY Recovery ride 0:30
SUNDAY LSD ride 3:00
TOTAL HOURS: 6:30

Week five
MONDAY Rest
TUESDAY Hilly tempo ride 1:30
WEDNESDAY LSD ride 1:30
THURSDAY LSD ride 1:30, including long steady climbs
FRIDAY Fartlek ride 1:30
SATURDAY Recovery ride 0:30
SUNDAY LSD ride 4:00
TOTAL HOURS: 10:30

Week six
MONDAY Rest
TUESDAY Hilly tempo ride 1:30, including 3 or 4 sprints
WEDNESDAY LSD ride 1:30
THURSDAY LSD ride 1:30, including long steady climbs
FRIDAY Fartlek ride 1:30, including 3 or 4 sprints
SATURDAY Recovery ride 0:30
SUNDAY LSD ride 4:00
TOTAL HOURS: 10:30

Week seven
MONDAY Rest
TUESDAY Hilly tempo ride 1:30
WEDNESDAY LSD ride 1:30
THURSDAY LSD ride 1:30, including long steady climbs
FRIDAY Fartlek ride 1:30
SATURDAY Recovery ride 0:30
SUNDAY LSD ride 4:00
TOTAL HOURS: 10:30

Week eight
MONDAY Rest
TUESDAY LSD ride 1:00, including spinning drills
WEDNESDAY LSD ride 1:00
THURSDAY Rest
FRIDAY LSD ride 1:00
SATURDAY Recovery ride 0:30
SUNDAY LSD ride 3:00
TOTAL HOURS: 6:30

Week four
A typical recovery week, following the hard three weeks that have gone before. Don't be tempted to train harder during this week, even if you think you can handle it. Your body needs to recover in order to be able to work harder later.

Week five
Training reaches a maximum volume of 10½ hours for the next three weeks. This is a large amount of time, so keep an eye on your general fatigue levels and note them down in your training diary.

Week six
The hours are similar to those on the previous week, but on Tuesday and Friday's rides, increase the intensity by working really hard on the hills and going for three or four sprints. Sunday's 4-hour session is the longest you will need to ride.

Week seven
Try to increase the intensity a little more from week six onwards. Your efforts should all be similar to those you will have to make in a race or sportive.

Week eight
Finally, you can rest and recover. If your main goal of the season is coming up, keep yourself ticking over now that you have achieved maximum fitness and are in top shape.

RACING

For some people, racing is the purest expression of bicycle riding. The bicycle was invented to be an efficient machine, and nowhere is this more important than in a bike race, when man and machine strive to be the fastest and best. No sooner had the bike been invented than people began to wonder how fast they could be pedalled and who could pedal them the fastest. As technology improved, other branches of bike racing evolved. With the advent of mountain bikes has come off-road racing. Track racing is one of the centrepieces of the Olympic Games. Racing demands specific skills, and the next section explains how to develop them.

Left: Bike racing on- or off-road takes dedication and determination.

ROAD RACING

The thrill of the road race has few equals in modern
sport. As part of a multi-coloured pack, riders fly up hills
before swooping down the other side, and cruise at
great speeds for miles before unleashing a fearsome
dash for the line. Finishing a road race takes more
than great speed and stamina. A number of riding skills
are needed to survive in a road race – how to climb,
how to descend, how to infiltrate a breakaway,
how to outsprint your rivals, and how to use team
tactics to your advantage.

Above: Road racers round a sharp bend in a mountainous race.
Left: Professional bike racers are among the fittest athletes on the planet.

The Road-racing Bicycle

Road-racing bikes are sleek, lightweight and fast. Ergonomic and aerodynamic principles are used in design so that everything possible is honed to a minimum, in order for the rider to be able to generate more speed.

Each element in a racing bike has been designed to be lightweight so that the rider can achieve maximum speed and responsive handling.

Frames

Carbon fibre or aluminium are used to make frames, or even a combination of the two, in which the main triangle of the frame is stiff aluminium, while the forks and seat stays are carbon fibre, to absorb some of the road shock. Frame tubes are wider than traditional steel bikes because aluminium is so much lighter than steel. Larger diameter tubes are stiffer, but even though more material is used in their construction, they are still much lighter than a comparative steel frame.

Right: A lightweight front mech (mechanism) on a racing bicycle.

Anatomy of a racing bike

❶ Wheels: size 700x20c, with 24 spokes and slick, lightweight tyres. Having a narrow section is much more aerodynamic.
❷ Frame: Carbon fibre or aluminium, with compact design and sloping top tube.
❸ Brakes: High performance dual pivot calliper. Carbon fibre brake levers to save weight.

❹ Chainrings: 53–42, attached to hollow bottom bracket axle and hollow cranks to save weight.
❺ Sprockets: 10-speed freewheel with 12–21 block.
❻ Gear changers: Brake levers also function as gear changers when they provide instant gear-changing ability.

❼ Saddle: Narrow and hard, with titanium seat rails to save weight.
❽ Handlebars: Dropped carbon fibre handlebars with ergonomically designed tubes for more comfortable and effective riding.
❾ Pedals: Lightweight pedals with special bindings for shoeplates to clip into.

The modern trend is for sloping top tubes and compact frames, which are smaller than traditional frames. A compact frame is stronger, because the tubes are shorter. They also allow frame manufacturers to make frames in fewer sizes, with most compact frames coming in three different sizes. Individual riders can tailor their position with precision using seatpins, stem, cranks and handlebars. Clearances between wheels and frame are reduced to almost nothing, and the profile of the bike is as narrow as possible, for better aerodynamics.

Specifications of wheels

Wheels are narrow – 700x20c, with 24 spokes, or fewer for the front wheel, depending on the model and spoke pattern. Tyres are slick and lightweight, with little or no tread – with such a small area of the tyre on the road at any one time, this actually offers the best grip. The fastest tyres used to be one-piece tubulars, which were extremely lightweight and glued to the wheel. However, the performance of traditional tyres, with a wire-on outer layer and inner tube, is now similar to tubular tyres. Wire-on tyres are easier to mend.

Components

Gearing in a racing bike is higher than the bikes that have been covered so far – road-racing bikes need to travel at high speeds, and the pace is rarely slow enough in a road race to justify using very low gears. Even on climbs, the riders try to go up so fast that their bottom gear doesn't need to be super-low. A typical racing bike has 52 or 53–42-tooth chainrings on the front, although this can be adapted to 53–44 if the course is less hilly, or 53–39 if it is especially hilly. At the back, a typical block would be 12–21 or 12–23, depending upon the type of terrain. Professional sprinters use an 11-tooth sprocket, but you should be very fit and strong before you attempt to turn over such a large gear. Brakes are lightweight and high performance.

Road-racing bikes feel very stiff, with all effort going into moving the bike forward. Most road races are

Above: Brake levers on a racing bike combine brakes and gear-changing functions at the same place.

Above: Brakes on a racing bike are light, but strong, making it easy to control your speed on a fast descent.

Above: Modern racing bikes have as many as 11 sprockets on the rear wheel, giving a total of 22 gears so that riders can travel at high speeds.

Above: Racing saddles are narrow, for improved aerodynamics. Choose a saddle that is comfortable for you by testing as many as possible.

shorter distance events, taking between 1 and 3 hours to complete, so that for this distance it is possible to sacrifice a little comfort for stiffness and responsiveness.

Tour de France riders, however, can sometimes spend as much as 6 hours at a time on a racing bike so for the long distances they ride, comfort is of paramount importance.

Choosing a Racing Bike

Which racing bike are you going to buy? You will probably want a bike that is light, fast and responsive but your choice should depend on your current ability, your potential ability, your ambitions and the depth of your wallet.

By choosing to buy a good quality racing bike, you are already demonstrating that you are serious about riding fast and racing. To help achieve your maximum potential, the better the bike you buy, the faster you will ride.

As a rule of thumb, you should always buy the best possible equipment that you can afford, without getting into the mindset that you cannot ride fast without it. By focusing too much on equipment you run the risk of relying too hard on it. Instead of working overtime to afford a titanium seatpin bolt, you might end up going faster by investing that time in training more effectively.

Matching components

It is important to buy a bike with a matching level of componentry and frame. If you spend all your budget on a professional level frame, and only have

Right: Buy the racing bike that best suits your needs and level.
Below: Carbon fibre is one of the lightest and strongest materials for making racing frames.

Carbon fibre or aluminium?

Bicycle technology has reached a point where there is so much choice that nearly everybody can find a racing frame that suits his or her needs and abilities perfectly. Deciding between carbon fibre and aluminium can, however, prove to be a difficult choice. Both are light, corrosion resistant and strong. Both give a stiff, responsive ride. The best way to choose is to test ride a model made in each material and see which you prefer.

Some people believe that a full-carbon frame tends towards a harsh ride. A good compromise is an aluminium frame that has carbon forks and seat stays.

enough left for a cheap groupset (the brakes, gears and drivetrain), there will be a compromise in performance.

For high-level racing, most riders choose between Shimano and Campagnolo groupsets. Shimano Dura Ace and Campagnolo Record are the

Above: Check that the distance from the saddle to the pedals is correct for you. Right: When setting up your bike, make sure that the reach is set at the correct distance for your size.

top range, and are highly engineered and reliable. As with choosing between carbon fibre and aluminium frames, the performance of both is so good that selecting one over the other is a matter of preference. The gear-changing system is different, and Campaganolo offers a more definite 'click' in between gears.

Wheels should have hubs compatible with the gearing system, and light, good quality rims. Advances in design, materials and spoke patterns ensure that there is a wide choice. For top level racing, a deep-section carbon rim is the best, but these are very expensive.

Left: An aluminium road and mountain bike frame is preferred by some riders.

Road-racing Skills: Breaking Away

Winning road races isn't easy. You share the start line with 150 other riders, who all want to win. Some are great climbers and others are great bunch sprinters. In a hilly race, if you are a good climber or a sprinter, you should make the most of these skills.

If you do not excel at sprinting or climbing, try to get into a breakaway. It's a rare road race in which the entire field rides round and waits for a group to sprint together (the bunch sprint). Attacks often go from the gun, and it takes special circumstances for the attack to be the right one.

Leading the charge
Attacking is energy-consuming. It is better to attack once, successfully, than four times unsuccessfully. The energy consumed in four unsuccessful attacks could make you miss the fifth, which is the one that disappears up the road. On the other hand, it might take those four attacks to succeed – the bunch may tire of chasing you down and let you go. Each race is different in this respect. But don't ever attack just for the sake of it. Choose your moment.

The best times to go are when the bunch slows down, either due to a corner, a hill, the fact that another group has just been chased down, or simply because the riders at the front stop riding hard. When you notice this happen, go as hard as you can. You may escape on your own, you may be followed by a small group in counterattack, or you may get chased down. After a few minutes, turn around and see which of these has happened. If you are on your own, but can see a small group working together to catch you 20 seconds behind, while the bunch is at a minute farther back, you are better off waiting for the small group to catch you. The short-term sacrifice of a handful of seconds is worth the long-

Right: The joy of victory – get it right and the win is yours.

Above: In a race, getting into the right breakaway is a crucial tactical skill.

term gain of being in the breakaway group and getting farther from the bunch than you could on your own. Be careful of who joins you, however. If the best sprinter in the race has made the bridge, there is little point in working well together – you might want to sit up and wait for the bunch to catch you. It may be a waste of energy, but so is towing a superior sprinter to the line, unless you are confident you can drop them before the finishing straight.

If you see somebody else attacking, your reaction must be fast. Every moment of hesitation means that there is a bigger gap to cross. When you see the telltale sign of a rider lifting themselves out of the saddle, try and make it a reflex to do exactly the same and put yourself right in their slipstream.

Individual riders often get away, but the most common breakaway is a small group, of between three and ten riders. Initially, these groups tend to work hard together to ensure that they are building a healthy lead over the pack.

You also need to know what the bunch are doing behind you. If they start chasing harder, it is worth marshalling the group to ride especially hard for 10–15km (6–9 miles). It's harder work, but if you can keep the gap at a constant level the bunch may become demoralized and back off. You will be more tired, but when the bunch slows, you can too.

Playing the field

Once groups have a minute or two of lead, riders work together, either by putting the lead at risk, or letting one or more riders do less work than the others. These riders will be fresher at the finish. There may be two riders from one team in the group. It may be your team. If there's a good sprinter in the group, you will need to get rid of them before the end. If you have superior numbers from your team, you can start to dictate things. If you or your team-mate is a good sprinter, it's worth the other rider sacrificing their chances in order to chase down attacks, lead the group at a fast pace to prevent attacks, and to do more of the work in order for the

Above: Solo breakaways are the hardest way to win, but the most spectacular.

sprinter to stay fresher. Or you can take turns in attacking, forcing the other riders to chase you down. If you attack enough times between you, it's a matter of time before an attack is successful.

Up against these tactics, you have to ride cleverly. If you are isolated you will have fewer opportunities to make an effort, but when you do, make sure it is the successful move. If another rider is pulling their team-mate to a sprint victory, make sure they are doing all the work and tiring themselves out, then launch a surprise attack near the finish. When two team-mates are attacking in turn, allow others to chase them down the first time at least. When the second or third attack happens, react at once, get into their slipstream and wait. If you are away, you now have a 50 per cent chance of winning. If you get chased down, go with the counterattack from the other team-mate.

In a breakaway situation, your main aims are working hard to ensure the break stays away, then using as little energy as possible when the tactical games start. Relax, watch your breakaway companions, and make your race-winning effort at just the right moment.

Left: Share the work with your breakaway companions, but be careful to watch them all the time.

Road-racing Skills: Climbing

Climbing is the hardest part of bike racing. Even good climbers suffer when they ride uphill, while for bad climbers, hills can be the difference between winning and losing a race. It is important to know how to climb.

A strategically placed hill can blow a race apart, so you need to know how to deal with them in a race.

Some people are born climbers. They are generally light, skinny and small, with a large power-to-weight ratio. For these lucky people, hills are where they can really put pressure on the rest of the field. If they also have good technique and tactical sense, they are very hard to deal with in a race.

Others don't climb so well. Larger, heavier riders have more weight to carry up the hills. Others find it difficult to react to changes in pace on uphills. However, even poor climbers can greatly improve their performance by using the best tactics in each situation.

In a race, whether you are a good climber or bad climber, it is important to be at the front when the climb starts. Poor climbers hope that by doing this, they can slip back through the bunch, and still be in contact as the race passes over the top. If these riders start the hill at the back, that is where they will stay. Good climbers need to follow the same tactic, so that they are in position to

dictate the race or react to others trying to do so. It can take several kilometres of racing to get to the front in time for the bottom, so be prepared.

Hitting your stride
On a long climb, cadence and rhythm are important. Pushing a big gear slowly is an expensive way of riding, and increases the chances that you will tire before the top. The best way of riding is to train yourself to ride in a much lower gear. This gives your legs greater 'snap' when making or reacting to an attack.

Breathing is difficult when climbing, so when climbing sitting down, try and sit more upright, holding the tops of the handlebars, thereby opening up the chest. Sometimes, when the speed

Left: Climbing in a race can be intense and painful – always maintain focus, as this rider is doing here.

Above: The easiest way around a hairpin bend is towards the middle of the road. Follow this line and you could save crucial energy for later on.

increases, or just to stay on top of the gear, you will need to stand up. A good climber can vary their position and rhythm between seated and standing climbing – train yourself to do this so that when you need to do it in a race you are ready.

The best line to follow through the corners on a climb is not necessarily the shortest one. Road corners are often much steeper on the inside than the outside, which could force you to work harder than you need to to maintain your speed. The most advantageous way is halfway between the two sides of the road, unless the corner is really steep, in which case it might be more efficient to move out farther. The important thing is

to conserve as much energy as possible, and spinning through the less steep part of a corner enables you to do this.

What is necessary while climbing, for good and bad climbers alike, is having the self-knowledge to know your limits and how you react to riding at certain speeds, and to be able to focus through periods of great discomfort. Train yourself in both of these, and your climbing will improve.

Tactics for a good climber

The best climbers use three methods to make life exceedingly miserable for everybody else in a race. The first is the most straightforward and involves going to the front and gradually accelerating until they are riding as fast as they can. Hanging on to them in this kind of situation is difficult.

The second is by attacking hard, and quickly accelerating away. The third method is, perversely, slowing down. Climbers can deal with changes in rhythm much better than non-climbers can, and by slowing things down they are making the other riders vulnerable to attacks.

If you are a good climber, practise all these methods and try to use them to your advantage.

Tactics for a bad climber

Bad climbers will have to come up with ways of dealing with the methods employed by good climbers to put them to the back of a race. By training hard and being confident of your tactics you may be able to neutralize the climbers.

Left: If you get attacked on a climb, respond, and it may help to discourage further attacks.

Left: If you are a good climber, attacking uphill can put dangerous rivals out of contention.

If they increase the pace slowly, go with it. It is going to hurt, but you will be maintaining a rhythm, which is more straightforward than responding to varying pace. If they attack suddenly, don't attempt to follow them, as you would an attack on the flat. Remain calm, and slowly increase the pace. Unless they are in super shape, an attack by a climber will be followed by a deceleration. Accelerate slowly to the point where you can bring them back. By catching them, you can make them doubt their ability to get away. If a climber is varying the pace, try to ignore them and ride at your own rhythm.

When climbing gets really painful, it can help to use mental techniques to master the pain. Counting to 10 over and over again will help you focus through the pain. If the climb is a long

Above: On long, steady climbs, stay as relaxed and focused as possible and hold your pace.

one, focus on getting to the next bend. Break the climb into smaller sections, which are mentally easier to deal with.

Bad climbers are especially vulnerable on races with hilltop finishes. There is no way you can hope to compete with a good climber here. Instead, you should work on getting into a break, giving you a head start.

Road-racing Skills: Cornering and Descending

Taking a corner fast, either on the flat or riding downhill, takes skill, balance and confidence. Deficiencies in any of these areas can lead to a rider being dropped. All these skills are easy to work on, and can be used to advantage in a race.

Your bike can only lean over through a corner so far before one of two things happens. Either your pedal will scrape the floor (if you are pedalling), with dire consequences, or your tyres' traction will be lost, which would be equally catastrophic. On a gravelly surface, this can happen at a very slight angle.

Dealing with a corner in a bike race involves three phases. First comes the approach, during which you adjust your speed to the level necessary to go through the corner. Next is the apex, which is the sharpest part of the corner. And finally there is the exit, which is where you can accelerate out again.

Cornering

In a bunch, the first rider will choose the racing line around the corner, generally swinging out in the approach, then turning their wheel and passing close to the apex. Finally they will swing out again as they accelerate away. If the bunch is strung out in a single line, follow the rider ahead, using the same line, trying to lose as little speed as possible. Do not attempt to overtake on the inside, where you are vulnerable to crashing and also disrupting the flow of the line of riders. By cutting up the inside, you are effectively moving into the racing line of other riders as they cut into the apex, which will make you unpopular. If riders are bunched up, follow close to the racing line and adjust your speed to match the riders around you.

When going around the apex, keep the outside leg down, and lean your bike, while keeping your head upright, to maintain the maximum speed possible. The idea is to cut from the outside of the road to the inside through the apex, then swing wide again once you have passed it. As soon as your bike

stops swinging wide, you have entered the exit phase and are ready to start pedalling again.

In a race, you can make others work harder through corners by getting to the front, keeping the speed high, and then accelerating hard out of the corner. This has the effect of stretching out the bunch, and riders have to work hard to close gaps that have opened up. Repeat this a few times, and your rivals may not have the energy to chase an attack.

Above: Descending fast and safely is an essential skill in bike racing – getting the racing line right is crucial.

Some bike races are flat, but most include hills for the sake of variety and to add a challenge. Going up the hill is not the only challenge – bunches race fast down the other side, and this is where the less confident descenders get found out.

If your race is taking place on open roads, your first priority should always be safety in the case of meeting cars or other

Cornering on the flat

Approach: *During the approach, adjust your speed to go around the corner.*

Apex: *The sharpest part of the corner is the apex. Lean into it as you go around.*

Exit: *The exit is the final part of the corner where you begin accelerating out.*

traffic. Stay on the correct side of the road in case there is a car around a blind corner. The same warning applies for training rides.

Descending

The first rule of descending is to keep your head up, look ahead and anticipate what is going to happen in front of you. Unless you are leading the bunch, you may have to react to the movements of other riders.

Effective descending means having a comfortable and aerodynamic position on the bike. Always hold the drops of your handlebars, with one or two fingers on the brake levers, so you can react fast to obstacles. Keep your centre of gravity low,

for better balance and aerodynamics. If you can see a long way ahead, you can go into a tuck position, with your hands on the tops of the handlebars and your chin almost touching your wrists. Use your legs as shock absorbers by putting more of your weight on the pedals and sitting on the tip of your saddle.

It is important to corner well going downhill. Slow down before you hit a corner, to a speed that will allow you to go around the bend without crashing. If you are in a bunch, don't make sudden movements if you want to change your position, but do signal your intentions clearly in case somebody in turn is trying to get around you.

Above: To enter a bend, swing wide, then cut in to the apex of the curve.

Cornering on a descent

Approach: *To begin, swing wide, and accelerate towards the corner.*

Apex: *Follow a natural line, stay relaxed and look forward with head up.*

Exit: *Start pedalling as you hit the exit with the bike starting to straighten.*

Road-racing Skills: Sprinting

Sprinters win far more bike races than any other kind of bike rider. They have the advantage of being able to wait until the finishing line is in sight and then unleashing their primary weapon. Various tactics can be employed to win the day.

Field sprinting demands nerve, speed, strength, determination and timing. When a rider has all of these attributes, he or she is very difficult to beat.

Sprinting, at a basic level, involves riding as fast as possible over a short distance, but there is more than one way of doing this.

Some sprints are won by a rider jumping to the front early in the race and holding their speed all the way to the line. Others are won by a rider getting into the slipstream of the rider who has made the early jump, taking advantage of the wind protection offered by their rival, then overtaking them in the final 50m (164ft).

Strength or speed?

Some riders rely on sheer brute strength in their sprint. If they can turn a bigger gear than anybody else, they can go the fastest. These riders favour a long,

drawn-out sprint. Riders at the opposite end of the sprinting scale rely on leg speed. They don't need to use as high a gear as the power sprinters, but instead turn a smaller gear faster. The advantage of this method is that their acceleration is far quicker, enabling them to speed away from other riders very quickly.

In a race, the preparation for a sprint starts as far as 20km (12.5 miles) from the finishing line. If you want to be involved in the sprint you need to make sure you are riding near the front well before the finish. Take time to move up the bunch, staying out of the wind as much as possible. Ideally, you will have a team-mate or two to help you do this.

In the Tour de France, the sprinters' teams maintain a very high speed at the front of the bunch for the final 10km (6 miles), to discourage breakaways from spoiling their leader's chance of a win. In smaller races, the run-in tends to be

more of a free-for-all. Stay near the front without going into the lead, so you can watch the way the race is developing.

Jockeying for position

With 3km (1.8 miles) to go, the real manoeuvring starts. Riding behind another rider saves energy, so the sprinters bump and barge each other to defend their position behind another rider. If there is a strong sprinter in the field, other riders keep close to their wheel, following them in the sprint and jumping around them to steal the win. There is only one place on his wheel, even if four or five riders are fighting for it.

As the race enters the final 500m (1,640ft), the riders start to fan across the road as the sprint is launched. Although every sprint is different, you should be aiming to start your final sprint with about 200m (656ft) to go. Try to stay on another sprinter's wheel until this point. Accelerate hard at this point and spend the next 50m (164ft) building up to speed. Then try to hold your top speed all the way to the finishing line.

Phases of sprinting

Acceleration and speed maintenance are the two phases of sprinting. Acceleration has to be a sudden increase in speed to reach top speed as fast as possible, to get around riders in front of you, and to shake off riders who are on your wheel. If gear selection is too high, it will take too long to accelerate; too low, and you will not be able to reach top speed. Terrain and wind direction must be taken into consideration. Grip the drops of the handlebars firmly, stand up on the pedals and jump as hard as you

Left: Bike races are often decided with a fast and furious bunch sprint. Good tactics make all the difference in a sprint.

How to sprint

1: *To sprint, jump hard, holding the handlebars firmly.*

2: *Push down with one leg; pull up handlebars with the opposite hand.*

3: *When your reach maximum speed, maintain it as long as you can.*

4: *Bend your arms. Use the upper body to best effect.*

5: *Extend arms and legs to push the bike over the line.*

can, putting as much force through the pedal stroke as you can, again and again. Use your upper body and each arm in turn to pull the handlebars up as you push down on the pedal with the opposite foot. Initially your acceleration will be slow, but as momentum builds up, you can get towards your top speed.

Finishing the sprint

Once you hit top speed, your aim is to maintain it to the finishing line. If you start to slow, other riders who have timed their sprint better will come past you. Keep your eyes forward, ignore other riders, and maintain a straight line to the finishing line to avoid obstructing other riders, for which you can be disqualified.

It is also the shortest distance. Don't slow in the final metres, even if you think you have won, but pedal hard through the finishing line, with the final strong thrust of the pedals coinciding with straightening your arms to 'push' your bike ahead. This is called 'throwing' the bike, and it can be the crucial skill that gains you victory.

Road-racing Skills: Strategies and Teamwork

It is often said that cycling is a team sport for individuals, and it is true that only one rider can win the race. However, that victory may well be partly due to the sacrifice and hard work of the rider's team-mates.

Getting into the right position in a race involves thorough pre-race planning, and clever decision-making during a race. Team tactics must be well thought out and flexible enough to allow unpredictable events to be dealt with.

Before the race

The most important part of preparation for a race is to train properly for the weeks and months leading up to it. Turning up at a race unfit is a waste of your time. If the race is an important one, ease off your training in the run-up to it, so that you are in tip-top condition on the morning of the event.

Well before the race, you should research its route. Knowledge of the roads you are racing on is a huge advantage. If the race is local, you can train on the route, get used to the corners, decide which gears you need to use, find out where the course might be exposed to crosswinds, and notice subtle variations in the gradient of the finishing straight. All of this information is a powerful tool in riding a good race.

Knowing that there is a hill might not be good enough. You need to know if it is steep at the bottom, or steep at the top. Is there a descent straight away, or does it emerge on to a plateau, which will be windy and could split the bunch up even more than the climb? Is there a sharp corner just at the bottom of the climb? If so, going around it in first position will enable you to accelerate and gain distance on your rivals, who will have to work hard to chase you down. Does your race finish on a hill,

Above: Lance Armstrong was helped to seven Tour de France wins by his US Postal and Discovery Channel teams.

and if so, who is your team's best climber? Is there a sharp corner 400m (1,312ft) before the finishing line? No detail is too small to help in your preparation. By knowing the course, you can also train specifically for its challenges, which will stand you in good physical stead.

Know your enemy

The course is one area that you should research well before the race; another is your rivals. They want to win the race as badly as you do, and they have their own plans for doing so. Good climbers need to be neutralized during the flat part of the course. Good sprinters need

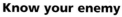
Left: Researching the route and working out strategies with team-mates ahead of the race can give a team an advantage.

to be kept to the back in the hills. If there is a particularly strong team taking part, rather than trying to beat them single-handedly, it might be better to apply the old saying, 'if you can't beat them, join them.'

Try to get into breaks with their riders and work with them, which effectively makes them, and the riders they have in the bunch, your temporary team-mates. You can work out how to beat them once you have carved up the race between you.

Lastly, look at the weather forecast the day before the race and bring the correct riding clothes for the conditions.

During the race

You should have formulated 'Plan A' before the race. This might involve getting a specific rider in your team away in an early attack on the first climb of the race. Or it could involve waiting for the finishing sprint.

Because these plans are fairly inflexible, and could be compromised by the actions of other riders in the race, you also have to react well to the prevailing circumstances. You might designate one or two riders who are under instructions to make sure that at least one of them is in every early break. This takes the pressure off the rest of your team to chase breaks down.

If you find yourself with a team-mate farther up the road in a break, your job is twofold. First, there is no need to expend energy in chasing down the break – you can leave this to others. Second, you should be vigilant for counterattacks, which might put your

Above: If you are a strong climber, use hills to get ahead during a race.

escaped team-mate in a weaker position. If counterattacks happen, it's worth trying to get another team-mate into them. If the tables are turned and your team has missed the break, it will be your responsibility, along with other teams who missed the break, to chase it down. If this is the case, don't use the whole team to ride as hard as possible on the front, or you will all be burned out by the finish. Instead, try and share the work with another team, using just a couple of riders to up the pace gradually and eat into the break's lead.

Apart from these strategies, the main aim of the race is to expend as little energy as possible so that you are still strong at the end. Stay close behind other riders as much as is practical. Don't panic as events unfold, but react to them calmly.

Left: By sheltering their leader (in the middle) from the wind, team-mates help him to save vital energy in a race.

Road-racing Skills: Time Trialling

The ability to time trial is one of the most important skills in cycling. Being able to ride fast and maintain a fast pace is a necessity not only in time trialling but also in road racing, when you are in an escape, or when chasing down a break.

Time trialling involves riding at a steady and consistent rate. The aim is never to ride so fast that you are unable to maintain your pace, and not to slow down – a feat which requires concentration, nerve, resistance to pain, endurance and strength.

Some riders are naturally better at time trialling than others. It is also a trainable skill. By working hard on your body position and endurance, and practising a lot, you can bring about improvements in your time-trialling results.

Time trials can be individual races, or part of a stage race. In the latter, you can afford to lose a little time if you know you can gain time in another stage. In an individual race, the fastest man or woman wins. It involves getting up to speed quickly and steadily, then maintaining the effort until the finish.

Your starting effort in a time trial should not be the same as an attack in a road race, or a jump in a sprint. Instead, accelerate gradually so that you don't overwork your muscles. At the same time, don't relax too much at this point – you need to be at cruising speed sooner rather than later.

Pacing yourself
Finding out what pace you can sustain over a long time trial involves training with a pulse monitor and working out

the percentage of your maximum heart rate you can ride at without becoming exhausted. This takes experimentation. Maintaining this pace should not be a comfortable process. During a time trial, your body will be in a great deal of pain, and you need to focus through this and be confident that you can maintain the same level of effort.

Riding at the same pace during a race is often made difficult by corners, hills and weather conditions. Some riders make the mistake of trying to maintain speed up hills and into a headwind; the extra effort will make them collapse later. The effort should be the constant, not the speed. There is no need to panic if it feels like you are riding slowly – your rivals will be doing the same. As with road races, knowing the course will

Top: Good time trialling requires an aerodynamic position, good equipment and the ability to endure pain.

assist in planning your race. If you have paced yourself correctly, you should be feeling weary in the second half of the course. This is the time to hold your nerve and focus. If possible add a little extra effort, without crossing into the red zone, ensuring that by the finishing line you are at your peak output.

Left: Time-trial bikes need fewer gears than road bikes, especially on the flat.
Right: Time-trial bikes handle less well than road bikes, so you have to take care to avoid crashes.

Time-trialling bikes

Road-racing bikes and time-trialling bikes are different. Aerodynamics are important for time-trialling bikes, since the speed will be greater than in other kinds of race. The bike is narrow, and puts the rider in a position in which the arms are ahead of the body, the back and head are as low as possible, while still letting the legs turn at maximum capacity.

Frames are stiffer than for bikes for road-racing. The greater distances in road racing mean that stiffness has to be balanced against comfort. Time trials tend to be shorter and comfort is not so important. By making the frame stiffer, less power is lost by the frame flexing, resulting in a faster ride.

Above: Time-trialling handlebars are arranged so that they put the arms and body into an aerodynamic tuck, with the head and back in a low position.

Anatomy of a time-trial bike

1 Rear wheel: Solid disc wheels are more aerodynamic than spoked wheels.

2 Front wheel: Deep rims cut down on the length of the spokes, which are flat, to reduce drag.

3 Frame: Moulded carbon fibre frame with flatter tubes. Extremely stiff, at the expense of long-distance comfort.

4 Handlebars: Special low-profile 'tri-bars' allow the rider to rest on their elbows with the arms stretched out ahead, giving a far more aerodynamic profile.

5 Chainrings: 53–44 or even less discrepancy in size, unless the bike is to be used on a very hilly course.

6 Sprockets: 8- or 9-speed freewheel with 12–19 or 12–21 block.

7 Gear-changers: These are mounted on the end of the tri-bars for ease of access.

8 Clothing: One-piece tight-fitting skinsuits and profiled helmets catch less wind than regular cycling clothing.

Racing Skills: Triathlon

Triathlons involve sandwiching a bike race between a swim and a run. For many cyclists, they are an extra challenge that also contribute to greater all-round fitness. The training discipline for a triathlon is very similar to that for cycling.

Triathlons are almost a pure endurance sport, in which judgement of pace and resistance to fatigue are the most important skills. The three sports are difficult enough on their own, but together they form a unique challenge.

When cyclists start triathlon training, the greatest challenge is forcing the body to work with different muscle groups. When making the transition, it is recommended that you spend a few months just getting used to swimming and running without going into any structured training routines.

Once your body is used to working in these different ways, it is a good idea to work with a swimming coach, who will improve your technique. The typical swim for an Olympic-distance triathlon is 1,500m (approximately 1 mile) – bad technique over this distance will slow you down and tire you out, and good cycling may not be enough to compensate. Better technique will greatly improve your swimming times.

If you are an experienced cyclist going into triathlons, work on maintaining your cycling economy and fitness – this

Above: Triathlons often begin with a massed start swim in which positioning is a crucial factor.
Below: Experienced cyclists have an advantage over their competitors in the bike leg of a triathlon.

Triathlon bike

At first glance, a typical triathlon bike looks very similar to a time-trial bike. However, the special nature of the exertion in the course of a triathlon means that the athletes have some needs not shared by time triallists.

First, the position of a triathlete is not as low down as a time triallist. The saddle should remain at the optimum height for maximum performance, but the handlebars should be raised so that the position is not so extreme. The bike section of a triathlon is followed by a run, which puts strain on the hamstrings. If the triathlete uses a low position, he or she risks injury during the run.

Second, there are two water bottles carried on the frame. The athlete will not have had a chance to rehydrate during the swimming leg. The bike is a good time to refuel and ensure consumption of enough energy to get through the run. Both bottles will probably be necessary.

is the part of the race in which you will have an advantage over swimmers who are starting the bike stage ahead of you.

The running stage is an unusual kind of exertion. Although running training is absolutely necessary, you also need to train yourself to run after a long bike ride. Your body is tired by now and this will slow down your running, so, as well as swimming, cycling and running training, you also need to incorporate what are known as 'brick' sessions into your training routine. These involve a training session linking two of the disciplines, most often cycling and running. A typical brick session might involve a 30-minute warm-up followed by 10-minute sets alternating between the bike (on a stationary trainer, unless you have an exact training route) and running. Cycle at 75 to 80 per cent of MHR for 10 minutes, then run at the same intensity for 10 minutes. Then repeat, before warming down. These sessions are essential if you are to achieve your potential in a triathlon.

Quick changes

The other challenge facing triathletes is to 'transition' as quickly and efficiently as possible between the three stages.

Right: Save time in the transition zone by having your equipment prepared exactly as you want it.

Above: The run leg of a triathlon is extremely arduous because of the fatigue after the swim and bike legs.

This is complicated by the fact that competitors often wear a wetsuit for the swim (if it is in cold, open water), and need to change shoes for both the cycle and the run. Organization and relaxed focus is necessary to do this as quickly as possible. When you leave the water, start to unzip your wetsuit as you jog towards the bike pen. Take your wetsuit off carefully but fast, so your feet don't get caught, then run with your bike

Above: During the transition time, take the opportunity to refocus on the next discipline.

(with shoes attached to pedals) out of the bike pen to the start of the bike leg. Mount the bike and put your feet into your shoes as you move off.

For the next transition, take your feet out of your shoes at the end of the ride and dismount the bike, running to the pen. Get your running shoes on as quickly as possible, and you are set. Transitions are an easy process, but rushing can add minutes to your finish time.

Great Road Races: The Tour de France

The Tour de France is the greatest race in cycling history. Because it is the first and oldest of the Grand Tours, with the best slot on the cycling calendar in mid-July and terrain perfectly suited to bike racing, it captures the imagination of the cycling world each summer.

The Tour is a stage race. The approximately 3,000km (1,865-mile) route is divided into daily stages, generally between 150 and 250km (93–155 miles), with time trials on some days. The riders start each stage together, and their accumulated time is added into the general classification.

Yellow jersey

The leader of the general classification wears a yellow jersey. There is also a points classification, for the rider who consistently gets the best stage placings, and a red and white dotted jersey for the best climber, known as the King of the Mountains. The yellow jersey is that colour because the original sponsoring newspaper, *L'Auto*, was printed on yellow paper. In the early years of the race it was pointed out that nobody knew who was winning the race, and the tradition of handing them a yellow jersey at the end of each stage was born.

Test of strength

The race is extremely arduous, with only two rest days during the three weeks. The route is different every year and in recent times has followed a clockwise direction one year and the next year, an anticlockwise direction.

The race always spends five or six days in the high mountains, crossing the Alps and Pyrenees. Riders can lose huge amounts of time in these stages, and many are forced to pull out.

In some years, when the organizers want to make the event particularly tough, the race goes into the Massif Central mountain range in central France for a day or two. The race has a different start – known as 'Le Grand Départ' – every year, but always finishes with a well deserved celebration stage on the Champs Elysées in Paris.

Above: Fans flock to the Tour de France in their thousands every summer, hoping for a glimpse of their cycling heroes.

1952

The most impressive Tours are the closest ones, and those that are dominated by a single rider. The year 1952 saw an Italian climber at the peak of his powers, with his rivals simply unable to keep up with him.

Fausto Coppi probably would have won whatever the route in 1952, but the organizers blessed him with a mountainous route including the first ever summit finishes – three of them, at Puy de Dôme, Alpe d'Huez and Sestrières. He won each of these stages, as well as a long time trial early in the race. Journalists, with very little to write about in the way of a close race (second-placed Stan Ockers was at least 28 minutes behind, which was a massive margin), waxed lyrical about Coppi's win, seeing it as nothing short of legendary.

Below: Fausto Coppi was one of the first heroes of the modern era, winning the Tour de France three times in the 1950s.

Above: Frenchman Jacques Anquetil, who was the first man to win the Tour de France five times.

Above: Eddy Merckx, who won five Tours in dominant style during the 1960s and 1970s.

Above: Greg Lemond time trials his way to victory in the 1989 Tour de France, the closest race ever.

1964

In 1964, the race was a battle between two Frenchmen – four-times winner Jacques Anquetil and his great rival Raymond Poulidor. Anquetil was the more successful on the bike, while Poulidor was more popular with fans.

In 1964, Poulidor came very close to toppling Anquetil. On the climb of the Puy de Dôme, the two rode side by side, elbows clashing, weaving up the road as they fought to win. Unbeknown to Poulidor, Anquetil was feeling terrible, but he bluffed his way up, fighting the agony to stay with Poulidor. Poulidor only realized too late that Anquetil was vulnerable and he attacked with sufficient time to drop Anquetil, but not enough to take the yellow jersey, which Anquetil eventually won by 55 seconds.

1969

As in 1952, 1969 saw a single rider dominate the race. His name was Eddy Merckx, and he was about to take the first of his five Tour de France victories. His nickname was the 'Cannibal', which referred to his voracious appetite for winning races and destroying the opposition. In 1969 the 24-year-old Belgian was unrivalled. He took the yellow jersey as the race entered the Alps in the first week, and held it to the finish. He took a brilliant solo victory on the 17th stage in the Pyrenees, attacking early and spending the day on his own at the front. He won by almost 20 minutes.

1989

This was simply the most dramatic race in Tour history. The excitement started when defending champion Pedro Delgado turned up late for the first stage and lost almost 3 minutes before he had began turning the pedals. The lead swung between Greg Lemond, on the comeback after a hunting accident, and two-times winner Laurent Fignon through the flat first week and the Pyrenees. Delgado began to claw his way back into contention.

In the Alps, Fignon looked the stronger, and two attacks on successive days put him 50 seconds into the lead with only a 30km time trial into Paris to go. Lemond beat him by 58 seconds, gaining the yellow jersey by 8 seconds.

2003

Lance Armstrong had dominated the race for four years previously, but in 2003 he almost failed. He was unable to stamp his authority on the race in his usual style, and although he wore the yellow jersey through the Alps and Pyrenees, his lead was slim, and he looked vulnerable to the attacks made by his rivals. He took a beating in a long time trial. On one day, one of his closest rivals, Joseba Beloki, fell off directly in front of Armstrong on a steep corner in the Alps. Armstrong was forced to take spectacular evasive action, and ended up riding across a field, jumping off his bike and carrying it back on to the road. In

the Pyrenees, his handlebar got caught on a spectator's bag strap, pulling him off his bike. He still managed to put in a race-winning attack farther up the road, defending a slim lead in the final time trial.

2008

The Tour in 2008 was one of the most tactical and closest ever. There were no outstanding favourites, and with only days left to race, there were still six riders within a minute of the lead, an unprecedented situation. In the Alps, in the last week, Spanish rider Carlos Sastre made an all-or-nothing attack on the Alpe d'Huez climb, and gained enough time to win the Tour.

Below: Lance Armstrong, the absolute record holder in the Tour, with seven wins.

10 Best-ever Tour de France Riders

The Tour de France is one of the most important stage races for cycling aficionados. It is a tough race, taking around 23 days and covering more than 3,000 kilometres (1,865 miles). To be the best, riders need endurance and great physical strength.

1) Lance Armstrong (USA)
TOUR WINS: SEVEN
Armstrong dominated the Tour de France between 1999 and 2005. He won seven on the trot, and in six of these he was unchallengeable. The exception was 2003, when he started tired, and struggled all the way to victory only 1 minute ahead of German rival Jan Ullrich.

2) Eddy Merckx (Belgium)
TOUR WINS: FIVE
Merckx won five Tours between 1969 and 1974, as well as virtually every other race on the calendar. His insatiable appetite for succeeding ensured that he won more stages than any other rider and spent more days in the yellow jersey than anyone else.

3) Bernard Hinault (France)
TOUR WINS: FIVE
The last indomitable French winner of the Tour de France took his fifth title in 1985. Hinault had an aggressive, confrontational style, in life as in racing, and didn't suffer fools gladly.

4) Miguel Indurain (Spain)
TOUR WINS: FIVE
Indurain was the first rider to win five successive Tours, between 1991 and 1995. He was an awesome time triallist, building a big lead in the individual tests, and hanging on to the best climbers in the mountains.

5) Jacques Anquetil (France)

TOUR WINS: FIVE

Anquetil was the first rider to win five Tours, taking his first in 1957, then another four between 1961 and 1964. His career was defined by his great rivalry with the more popular Raymond Poulidor, whose nickname 'the eternal second' revealed which of the two riders was faster on the bike.

6) Greg Lemond (USA)

TOUR WINS: THREE

Lemond was the first American rider to win the Tour de France. His career was interrupted by a hunting accident in which he nearly lost his life. On recovering, he showed his ability in an amazing comeback, and stormed through to win the 1989 race by only 8 seconds, which was the closest race in history.

7) Louison Bobet (France)

TOUR WINS: THREE

Bobet won three successive Tours between 1951 and 1953, starting a golden age in French cycling. Including his wins, French riders won 11 out of 15 Tours, a record they have rarely approached since. His performance in the 1953 Tour was considered to be one of the finest ever because the conditions were so difficult.

8) Philippe Thys (Belgium)

TOUR WINS: THREE

The first triple winner of the race, Thys would probably have won a lot more Tours if his career had not been interrupted by World War I. Although he started off as a cyclo-cross champion, he went on to win the Tour de France in 1913, 1914 and 1920. He won five stages in 1922 and two stages in the tour of 1924.

9) Fausto Coppi (Italy)

TOUR WINS: TWO

As with Thys, war took Coppi's best racing years from him and his racing career took place when travelling across borders was not particularly easy. He dominated the Tour in the mountains in a way rarely seen in the history of the race. His 1952 win has been described as the best Tour de France victory.

10) Laurent Fignon (France)

TOUR WINS: TWO

Fignon won the Tour at the age of 22 in 1983, and after thrashing Bernard Hinault the following year, it was expected that he would go on to win many more Tours. But plagued by injury, poor morale and a spate of bad luck, the rest of his career was blighted, and he missed out on winning in 1989 by just 8 seconds.

Great Road Races: The Giro d'Italia

The cycling season doesn't begin and end with the Tour de France. There are two other Grand Tours, the Tour of Italy and the Tour of Spain, as well as a whole host of stage races and one-day races from February through to October every year.

The Giro d'Italia, or Tour of Italy, is the first Grand Tour of the year, taking place in late May and early June. Like the Tour de France, it is three weeks long, and is contested in the same way, with daily stages and a general classification. The leader of the race wears a pink jersey, known as the 'maglia rosa', in the same way as the Tour de France leader wears a yellow jersey.

The race is as tough as the Tour de France, with stages in the Alps and Dolomite mountain ranges. In recent years, the Giro d'Italia organizers have tried to design ever-tougher mountain stages, to make it the hardest race in the world.

1949
Just like in the 1952 Tour de France, Fausto Coppi dominated the 1949 Giro with superb lone attacks in the mountains. His closest rival was Gino Bartali, who finished 24 minutes behind.

On a sporting level, it was a one-horse race, but the rivalry between Coppi and Bartali divided the nation. As Italy emerged from the chaos of World War II, it stood at a crossroads between the old ways, and the modern ways of the Western world. Bartali was a pious Catholic, who attracted the older, more conservative fans, while Coppi, divorced and conducting a public affair with another woman, represented the secular,

modern world. The fans played out the cultural war using Coppi and Bartali as symbols of their beliefs.

1987
The 1987 Giro d'Italia was possibly the most entertaining Grand Tour of them all, with a bitter feud raging at the heart of the race. Irishman Stephen Roche was the winner. He took the lead midway through the race, with an attack on a mountain stage. That might not have been a problem in itself, except that he was riding for an Italian team, in Italy,

Below: The Irish cyclist, Stephen Roche, who won the 1987 Giro d'Italia.

Above: Andy Hampsten, winner of the 1988 Giro d'Italia. He won the race in terrible conditions in the mountains.

Above: Fausto Coppi, who became a hero for Italian fans by winning the Giro d'Italia five times in the 40s and 50s.

and the rider he relieved of the pink jersey was his Italian team-mate Roberto Visentini. It caused a scandal.

Visentini spent the rest of the race conducting a war of words in the press with Roche, who could no longer rely on the support of his team-mates. The crowds by the roadside yelled abuse and threw missiles at Roche as he rode past, while Visentini tried to knock him off his bike. Roche prevailed and went on to win a historic triple in the same year – the Giro, the Tour and the World Championships.

1988

After the drama of 1987, it was only a year before the next big drama in the race. On a mountain stage to Bormio, in the Dolomites, the weather took a turn for the worse. It was raining in the valleys, but the stage was going over the 2,600m (8,500ft) Gavia pass, where the rain turned to snow. In apocalyptic conditions, the organizers refused to stop the race, forcing riders to struggle up through

the blizzard, then, which was worse, ride down the other side. American Andy Hampsten and Dutchman Erik Breukink handled the conditions the best, putting almost 5 minutes between them and the next rider, and Hampsten went on to win the race.

Above: The 18th stage of the Vuelta a España in 2007.

The Vuelta a España

The Tour of Spain, known as the Vuelta a España, is the third Grand Tour of the cycling season. It is not as big or brash as its counterparts in Italy and France, and suffered from a crisis in confidence when it was moved from May, when it used to attract good quality international stars, to September, towards the end of a long and tiring season. It is said that there are two kinds of riders at the Vuelta – those who want to win the race, and those who have been sent there as punishment. The Vuelta is a three-week stage race and the route changes each year but usually includes steep climbs. Nevertheless, it is still an important race. Spain emerged as a powerful cycling nation in the late 1980s and 1990s. Pedro Delgado and Miguel Indurain's Tour de France wins brought more fans to the Vuelta.

Nobody has ever dominated the Vuelta like Merckx dominated the Giro and Armstrong dominated the Tour – the record for victories is three by Swiss rider Tony Rominger between 1992 and 1994, and even Merckx only managed to win it once. Indurain famously never managed to win it, claiming it came at a time of the season when allergies affected his form.

Great Road Races: The Classics

As well as the Grand Tours, there are also many one-day races throughout the cycling year. The biggest and oldest are the five major Classics held at venues in Europe. The only other one-day race that comes close in terms of prestige is the World Championships.

For many riders and fans, the five Classics and the World Championship races are the ultimate prize – even more important than the Tour de France. For each Classic, there is an outstanding race or a rider that fought against all the odds to win. These races will never be forgotten.

Milan–San Remo

Known as 'La Primavera', Milan–San Remo happens as spring reaches northern Italy. It is a mainly flat race, which attracts the bunch sprinters, but two strategically placed hills near the finish always have the potential to stir things up. The most memorable race took place in 1983. This race has a fond place in the hearts of Italian cycling fans. The home favourite, Giuseppe Saronni, was the winner. He was wearing the rainbow jersey of world champion, which simultaneously heaped the pressure on to his shoulders, and made his victory all the more worthwhile. He attacked alone on the Poggio, the final climb into San Remo, and held off the bunch on the descent to the finish line.

Tour of Flanders

The whole of Belgium stops what it is doing on the day of the Tour of Flanders. Belgian cycling fans are among the most passionate in the world, and if they get a home winner, the excitement is comparable with a national holiday.

The race includes several steep cobbled climbs, called 'bergs', and rutted, sometimes muddy tracks, where the atmosphere is second to none. The race is usually decided on the climbs.

Belgian cycling fell into something of a decline when Eddy Merckx retired in 1977. The country embarked on a fruitless search to replace their hero, whose ability and wins will probably never be equalled in the sport.

In 2005, however, a new national hero emerged in the form of sprinter Tom Boonen. He dominated the race, making his rivals look second-rate with a searing attack in the final 10km (6 miles).

Left: Andrei Tchmil wins the Paris–Roubaix, the best performance of modern times.
Right: Giuseppe Saronni, who won the unforgettable 1983 Milan–San Remo.

Above: Tom Boonen (left), the Belgian rider who won a famous Tour of Flanders in 2005.

Paris–Roubaix

Famous for the cobbled farm tracks that appear with increasing frequency in the second half of the race, Paris–Roubaix is a hard race to ride. The rough tracks turn the race into a war of attrition,

which only the strongest can survive. Riding on cobbles is hard enough – it is atrociously difficult even for the strongest professional cyclists. In 1994 persistent rain added to this difficulty, turning the roads into quagmires, covering the riders in thick mud and causing crash after crash. The formidable Russian Andrei Tchmil emerged from the chaos to take victory, riding away from the other favourites with 50km (31 miles) still to ride.

Liège–Bastogne–Liège

The oldest of the Classics is a hilly race in the Ardennes region of Belgium. It tends to attract the type of rider who is also a contender for the Tour de France – the constant climbing whittles down the field until only the strongest climbers are left.

Above: Bernard Hinault en route to winning the 1980 World Championships in dominant style.

Above: Hinault, this time battling through arctic conditions at the 1980 Liège–Bastogne–Liège.

Frenchman Bernard Hinault won the 1980 Liège–Bastogne–Liège in a terrible blizzard that besieged the riders throughout the race and subsequently wiped out more than half of the field. As rider after rider abandoned the race, Hinault forged ahead on his own, finishing 9 minutes ahead of the next rider. The cold was so terrible that Hinault never regained the feeling in one of his fingers.

Tour of Lombardy

The 'race of the falling leaves' takes place in northern Italy at the end of the cycling season. The race winds through the scenic wooded hills surrounding Lake Como – the biggest climb, the Madonna del Ghisallo, is named after the chapel at the top. Cycling fans consider this to be the most beautiful race of the season.

A race as hard as the Tour of Lombardy is usually won by solo escapers, but in 1983, a group of 13 riders poured into the finishing straight, including recently crowned world champion Greg

Lemond, and Irishman Sean Kelly, who would become one of the most prolific Classics winners of them all.

As the group sprinted towards the line, there was a blanket finish, with four riders flashing across the line. In first place was Kelly, only half a wheel ahead of Lemond.

The World Championships

Held at a different venue every year, the World Championships take place over a course based on laps of the same circuit. Unusually, riders compete for their country, rather than the professional trade teams they represent the rest of the year. The winner of the race is presented with a white jersey with rainbow stripes, which he has the right to wear in races for the next year.

In 1980 the course was more mountainous than it had ever been before, based at Sallanches in the French Alps. This coincided with French cyclist Bernard Hinault, a notoriously prickly character, coming back from injury, during which he had been written off by the media. He took his revenge by thrashing his rivals, attacking on the climb on each lap until he was on his own.

OFF-ROAD RACING

The next step up from riding off-road trails is racing along them. With the boom in mountain biking, off-road racing has grown along with the popularity of the bikes themselves. Mountain bike cross-country racing is now an Olympic sport, while thousands of people enter long-distance enduro races.

The sport of cyclo-cross, which developed along with the sport of road racing, has enjoyed a mini-boom on the back of mountain biking. As people discover the fun of racing mountain bikes, cyclo-cross gives them a different opportunity to race off-road.

Above: Cross-country racing on mountain bikes has become more and more popular.
Left: Off-road racing is a tough but rewarding sport.

The Cross-country Race Bike

A good cross-country bike has to meet many requirements. Cross-country racing is technically demanding, testing physical strength and stamina and bike-handling ability across a wide variety of terrains.

In a cross-country race held on a small or medium-sized circuit, a rider can expect to encounter steep uphills, technical sections demanding occasional dismounting, twisty descents and long flat sections. Added to all that, the prevailing weather must also be taken into consideration. If it is raining, wet surfaces can completely change the character of a circuit. What is perfectly acceptable to ride on in the dry might be a totally different proposition in poor weather or in muddy conditions.

There is a perfect cross-country bike for each course, but most people cannot keep a stable of mountain bikes, all set up differently, to take down when they are needed. Sometimes, a compromise is necessary, in which case you should simply get a bike that you feel comfortable with and that suits you and your riding style.

Most cross-country courses include punishing technical sections that make great demands on both bike and rider, so it is also a good idea to emphasize reliability.

Anatomy of a cross-country race bike

1 Suspension fork: Medium or short travel or 'give' – some shock absorbency is needed.

2 Full-suspension frame: Greater shock absorbency is needed for technical sections of the races. Some models can lock out the suspension system for better conditions and easier terrain.

3 Brakes: V-brakes are the lightest, most efficient option, and they provide good stopping power.

4 Wheels: 26in spoked wheels.

5 Tyres: Knobbly tyres are good for maximum traction. If the course has less in the way of loose surface, such as stones, semi-slicks can be substituted instead.

6 Gears: Nine-speed freewheel. Gear levers are integrated with brake levers.

7 Chainset: Triple chainset for a wide range of gears – some technical and steep sections need very low gears to prevent stalling.

8 Pedals: Clipless pedals to be used with off-road shoes. Shoeplates can clip into either side of the pedal.

Choosing a cross-country bike

The first question is whether to go for hardtail or full suspension. The hardtail will be lighter uphill, but is much less comfortable and manoeuvrable down the other side. Until full-suspension bikes are made lighter, this choice will have to be made. With suspension, both at the forks and rear of the bike, travel is an important factor. For leisure riding, greater travel in the suspension gives a more comfortable ride. But racing riders want speed rather than comfort. Ideally there will be minimal travel in the forks and just enough travel in the rear to take the shock out of bumpy downhills.

Left: Suspension forks are needed for all but the easiest of cross-country courses, dampening the shock of hitting bumps, rocks and tree roots.

Top left: Many cross-country courses have technical sections that test riders' abilities to the limit.
Top: Powerful disc brakes help control speed.
Above: Thick, knobbly tyres are necessary for grip and traction.

Sizing is important. Cross-country racing bikes have a long top tube for aerodynamics and efficiency on long hills but a shorter bike is easier to pedal up short steep hills. Cross-country bikes use 26in wheels, with a width of between 1½ and 2in. The narrower the wheel, the lighter, but a 1.5in wheel will be a compromise between lightness and durability. Tyre pressures need to be higher, so rough terrain is hard to ride on. On a fast, dry course, less tread gives a more efficient ride.

Cross-country Race Skills

Cross-country races can be won on your ability to go up and down hills successfully. Practice can really pay off in this situation. If you cannot climb, you will find it difficult to win a cross-country race because most courses are hilly.

By training for climbs and riding them effectively, your chances of victory or a top-ten finish will be increased. Even if you are well behind the leaders, riding to your own potential is a satisfying experience. While most hills will probably be short, steep sprints, there will still be significant amounts of climbing in most courses.

As well as training, there are two things you can do to lighten the load and increase your climbing speed – losing weight yourself, and losing weight from your bike. At the same time, work on your climbing technique and you will see big improvements.

The longer top tube typical on racing cross-country bikes is an aid to climbing – it stretches your upper body out and gives you a lower centre of gravity. Bar-end attachments will get you even lower.

Depending on the steepness and the surface, move backward and forward on the bike to maintain traction. A steep

climb needs more weight forward, while you can stay back for a steady climb. It may sometimes be necessary to climb out of the saddle but this reduces traction in the back wheel, so you must judge whether the terrain is suitable. Climbing out of the saddle can be useful when a hill is very steep or if you are trying to get to the top ahead of another competitor before reaching a technical section you want to lead.

Descending and cornering

While cross-country races can be won on the uphill sections, they can equally be won or lost in the downhills. Descending fast is an essential part of cross-country racing – you will need to be able to relax and stay controlled.

If you have a full-suspension bike, your job is already easier – by taking some of the shock out of the bumps,

Left: On less technical descents, keep your weight back and stay in control of your bike.

Above: Be careful of letting gaps go during uphill sections, and always be on the lookout for overtaking chances.

the suspension will allow you to control your line and bike much better.

To ride down steep hills fast, you need to allow the bike to do some of the work while you stay supple and relaxed. Get your weight back – on some very steep hills, you need to be well over the back wheel, with your stomach touching the saddle. Check your speed by feathering the back brake, and pick your line well ahead.

In corners, depending on your speed, the angle of the track and how sharp the bend itself is, the correct technique is to use shifts in your weight, as well as steering, to get round. With more body weight over the front wheel, you can gain traction and control.

Many bends are banked, which helps in getting round them – moderate your speed before you hit the bend, lean the bike over, keep your head at 90 degrees

Above: During complicated sections, keep your fingers over the brakes in case of sudden obstacles.
Left: Tackle descents that have obstacles with care. Stay relaxed and balanced.

to the ground, steer as much as you need to and let the banking and centrifugal force do the rest.

Planning and fuelling
For longer races, it is not enough to simply turn up and ride. Since no external assistance is allowed in cross-country racing, you have to help yourself in the case of mechanical trouble. You are also responsible for making sure that you eat and drink enough to prevent yourself running out of energy.

It is your choice how much mechanical gear you take with you in a race, but if finishing is a priority, then you will need to carry spare tubes, tyre levers and a chain breaker. With these tools you can improvise a repair that will get you up and running again.

For race food, modern energy bars and gels are light and take up very little space – in a long race you need to eat at least one energy bar or gel an hour.

They can be carried tucked into a pocket. Drink plenty of fluid, depending on the weather: experience will tell you how much you need.

Above: Aim to control your line and your bike when riding down a bumpy or rocky descent.
Above left: In longer races, riders have to refuel on the go. It's a good idea to keep an energy gel tucked in the shorts for easy access.

Cross-country Race Strategies

The difficult terrain of cross-country events is such that technique and tactics throughout the race really count if you are to win. As with most cycle races, trying to have a plan for every eventuality is the best bet.

At the start of a cross-country race it is crucial to get to the front as soon as possible. Courses tend to narrow down to a singletrack fairly quickly, making overtaking very difficult. The more people get in front of you at the start, the harder it is to make any headway on the leaders. Some starts are organized by race number or seeding, with the best riders on the front row, and the others in lines behind them. Others are based on order of arrival.

There are two things that will affect your initial placing in a race – your grid position, and yourself. If you are on the front line, you will have a clear run at the first corner. If you are back on the third row, you'll be fighting for position.

A good start, in either position, will significantly help your chances. Before the start, warm up thoroughly – your legs have to be ready for an immediate big effort. A physical warm-up is not the only necessity – go through the first

minutes of the race mentally, which will get you focused on what you need to do.

When the starting gun goes, get clipped in quickly and go as hard as you can to get to or stay at the front. The sprint for the first corner, or the first narrow section, is as important as the sprint for the finish line. You need to be strong and determined, and able to recover quickly from the effort.

Pacing

Cross-country races, even short ones, are extremely hard work. Uphill sections build up lactic acid in the muscles. The start puts you into oxygen debt. Long technical sections of singletrack force you to constantly brake and accelerate. Even supporting your body weight and absorbing the shocks on the downhill sections is very hard. Fitness is crucial, and so is the ability to pace yourself. Trying too hard in the first half of a race can leave you with no energy in the second

Above: Cross-country mountain bike races start with all the riders in a group.

Above: Cross-country races involve consistent and intense efforts.

half but sitting back to save yourself for the second half will leave you well down the field, with stragglers blocking up the singletrack. Experience will tell you how hard you can go. But cross-country is not a time trial – it is a race against other people. Sometimes it is important to go harder or ease up. If you are a handful of seconds ahead of the rider behind and you know that there is a stretch of singletrack coming up, try to get there first. It's worth making the effort to stay ahead – they will find it difficult to get past once the singletrack starts, and you can recuperate there. If you are in second place, you know that a really hard dig for a few minutes will be worth it if you can get past.

Overtaking

Singletrack is great for technically skilful riders. During a singletrack section of a cross-country race, good bike handlers and trail riders come into their own.

On a singletrack, having the skills needed to overtake when you get stuck behind a slower rider is crucial. You could always wait until the next climb or wider track to overtake, but that might be several minutes away. Instead, you should press for a chance to overtake.

To overtake on singletrack takes acceleration and foresight. Follow your opponent's wheel, assuming he or she is on the racing line, and look past them for small gaps, or wider sections. Keep pressing, staying as close as possible,

Top left: Don't lose concentration during downhill sections.
Top middle: Always keep your eyes open for overtaking opportunities.
Top right: When you start to get tired, try to keep going and pace yourself.
Above left: The start of a race is a crucial time for getting into the best position.
Above: With luck, fitness and ability, comes victory.

so that when the opportunity presents itself you will be ready for it. When it comes, attack hard and try to surprise your opponent. If you can get your front wheel in front of theirs, you can dictate the racing line. The openings will be brief, but they are there to be taken.

Great Mountain Bike Races

The World Cup, the World Championships and the Olympics are big events for mountain bike competitors. Attracting the elite of international mountain bike riders, they are popular with tourists and also with aspiring riders.

In a notable series of mountain bike events that are scheduled around the world during the course of a year, four stand out.

The World Cup
In this event, riders win points in each round, which count towards an overall title at the end of the year in a variety of disciplines including cross-country, downhill and four-cross racing.

Events attract huge crowds, and the World Cup has evolved into the most important mountain biking competition in the world, after the Olympic Games. The various events have proved popular as tourist races – amateurs can ride on the same terrain and courses as their professional heroes.

Right: Ned Overend, a formidable and successful competitor in many mountain biking events.

Above: The Dane, Henrik Djernis, has won countless races in his long career.

The World Championships
The mountain bike World Championships started in 1990 and are now a one-off event held annually in a different venue every year. Disciplines added from 1992 include cross-country, trials riding, downhill and four-cross. The blue riband event is the men's cross-country race, which was first run in 1990 and won by US mountain biking legend Ned Overend. Winners of the events receive a gold medal and are eligible to wear the rainbow jersey for similar events for a year.

The World Championships are arranged by nationality rather than by teams, and are usually held at the end of the mountain biking season.

The most successful rider at the World event has been Danishman Henrik Djernis, who won three world championships in 1992, 1993 and 1994. In recent years Julien Absalon also won a hat trick, between 2004 and 2006.

Above: French mountain biker Julien Absalon won the Olympics in 2004.

The Olympic Games

The cross-country race has been part of the Olympic Games since 1996, and is seen as the pinnacle of mountain biking competition. It is the only form of mountain biking discipline practised at the Summer Olympics, and the gold medal winners have gone down in history as legends of the sport.

The first Olympic cross-country race for men in Atlanta 1996 was won by Dutchman Bart Brentjens, while Italian Paola Pezzo took the women's race. The Americans hosted the event with expectations of victory, but the home of mountain biking came away with nothing except a bronze medal in the women's race. Their top finisher in the men's race was Tinker Juarez in 19th place. France has performed well since then, having taken two gold medals in the men's cross-country race. Miguel Martinez dominated the Sydney Olympic race in 2000, while Julien Absalon was the winner in Athens in 2004.

The Sea Otter Classic

One of the biggest off-road cycling festivals in the world is the Sea Otter Classic. The World Championships, the World Cup and Olympic Games have the official stamp of approval, while the Sea Otter Classic welcomes amateur racers as well as the top elites. Sea Otter takes place in Monterey, California, and hosts events such as dirt-jumping, slalom, cross-country, downhill and elite-level races as well as trials demonstrations. The Classic attracts more than 50,000 mountain biking enthusiasts, and spectators and riders alike enjoy one of the largest cycling events of the year.

Above: Miguel Martinez on his way to a gold medal in the 2000 Summer Olympics in Sydney.
Below: Bart Brentjens, who won bronze in the 2004 Summer Olympics.

Left: The popular Sea Otter Classic in Monterey celebrates the sport of mountain biking with several events for all levels and all ages.

Cyclo-cross

The winter sport of cyclo-cross is the original off-road racing – it was around for years before mountain bikes came on to the scene. Cyclo-cross is very different from mountain biking; both take place off-road, but there the similarity ends.

A cyclo-cross bike looks more like a road bike than a mountain bike, with dropped handlebars and minimal extras. In a race, riders get off their bikes during steep sections and run with their bikes on their shoulders, sometimes for significant distances. Unlike mountain bike races, which are predicated on self-sufficiency, cyclo-cross races allow mechanical assistance. Riders often use two bikes in a race – one to ride, while the other is cleaned and prepared by a helper.

Obstacles along the way

Cyclo-cross races are short and sharp. They take place on a circuit, upon which the riders do enough laps for the race to last an hour. Like a mountain bike race, overtaking is difficult, with many circuits offering enough room for only one rider to pass. Circuits can incorporate muddy sections, wooded paths, sand, steep hills, cambered sections and occasionally even stretches of road. Tree roots and rocks have to be cycled over, jumped or riders simply have to dismount. Many organizers incorporate short sections of boarded jumps, about 30cm (12in) high, which have to be crossed on foot, although the 1989 world championships were won by Belgian Danny De Bie, who developed a technique of bunny-hopping the obstacles and staying on his bike while others wasted time dismounting, running and remounting. Depending on the time of year and weather, there may be obstacles such as water and ice. Coping with these challenges will improve your chances in a race.

Right: Weary cyclists carry their bikes during the Three Peaks cyclo-cross event in Yorkshire, England, which is one of the longest and toughest events in the world. It covers 61km (38 miles) over three of the highest hills in the country.

Mud

Cyclo-cross is referred to as 'mud-plugging', which describes the conditions encountered in a cyclo-cross race. After rain, the course becomes stickier and more slippery. Sticky mud gets into the tyre treads and the workings of your bike, adding to its weight and detracting significantly from its performance. A bike change every lap can help, but the mud soon builds up again, sapping your strength. Slippery mud comes with more rain. Keeping your balance is difficult, especially on cambered surfaces or around corners.

The main technique to use when riding in mud is to put the bike into a lower gear, and sit more upright, putting more weight on the pedals so that you are still sitting on the saddle but also letting your legs take the strain. This will give more traction. This takes a little weight off the handlebars, which results

in a more relaxed riding style, and it leads on to another technique that is easier to do than explain. It involves letting the bike take some decisions for you – don't force it to follow a certain line. In really atrocious conditions, let some pressure out of your tyres to give more traction in the mud.

Dry conditions

You can approach a dry cyclo-cross course very differently from a muddy one, and the going will be easier and faster. Depending on the surface of the course, it might be worth putting on tyres with less tread and inflating them to a higher pressure. You will not need to change bikes so often, or perhaps at all – plan for this, and your race strategy will be more effective.

Roots and bunny hops

To ride over roots, lift your front wheel over them and let your back wheel follow. This way you can maintain maximum traction and acceleration.

To clear bunny hops, lift the front wheel first, pulling your arms up. Then, immediately pull up and backwards with your legs to get the back wheel over the obstacle. If they are too high, the only way is to jump off and run over them.

Ice and snow

The hardest surface of all to deal with is ice – the slightest deviation in your line, or on the surface, can have you off your

Left: Riders have to get off and run when bunny hops are too high to jump.

Above left: On muddy ground, riding becomes less efficient – sometimes it is faster to get off and run.
Above: When the weather is dry, races are much faster.
Below: Cyclo-crossers should be prepared for all kinds of conditions.

bike very quickly. Being able to avoid crashing on an icy course is a big advantage. The technique for riding on ice is to turn a big gear and sit low, to keep your centre of gravity nearer the ground. Fatter tyres, at a lower pressure, help to maintain grip.

Snow can be similar to mud and clogs up the workings of the bike, especially the brakes and the sprockets. For this you will need tyres with a deeper tread on the rear wheel and a file tread on the front.

The Cyclo-cross Bike

Cyclo-cross is a winter sport, so bikes are subject to constant abuse from rain, mud, sand and grit. Mud and dirt builds up in the crannies of the frame, in the brakes and in the gears, so to get a good performance from your bike, maintenance is essential.

Cyclo-cross bikes may look like road racing bikes, but they have a number of modifications that make them ideal for off-road racing. Bikes for cyclo-cross need to be as light as possible so that they are easier to carry. On a technical course, with steep hills, the riders will spend a great deal of time running with their bikes on their shoulders, and every extra gram counts. Comfort is a consideration, although most cyclo-cross events tend to be short at around an hour, so it is not as important as it would be with a mountain bike or a sportive bike.

Choosing a cyclo-cross bike

Cyclo-cross frames tend to be about 1cm (½in) shorter along the top tube than an equivalent road bike for the same rider. Aerodynamics are not as important, so riders sit more upright, with higher handlebars, and brake levers positioned higher up, giving a shorter position. Frame geometry differs – a shallower seat angle, and a moved-back saddle pushes the rider back so that their weight is farther over the rear wheel. This helps steering and control and adds traction over rough terrain.

Anatomy of a cyclo-cross bike

❶ **Frame:** Lightweight for easier carrying, with large clearances to avoid mud build-up.
❷ **Wheels:** Lightweight, for easier carrying. Mud builds up on spokes, so modern wheels have fewer of them. V-shaped rims are easier to clean. Size is usually 700x28C, but larger or smaller wheels can be used according to conditions.
❸ **Tyres:** Fat and knobbly for extra traction on loose surfaces. Pressures are lower than for road tyres, which also helps traction.
❹ **Chainset:** Single, double or triple chainrings, according to terrain. A triple offers more gears, but weighs more. Generally, double is most popular, using 39–48. Cranks are marginally longer than a typical road bike.
❺ **Sprockets:** Nine-speed freewheel with 13–26 sprockets.

❻ **Brakes:** Cantilever brakes avoid mud build-up. Brake levers incorporate gear levers for accessibility. Some riders ride with an extra pair of brakes on the top, with separate cables to the brakes.
❼ **Handlebars:** High handlebars for an upright position, with dropped ends, for use when accelerating.
❽ **Pedals:** Clipless pedals to be combined with an off-road shoe.

Above: Cyclo-cross bikes have to be set up to deal with clogging mud.
Right: Riders in cyclo-cross events need to be prepared to spend a lot of time running with their bike.

The clearances on a cyclo-cross frame are large, with no bridge between the chainstays, and the fittings are designed to take cantilever brakes. These have separate calliper arms attached to pivot points on the frame and forks, joined by a central cable that runs to the brake levers. The advantage of cantilever brakes is that they do not clog up with mud.

Wheels need to be lightweight. Carbon composite wheels can be used, which have fewer spokes and are very easy to clean. On these wheels, the braking surface is aluminium, for better performance. Carbon wheels are an expensive option, however, and a set of lightweight spoked wheels will also offer good performance. Deep, V-shaped rims are less likely to clog up around the spokes, and are easier to clean.

Tyres need good traction. Cyclo-cross tyres are knobbly to prevent slipping.

It is possible to ride cyclo-cross races with single, double or triple chainrings, according to the terrain. A single chainring saves weight, but there will be

Above left: Cyclo-cross bikes are similar to road bikes, but note the thicker tyres and cantilever brakes.
Above right: Stay upright when riding through challenging or technical sections.

fewer gears. Doubles are the best option generally, using a 39–48 combination, with 13–26 sprockets at the back. In very steep terrain, a triple might be necessary, but it is often easier to get off and run up steep hills because of the rough ground.

Cyclo-cross Skills

Racing cyclo-cross requires a wider set of skills than racing on the road. Accidents apart, road racers mount once and dismount once, before and after a race. Cyclo-crossers may do this 50 times or more in the course of a race so it's an important skill to perfect.

Running with the bike on your shoulder will be quicker than riding in many situations. You should learn to dismount and mount in relaxed, confident movements, making them part of the forward progress of your bike.

When and how to dismount

The reasons for dismounting are a steep hill, or an obstacle that you cannot jump the bike over or ride around. On a steep hill, first try riding out of the saddle with your weight back to maintain traction. If the hill is too steep, dismount from the bike. In the approach to the dismount, ride in an upright position, with your hands on the brake hoods. Unclip your right foot and swing it over the back of the saddle, and grab the top tube with your right hand as you jump off. Unclip the left foot. With the bike still moving, start running as your feet hit the ground, and lift your bike on to your shoulder. If the hill you are about to ride up is rideable at the bottom, don't

Handling on slippery hills

Cyclo-cross climbs are short and steep, and the fastest way up when they are rideable is to ride out of the saddle with your hands on the brake hoods. But the muddier the ground, the harder it is to gain traction. When it is especially slippery, stay out of the saddle, but try to put your weight back over your rear wheel to prevent it from slipping, and ride in as straight a line as possible.

Descending is straightforward – hold the drops, and relax, with your weight set back to keep traction, and staying out of the saddle so you can use your legs as shock absorbers. If you feel the bike slipping, or you can see an especially difficult section coming up, unclip one foot from the pedal and touch it to the ground for balance.

Dismounting from your bike

1: *Approach a dismount with your hands on the brake hoods.*

2: *Unclip your right foot and start to swing your leg over the saddle.*

3: *Unclip your left foot and jump from the bike.*

4: *Lift your bike on to the shoulder or, if you are tall, hold the frame.*

dismount until then. Try not to grind to a halt, but swing your right leg over, keeping both hands on the brake levers. Jump off, push the bike along the ground to maintain momentum, then pick the bike up. Running with a bike unbalances your natural rhythm and weighs you down. Carry the bike with the top tube on your right shoulder, with the wheel turned inward. Taller riders may find it more comfortable to hold the head tube with one arm, and the handlebars with the other. Shorter riders hook their arm under the down tube, and hold on to the drop of the handlebar. Most running sections are short, so concentrate on strong running.

How to remount

Once you have cleared the obstacle, remount. Grab the top tube with your right hand, and put the bike on the ground. Push forward to get moving again, at the same speed as you are running. Put both hands on the brake hoods and jump back into the saddle, with your right leg over the back wheel. Once you are on the saddle, look down to the pedals, and clip both feet in.

Climbing

Climbing: *When climbing, keep your weight back over the rear wheel.*

How to run with your bike

Running: *Lift the bike on to your shoulder, or if you are tall, hold it by the frame. Look ahead to where you are going and stay upright, relaxed and balanced.*

Remounting your bike

1: *Put your bike on the ground while you are still running.*

2: *Place your hands on both handlebars before remounting.*

3: *Jump back on, swinging your right leg over the saddle.*

4: *Land in the saddle as you clip in with your left foot.*

TRACK RACING

Track riding is bike racing at its purest. The bikes have a single gear, with a fixed wheel system that prevents freewheeling. They have no brakes – sudden braking is not necessary, and the legs can be used to slow the bikes down. Riders race around a velodrome – a steep, banked oval track, either indoor or outdoor. The banking helps keep the speed high by counteracting the centrifugal force that normally pulls riders out on bends. Track racing is fast and furious, with spectacular races and unique athletic challenges.

Above: In the Madison relay race, one rider propels another into 'play'.
Left: Specialized track races take place in a velodrome.

The Track Bike

Track bikes are the minimalist art of the bike world; they are pared-down lightweight models. The designs are highly specialized, and there are almost as many different types of track bikes as there are events.

Sprinters' bikes need to be as stiff as possible, to withstand the considerable force applied during acceleration. Pursuit riders add tri-bars to their bikes for more aerodynamic positions, and their frames need less steep angles than the sprinters.

It is impractical for most riders interested in riding track to own a different bike for each race, so most track bikes are capable of being used in all events, with small adjustments for each event if necessary.

Track bikes are built for speed and efficiency. While road bikes are often a compromise between the stiffness needed to ensure effective transmission of energy and comfort over long distances, there is no compromise with track bikes. The stiffer the better in this case, since you will not be doing any long rides on your track bike.

Specification of a track bike

Track frames have a shorter wheelbase, and positions are often set more aggressively than on road bikes, with lower handlebars for better aerodynamics. The biggest difference between track bikes and road bikes is in the gearing. Although component manufacturers have been adding more sprockets on to the back wheel of a road bike – from five in the 1970s to ten 30 years later – the track bike still has only one gear. Riders accelerate, cruise and sprint in the same gear, and a lockring on the rear gearing prevents freewheeling. Riders must choose a gear based on their experience and training.

The wheels are built for lightness and stiffness. Many riders favour a solid carbon fibre rear disc and spoked front wheel. The front wheels also may be

Above: Track bikes have a single chainring at the front and a single sprocket at the back, giving only one gear.
Below: Track bikes are pared down to the minimum, so that very high speeds can be reached.

carbon fibre, with deep rim sections and three or four spokes to reduce air resistance. Handlebars are deep and narrow. For racing, riders need only use the drops, so the tops of the bars are minimal. With bars set closer to the bike, riders can use their arms and upper body to pull up while pushing down on the pedals, to gain extra power.

Right: Track bikes don't have brakes – to decelerate, just slow down pedalling rate.

Anatomy of a track bike

❶ **Frame and forks:** Ultra-stiff carbon fibre one-piece frame. Frames are light, but low flexibility under acceleration is most important. Steep angles give a more responsive, albeit less comfortable ride.

❷ **Rear disc wheel:** Solid, and more stiff and aerodynamic than a spoked wheel. Attached to the frame with a fixed nut, rather than a quick release, to withstand the force of acceleration.

❸ **Front wheel:** Stiff, aerodynamic carbon fibre deep section rims with minimum number of spokes for less air resistance. Sometimes solid.

❹ **Tyres:** Lightweight tubular tyres for less rolling resistance and weight.

❺ **Chainring:** Single lightweight chainring.

❻ **Sprocket:** Single sprocket gives only one gear ratio, so gear selection is crucial. Hub is fixed to prevent freewheeling.

❼ **Handlebars:** Deep handlebars, set in close to the bike for greater aerodynamics, and to give maximum pull during acceleration.

❽ **Saddle:** Comfortable and supportive.

❾ **Pedals:** Clipless road pedals. For some events, in which acceleration is important, riders also strap their feet to the pedals for extra security and power.

Track Racing Skills: Getting Started

Track riding is a bit more limited than road riding in the sense that if you don't live near a velodrome, it is difficult to practise, whereas on the road, you can just go out and train. If your ambitions lie on the track, find your nearest velodrome and arrange to train there.

If you can only ride on a velodrome twice a month, make the most of the sessions on the track, and work on your endurance, speed and power on a road bike. Many countries boast velodromes and the sport is very popular in Europe, particularly in France, Germany, Belgium and the United Kingdom. Japan and Australia have also taken up track racing, and it is included in the Summer Olympic Games and also the Track World Championships.

Starting out

Even if you are an experienced bike rider, it is worth taking time and care over the transition to a track bike and

Right: When riding in a bunch on the track, keep your head up in case of riders changing direction in front of you.

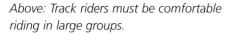

Above: Track riders must be comfortable riding in large groups.

Above: To attack, riders accelerate, then jump hard to quickly make a gap.

riding on a velodrome. When a rider wants to stop, the natural reflex, built up over years of cycling, is to stop pedalling and apply the brakes, but there are no

brakes, and it is impossible to freewheel on a track bike. The result of trying to do this can be undignified, at best, as the momentum of the pedals going

round throws the unsuspecting road rider off the bike. Stopping a track bike is an acquired skill. At the end of a race or ride, just slow down gradually, circling the track as you do so. As you come to a halt, lean up against the track wall or railings, so you can unclip safely. If you

Above: When riding around a bend in the velodrome, it is very important to maintain your balance.

need to stop more quickly, use your legs as brakes by fighting against the turn of the pedals. Keep your balance and make sure the upper body is providing a good anchor for your legs. After a while you will be able to control your speed with variations in pedalling technique.

Riding on a velodrome track for the first time can also be difficult. The banking on the corners, especially on smaller tracks, seems quite steep. It is important to ride positively into a corner, especially when you are inexperienced. The banking is there to guide you round

Above: Rebecca Romero and the UK team on their way to winning the Women's Team Pursuit in the Track World Championships of 2008.

the corner without losing speed, so concentrate on getting up to a good speed, then holding your line as you hit the bend. Do not be tempted to turn left (down), as you will come off the banking and lose speed. Instead, follow the bend round until the exit. It is an exhilarating experience, and the more you do it, the more your confidence will grow. If you follow the golden rule of holding your speed and line, your progress round the bend will be constant.

Gaining speed

Banking on a track not only keeps your bike in a straight line when you go around corners, it can also help you to accelerate in a race. If you ride in a straight line around the banking, you are essentially riding along the flat. By riding up the banking, to the top, you have ridden up a hill. Correspondingly, it is downhill from there to the bottom of the track. Sprinters often use this technique to gain extra acceleration. To do this, move to the outside of the track

Right: To perform a track stand, turn the wheel up the track and balance carefully.

before the corner, and follow the line round at the top of the bank. Once you are round the apex of the bend, accelerate hard, and turn inward so that you can take advantage of the downhill slope to boost your speed. You should not cross anyone's racing line while you are doing this, although professional track sprinters take their riding right up to the limit of this rule. One disadvantage is that by riding around the outside you are riding farther than your rival, but this is balanced by the extra acceleration. Experience will show you when to use this tactic.

Track Racing Skills: Group Riding

Most track events involve riding in a bunch. With limited space on the track, riders must co-operate, as well as compete with each other. When riding in a bunch, individuals must develop a keen sense of awareness, and anticipate what others are going to do.

Riding with other people is especially important in the keirin event, where six sprinters race against each other, and the team pursuit, where four team-mates have to work together to ride as fast as possible. In each case, you will be riding at great speed in close proximity to other riders, and your safety relies on everybody being capable of riding in a group situation.

Bunches of riders move efficiently around velodromes, if everyone rides in a straight line and holds that line around the bends. It gets complicated when, as often happens in a bike race, certain riders want to move past other riders.

Manoeuvres take place in a spirit of general co-operation, within certain boundaries. Riders are responsible for

Below: Riders must be aware of the situation of the whole bunch and look around to check where other cyclists are positioned.

Above: When the speed in a race increases, the group lines out into single file – riders must not let gaps go.

their own actions and for knowing what is happening around them. You should be constantly looking ahead and focusing on what is happening. You can hear riders behind you, and occasionally look behind with a small glance, just to make sure nobody is coming up fast. If you want to move up, once you are sure nobody is coming up fast behind you, give a small signal by flicking your elbow out on the side you want to move into. Then make your move. Communication is important. Riders shout to let each other know if they are coming up fast,

or if you move out too suddenly. Keep your movements flowing, rather than sudden – this maintains the speed and momentum of the bunch, avoids making enemies, and will allow for smoother, more efficient acceleration.

Sprinting

When sprinting, choose and hold your line, and respect that of other riders. In a scratch race, when sprinting for first place at the finishing line, 10 or 15

Above: One momentary lapse of concentration can cause a crash – take care to stay out of trouble.

riders, or even more, can be jockeying for position across the track. Never move across someone's line, and trust that they will not do the same to you. It's a good idea to get into a good position at the front before the final sprint starts, so you can avoid the jostling farther back. In a team pursuit, or during a breakaway,

Above: This shows the point in a race when riders are holding a straight line around bends.

Above: In a race, if you ride directly behind another rider, you will save yourself effort.

Golden rules of track riding

1 Keep pedalling
You should always keep your legs moving on your track bike – with no freewheel, you have no choice but to pedal while the bike is moving, and your legs control your speed. The constant pedalling can have a beneficial effect on your pedalling style for other forms of riding and on the suppleness of your legs.

2 Keep your line
You will obviously need to move from side to side occasionally in order to pass riders, but there is a definite etiquette to follow, based around the idea that no rider should put another rider in danger. When moving out, signal with a flick of your arm that you are going to do so.

3 Keep your head horizontal
When going around the bend, don't hold your head at 90 degrees to the sloping track; hold it horizontal to the ground. This will help you keep your balance and judge the steepness of the banking.

4 Be aware of those around you
Keep an eye on the riders ahead, and turn around every so often to check what is going on behind you. Know where the other riders are and what they are doing, and you can use this to your advantage.

5 Vary the pace
The greatest skills in track riding are being able to accelerate fast, and hold a high cruising speed. If you can do this in a race, your chances of success are much higher.

6 Concentrate
Things happen very quickly in track races, including crashes. Be ready to react to everything that happens in front of you.

riders work in groups as in a road race. The best way is to ride in a line, one behind the other, because there are no crosswinds to make group riding more efficient. Each rider does a turn, then swings up the banking, keeping the same speed, but adding distance so the others can move up on the inside. The first rider drops into last position in the line.

Track Racing: Scratch Race, Points Race and the Madison

Track racing has evolved an esoteric and unusual group of events, perhaps because tracks are so uniform across the world. To provide entertainment and variety for the crowds, different styles of racing have developed.

Track racing is basically divided into two types of event – endurance and short distance. The short-distance events are the explosive ones – sprinting, kilometre time trials, and an event that originated in Japan called the keirin.

Endurance events include the pursuits, individual and team, and races such as the points race, scratch race and the Madison.

Scratch Race

The most straightforward on the track, the scratch race is a distance race that is held over a number of laps or of kilometres, and the first rider across the line is the winner. The bunch does not ride the distance and just wait for the sprint finish, however. Like riders in a road race who want to neutralize a sprinter by attacking early, track riders don't want to pull a fast sprinter all the way to the last corner and see them sweep to victory. The scratch race is often full of attacks, counterattacks, splits and politics.

When racing a scratch race, it is a good idea to do your research first. Find out who is riding, who is a good sprinter and who is better at long drawn-out efforts. Make sure the sprinter is not in a position to go for victory, and watch for meaningful attacks by the latter kind of rider. There is no need to follow every attack through the race, but when a good long-distance rider goes, try to get into their slipstream, and see what you can do to gain a gap by working with anybody else who has made the split.

The advantage of racing in a velodrome is that once you have a gap of 100m (330ft) or more, you can see your pursuers on the other

side of the track. Keep an eye on them. When they string out it means that they are going faster, so inject a little more effort into your breakaway work, sharing to maintain the gap. If your break proves to be successful, you'll be in the sprint for the win. If it does not, just sit back in the bunch and gather your resources before making your next attack.

Above: In a scratch race, the first rider across the line wins, and the race is full of attacks and counterattacks.

Points Race

The winner of the points race is not necessarily the rider who crosses the line first at the finish. Over the course of the points race, there is a sprint, usually every 10 laps, for which points are awarded to the first four riders over the line. Throughout the race, each rider accumulates more points, and the rider with the most points at the finish is declared the winner. Some sprints offer double points.

The best way of guaranteeing a win in the points race would be to win every sprint. Since this scenario is unlikely, tactics start to come into play.

The most basic tactic involves going for every sprint, so that you have at least some chance each time. This is highly energy-consuming, although it can be an effective way of racing. There is a risk of spreading yourself too thinly, however, and tiring yourself for the crucial sprints later in the race.

The other method is to sit back and not contest the first two or three sprints. Save yourself and keep your resources for a big effort at the last sprint before halfway. If you can win this, you have a good foundation for the second half of the event.

The riders who have spent energy going for the first sprints may be too tired to match you. However, you should be careful of letting anyone accumulate too big a lead. The points race demands that you think on your feet because you may have to change your tactics later.

The Madison

This is an unusual event that involves teams of two riders competing in a system similar to the points race. In the Madison points are awarded in certain sprints through the race, and the winning team is the one with the most points.

Where things differ from the points race is in the style of racing. One rider from each team is 'in play' at any one

Above: In the 2008 Olympics, Bradley Wiggins (right) and Mark Cavendish (left) won gold for Great Britain in the Madison event.

moment. Teams work in a relay, swapping over, with one rider in the race, and the other resting. While the rider 'in play' competes, the other rider circles the track at the top and waits for their partner to approach. Once the partner is within a certain distance they accelerate, drop down, and then, using a method known as a handsling, are catapulted into the race, becoming the rider 'in play'.

The Madison is often confusing to watch, because slower riders circling the track at the top can distract from the race, and while teams are swapping over, it can be difficult to follow where the bunch exactly is.

An effective Madison partnership usually involves a good sprinter and a good endurance rider. The sprinter can gain laps, by attacking and lapping the field. Then the endurance rider works hard at maintaining the lead.

Left: A Madison handsling almost completed – the higher rider of the pair will accelerate away with the momentum of the handsling.

Track Racing: Pursuits, Kilometre Time Trial, Sprint and Keirin

Different kinds of track racing demand very different tactics and skills. The pursuit events need pure endurance over a longer distance, while the kilometre time trial is a harder, shorter event. The sprint and keirin are tactical battles between riders.

Left: Bradley Wiggins of Great Britain speeds to victory and a gold medal in the individual pursuit race in the Beijing Olympics in 2008.

Team pursuit

Racing in a team pursuit works on exactly the same lines as the individual pursuit, except that there are four riders involved in each team. Team pursuit riding is as physically demanding as the individual pursuit, and imposes extra mental demands on the riders. A well-co-ordinated team rides in a perfectly straight line, with only centimetres between their front and back wheels. Riders work together, sharing the work to overcome air resistance. To change leaders, the front rider swings up the track on a bend, allowing the others to overtake on the inside. The leader then swings immediately back down, joining the line flawlessly in last place. Any error in judgement here can result in the rider dropping too far back, and not being able to keep up with the team. Although the time of the team is taken on the third rider to cross the line, a three-person team cannot easily match a four-man team.

Even start order is important in the team pursuit. Your slowest starter should be last in line for the first lap – they will start at the top of the track, and the slight banking in the straight will give them a small downhill, making up for their slower acceleration.

Unlike the races on the previous pages, the pursuit events, kilometre time trial, sprint and keirin don't involve large bunches of riders. The individual pursuit pits two individuals against each other, usually over a distance of 3 or 4km, while the team pursuit does the same with two teams of four riders, over 5km. The kilometre time trial is an individual race against the clock, while the sprint and keirin pit two and six riders respectively against each other in a dash to the line.

Individual pursuit

The individual pursuit is a 4km time-trial event in which two riders start on opposite sides of the track, and set off at the same time. They are racing both against each other and against the clock.The race is over when both riders

complete the 4km. If one rider can manage to catch up with the other, the race is declared over.

In major championships, the competitors ride a timed heat over the distance, with the top eight going through to the knockout round, where they are seeded according to their result. The pursuit attracts thoroughbred endurance riders, and many pursuiters develop into very good road riders. The distance is long enough that pace judgement, gearing and pain tolerance are very important. Of all the events on the track, it is easiest to start too fast in the pursuit. This results in a gradual and painful deceleration over the course of the 4km. Ideally, the 1km splits in a pursuit should be more or less identical, save for a slower first lap which takes into account accelerating from a standing start.

Kilometre time trial

For this race, riders are timed individually over a distance of 1km – the fastest rider wins. While the concept is simple, 1km is an extremely difficult distance to judge pace at. It is farther than the body is capable of maintaining at a sprint, but is not far enough to settle into a rhythm. It is one of the most painful disciplines in cycling, because of this difficulty. Riders often start too fast, resulting in cramping during the last lap as lactic acid builds up in their muscles.

The best way to approach a kilometre is to start fast, hold speed through to the last quarter, then do everything you can to hold on as the pain really kicks in.

Sprint

The sprint is a head-to-head event between two riders over a kilometre, although only the last 200m is timed. The riders circle the track, watching each other closely, before one of them launches their sprint, which can happen at any time, but tends to be in the latter stages of the race. The first across the line is the winner.

Sprinting gains its tactical subtleties from the fact that it is usually easier to win a sprint from behind another rider, thanks to the shelter from air resistance.

Below: Competing in the tough team pursuit event at the 2008 Olympics in Beijing resulted in a gold medal for the cycling team from Great Britain.

Riders will do everything they can to avoid having to lead out. As they slowly circle the track, the rider in the lead might try and force the other into the lead by jumping suddenly. The opponent, in order to prevent being left behind, will react. The original leader slows down dramatically, while the opponent goes past him, taking the lead. Some sprinters start the sprint from a long way out, hoping that their rival does not have the endurance to be able to hold their speed to the end. Others prefer to wait, using devastating acceleration over a short distance to win.

Keirin

This is a race for a pure sprinter. The keirin originated in Japan. It is a sprint event in which a line of six r iders is brought up to speed using a pacing rider, or more commonly a motorized bike called a 'derny'. Riders jockey for position following the derny – as the derny is providing shelter, there is no disadvantage to leading. With a certain distance to go, the derny peels off, and the riders are left to fight out the sprint.

Above: Chris Hoy of Great Britain wins the battle of the sprint, and the gold medal, at the 2008 Olympics in Beijing.

Track Racing: The Hour Record and Six-day Racing

The hour record is the blue riband of track racing. It is one of the hardest experiences riders can put themselves through on a bike, requiring immense skill, stamina and strength, as well as willpower, yet it also one of the simplest.

Two events that rate as the most popular on the track are the hour record and six-day racing. The hour record is extremely arduous, while the six-day racing is very entertaining.

The hour record

Riding the maximum possible distance in an hour, around a velodrome, is called the 'hour record'. It demands constant, all-out exertion for the entire hour, with no chance to rest or freewheel. Because of its difficulty, very few riders attempt it, and winners gain great prestige. Sometimes the hour record is ridden at high altitudes, which confers an aerodynamic benefit on the rider because of the thin air. The design of the bike affects performance and innovative aerodynamic equipment has

Below: The UK's Chris Boardman on the way to setting the 'athlete's' hour record at Manchester velodrome in 2000.

Above: Graeme Obree in the contentious 'superman' position, which he invented for the arduous hour record, one of the most physically difficult events in cycling.

been specially built. The hour record has belonged to some of the finest riders in the history of the sport – Fausto Coppi, Jacques Anquetil, Eddy Merckx and Miguel Indurain have all held it. These riders won 17 Tours de France between them. Merckx described the hour record he set in 1972 as the hardest event he had ever ridden.

The hour record entered the modern era in 1984 when Francesco Moser beat Eddy Merckx's long-standing record. While Merckx rode on a normal bike, with normal wheels and handlebars, Moser used a low-profile time-trialling machine with disc wheels. British rider Graeme Obree broke Moser's record in 1993, using a radical new position on the bike, known as the 'tuck'. Obree famously constructed his own bike for the record, with bottom bracket bearings taken from the drum of a washing machine. His compatriot Chris Boardman broke the record next, followed by Indurain and Swiss rider Tony Rominger. When Obree's position was banned by the cycling authorities, he developed yet another new position, the 'superman'. Boardman used the position and rode an astonishing 56.375km (35 miles). Although the 'superman' was controversial, the authorities granted Boardman the record, but banned the position.

There is now an 'athlete's' hour record, for which riders have to ride bikes similar to Merckx's when he broke the record.

Below: Track racing attracts many spectators at events across Europe.

Right: The Madison is one of the staples of six-day racing, drawing large crowds and elite riders.

Six-day racing

A six-day is an unusual type of cycling event held at velodromes in the winter that is part bike race and part circus. Originally, a six-day was just six solid days of racing, including at night. Since this much exertion is unreasonable, even by the tiring standards of bike racing, it has evolved into a race meeting where riders compete every evening for six days, in a variety of events.

Crowds at six-day races are huge. The Ghent six-day event, which takes place in Belgium every November, is one of the most atmospheric experiences in cycling. The velodrome at Ghent is tiny – the track is only 166m (545ft), with steep banking, and crowds are allowed into the centre of the track as well as in the stands. The riders speed past, within inches of the audience. Events include sprints and points races, but the real draw for the crowds is the nightly Madison event, which attracts the biggest names. There is a Madison classification similar to that in a stage race, where accumulated laps and points are added to a total to find the overall winner of the six-day racing.

ADVANCED TRAINING

In order to improve top-end fitness, racing cyclists need to incorporate high-intensity workouts into their training regime. By using interval training, riders can achieve a specific kind of fitness that will enable them to compete at the front of races. It is important to look after the body, by rest and recuperation, and by refuelling and nutrition strategies. You should also know how to deal with injury, if it occurs.

Above: Serious racing requires serious training on a regular basis.
Left: A racing cyclist is all kitted out to do some high-intensity riding.

Advanced Endurance Training and Specialized Drills

Base-building is one of the most important parts of training for cycling. By building endurance through regular, long steady distance rides, you prepare your body for the more intensive training that is to come later on.

Even when you are concentrating on speed work, it is important not to forget to work on your endurance. If you have spent several months building it up, it would be a shame to let it slip back.

If you are not racing over a weekend, try instead to go for a varied long ride, with sprints, long periods of hard efforts and hard climbing. The difference between this and a fartlek ride is that you rest more during the latter. For this advanced endurance ride, keep your

Long, varied endurance ride
You can do this type of ride with a group or on your own. Go out for a ride that is as long as your longest LSD (long steady distance) ride, but really vary the pace. Once you have warmed up, do some long climbs, and then try some extended periods when you are cruising at a good tempo. Include a couple of sprints. Keep up a high level of effort throughout.

effort steady between the harder efforts. Depending on the length of race, sportive or enduro you are training for and riding, this ride might be as long as 4 or 5 hours.

When building distance up over a period of weeks, a gradual increase is far preferable to a sudden increase. It is a

Below: On a long training ride, build endurance by keeping a steady effort over varied terrain, including long climbs.

good idea to incorporate an increase into your weekly distance, or the distance of your longest ride, then follow that by a week with no increase. By plateauing in this way, your body will compensate and be ready for the next increase.

The reason it is important to maintain and increase your endurance is that it improves your body's ability to use the glycogen stored in your muscles and liver. Your body will become more efficient at using glycogen as fuel, while at the same time burning larger amounts of fat. Your muscles will also become efficient at producing the movements necessary for cycling. As endurance is maintained and increased, your capacity for more specialized training is maintained and increased.

Specialized drills

Regular endurance training and interval training are very good for boosting your body's physiological abilities. You also need to pay attention to the skills you use in a road race, especially sprinting and climbing. The physical effort is very important, but you also have to hone your technique, so that you are sprinting and climbing with as much economy as possible.

Sprint training

During a long ride, include some sprint drills as you normally would, but focus on technique as well as physical effort. Keep your bike in a straight line, and maintain a strong upper body and core, using the arms to pull up on the bars while your legs work at turning the pedals round. Especially work on your initial jump, by seeing how quickly you can accelerate to maximum speed.

Climbing training

On the hills, follow the correct line round all the corners, focusing on sitting upright and relaxing the body, while spinning a low gear at 90–100 revolutions per minute or more. Hold the bars firmly, without gripping tightly. Practise varying the pace, even if you are not a natural climber. Attack hard out of the saddle, sit back down again to recover, accelerate slightly, then ride steadily to the top before sprinting the final 50m (164ft).

Above: During sprint training, build a series of maximum effort sprints into a medium-distance ride.
Below: Training with a group for long rides can be beneficial in alleviating boredom.

Interval Training

The training schedules in the following pages of this book are designed for sportive, enduro and fitness-oriented individuals, and will build a good base for this kind of cycling. Interval training alternates high-speed intense training and rest or low activity.

The intensity of a short race is much higher than that in a sportive or enduro event. The reason many people get dropped in a road or mountain bike race is not because they are not fit enough to ride the distance, but because they are not fit enough to ride at the same speed as their rivals. The frustrating thing is that often, the intense periods in a race don't last that long, but by that time, inexperienced or less fit riders are off the back. Race training therefore has to aim to cope with these larger stresses on the body. To do this you have to imitate the efforts made in a race situation, and the best way to do this is through interval training.

Interval training basically involves riding hard for a set period of time, usually between 1 minute and 10 minutes or so, then resting for a set recovery period, then repeating three or more times. Confusingly, the 'on' phase of the workout is known as the 'interval'.

Most intervals are precisely set at or slightly above your body's lactate threshold (see box). They are very effective at increasing fitness, but you do need to have a solid base of steady miles in your legs before you attempt them. The greater your endurance, built up over time, the higher the level of fitness you can achieve through intensive training. You should always be flexible about interval training – if you are tired before you even start, doing a full set might be counterproductive. Go for a recovery ride instead, and postpone your intervals for a couple of days.

The improvement in fitness levels from interval training means that from one week to the next, you'll need to increase the length of your intervals, or the frequency. If you are going to embark on a programme of interval training, it is essential to buy a pulse monitor, which will help you measure your effort correctly. Going too hard or

Above: Sportive events can be gruelling so it is important to be fit to begin with.

too easily will defeat the purpose of the training. Don't overdo it. It's important to keep increasing the length or intensity of your intervals according to your schedule, to get fitter.

Classic intervals
These are the most straightforward intervals you can do, and are an ideal way of introducing your body to the stress of the harder training. Make sure that you have been doing tempo rides for several weeks before you start doing these intervals. Once you are ready for interval training, the most important thing to do on these sessions is warm up properly. Spin your legs at a level of effort between easy and moderate for 20 or 30 minutes. When your warm-up is complete, find a flat bit of road with no junctions or traffic lights. Increase your effort to your lactate threshold for 6 minutes. Concentrate on smooth pedalling style, relaxing your upper body, and maintaining a steady pace.

Lactate threshold

During exercise, your muscles release lactic acid, a by-product of the process by which carbohydrates are converted into energy. When glycogen, stored in the muscles and liver, is metabolized, it is converted into energy, in the form of a molecule called adenosine triphosphate (ATP). The waste product from this process is lactic acid.

Lactic acid is what causes the burning sensation and pain in your muscles when you are exercising hard. At moderate or low levels of exercise, the body is capable of getting rid of lactic acid as fast as it builds up – this means that the body can maintain the same level of exertion. This is known as aerobic exercise; it uses a combination of fat and carbohydrates for fuel, and oxygen is used in converting this fuel to energy. The higher the intensity of exercise, the more carbohydrates are used as fuel, and the more

lactic acid builds up. But at more intense levels of exertion, the metabolism converting your muscles' fuel into energy goes from aerobic to anaerobic – oxygen delivery can no longer keep up with the demand. Beyond this point, your ability to sustain the effort is limited – if you sprint up a hill, you will probably experience an oxygen deficit. Anaerobic exercise relies on burning carbohydrates for fuel. When the body switches to anaerobic energy production, lactic acid builds up faster than your system can get rid of it. The point at which this happens is known as the lactate threshold, and it happens at a certain percentage of your maximum heart rate, depending on the individual. Scientific testing to measure blood lactate levels can find what your lactate threshold is, and will enable you to train effectively, with workouts based on exertions that are at, or just beyond, your threshold.

Right: Training at high intensity gets your body used to the suffering it will encounter in a race.

Don't just push down on the pedals, but use these training sessions to work on pulling the pedals up and building a smooth pedal revolution.

After your 6-minute interval is up, recover for 3 minutes by riding at a similar pace to your warm-up. The pace should be moderate, but not slow. Then repeat the sequence three more times for a total of four intervals.

When you have done this workout twice, change the length of the interval to 7 minutes, but keep the rest period at 3 minutes. Keep adding a minute every two sessions until you can sustain the pace for four sets of 10-minute intervals.

High-intensity intervals
After a few weeks of regular classic intervals, you will be ready for some intervals of a higher intensity. For these workouts, always warm up well. Ride for 3 minutes just above your lactate threshold, and rest for 3 minutes before repeating three more times for a total of four intervals. Increase the length of these intervals by 30 seconds a week to a maximum of 5 minutes.

Right: Breaking away in a race involves riding at a hard effort over a long time. Far right: Cycling athlete and Olympic competitor Nicole Cooke in 2005, winning the Fleche Wallone, in the Ardennes town of Huy.

Super-high intensity intervals
Intervals are similar to sprints, but you'll hold the pace for a set amount of time. Ride for 90 seconds at your maximum cruising pace, which will be not far off your maximum heart rate. Rest for 5 minutes, then repeat twice. These are extremely tough sessions, and should be treated with caution. If you are having trouble holding the pace for 90 seconds, you are not ready.

Racing Training Schedule: Endurance Events

Peaking for a race, enduro or sportive is an important part of training and achieving long-term goals. For the final two months before a race, your build-up should include more and more intensive workouts as you reach a higher state of fitness.

This training schedule is designed to get you ready for a sportive or enduro that is five hours long. Complete the basic, intermediate and advanced training schedules described earlier before tackling this schedule, which extends over eight weeks.

Train smart

You need to be careful not to overtrain – enthusiasm for hard workouts is an admirable thing, but training smart always beats training hard. When you feel fatigue building to a point where you cannot complete workouts or intervals, it is time to add in some rest periods and recovery rides before tackling harder rides.

Recovery period

In the final week before the event, you can cut down on the quantity and intensity of your training, allowing your

Above: Tough and well-designed training schedules are essential to prepare you for the arduous conditions of road or mountain bike racing.

body to recover so that it is at peak fitness for your event. It should be noted that this is an extremely time-consuming schedule and is designed for people who are able, and wish, to devote more time to their cycling. It is best to choose the most convenient time to carry out this schedule, such as when you have two months in which you have no other major commitments that could deter you from your goal.

The training schedule is worked out to train your body to maximum fitness, then the intensity reduces prior to the event to allow you to recover before achieving your goal.

Left: Hill riding and some sprints can sharpen your legs and improve your general fitness in preparation for an enduro or sportive race.

Week one

MONDAY Rest

TUESDAY LSD ride 1:30, including
Classic intervals

WEDNESDAY LSD ride 1:30

THURSDAY LSD ride 1:30, including sprints
and long steady climbs

FRIDAY LSD ride 1:30, including
Classic intervals

SATURDAY Recovery ride 0:30

SUNDAY LSD ride 3:30

TOTAL HOURS: 10:00

Monday is a day off. If you are feeling good, go
for a recovery ride, otherwise, this is a good
rest to let you recover before starting the rest of
the week. Tuesday and Friday have medium
distance rides including Classic intervals.

Week two

MONDAY Rest

TUESDAY LSD ride 1:30, including
Classic intervals

WEDNESDAY LSD ride 1:30

THURSDAY LSD ride 1:30, including sprints
and long steady climbs

FRIDAY LSD ride 1:30, including
Classic intervals

SATURDAY Recovery ride 0:30

SUNDAY LSD ride 4:00

TOTAL HOURS: 10:30

Similar to week one, with a day of rest on
Monday. Sunday's ride is longer. On Friday, you
may be tired from four consecutive days of
riding, so be prepared to cancel the intervals
and go for a recovery ride instead.

Week three

MONDAY Rest

TUESDAY LSD ride 1:30, including
Classic intervals

WEDNESDAY LSD ride 2:00

THURSDAY LSD ride 1:30, including sprints
and long steady climbs

FRIDAY LSD ride 1:30, including
Classic intervals

SATURDAY Recovery ride 0:30

SUNDAY LSD ride 4:00

TOTAL HOURS: 11:00

Sunday's long ride stays at 4:00 to allow the
body to get used to the distance before
increasing again in two weeks. If you have
time on the Wednesday, add an extra half
hour to the ride.

Week four

MONDAY Rest

TUESDAY LSD ride 1:00, including
spinning drills

WEDNESDAY LSD ride 1:00

THURSDAY Recovery ride 0:30

FRIDAY LSD ride 1:00

SATURDAY Recovery ride 0:30

SUNDAY LSD ride 3:00

TOTAL HOURS: 7:00

After three very hard weeks, with very
long hours of training, it is time to have
an easy week, to allow your body to recover
its strength. Even if you feel full of energy,
do not be tempted to train hard through
this week, to avoid the risk of
overtraining.

Week five

MONDAY Rest

TUESDAY LSD ride 1:30, including
Classic intervals

WEDNESDAY LSD ride 2:00

THURSDAY LSD ride 1:30, including short
steep hill repetitions

FRIDAY Recovery ride 0:30

SATURDAY Long varied endurance ride 4:30

SUNDAY LSD ride 1:30

TOTAL HOURS: 11:30

The longest ride switches to Saturday, with a
long varied endurance ride of four and a half
hours, followed the next day by one and a half
hours of steady riding. This will improve
efficiency and endurance, while the intervals
and hill repetitions will boost top-end fitness.

Week six

MONDAY Rest

TUESDAY LSD ride 1:30, including
Classic intervals

WEDNESDAY LSD ride 2:00

THURSDAY LSD ride 1:30, including
short steep hill repetitions

FRIDAY Recovery ride 0:30

SATURDAY Long varied
endurance ride 5:00

SUNDAY LSD ride 1:30

TOTAL HOURS: 12:00

This is the hardest week's training of all. Hill
riding will sharpen your legs and there is a
long ride on Saturday. After this week, you
will start to reduce your training volume in
order to peak for your event.

Week seven

MONDAY Rest

TUESDAY LSD ride 1:30, including
Classic intervals

WEDNESDAY LSD ride 1:00

THURSDAY LSD ride 1:30

FRIDAY Recovery ride 0:30

SATURDAY LSD ride 1:30, including short
steep hill repetitions

SUNDAY LSD ride 2:00

TOTAL HOURS: 8:00

Reduce volume this week, with slightly shorter
long steady distance training rides on every
day except Monday, which is a day of rest,
but maintain the high intensity of Tuesday
and Friday's intervals. Include short steep hill
climbing repetitions on Saturday.

Week eight

MONDAY Rest

TUESDAY LSD ride 1:00, including
spinning drills

WEDNESDAY LSD ride 1:00

THURSDAY Recovery ride 0:30

FRIDAY Recovery ride 0:30

SATURDAY Recovery ride 0:30

SUNDAY EVENT

TOTAL HOURS: 3:30

Another easy week with the shortest hours
put into training. The training you undertake
this week should see you ready for your event
on the Sunday. Long steady distance rides
and a recovery ride will leave you ready to
go. Just spin the legs nice and easily during
your rides this week.

*Above: Your training schedule will help
you to acquit yourself well in the event.*

Racing Training Schedule: Short-distance Events

For a shorter race, such as a local-level road race or mountain bike race, the volume of training need not be so high, but the intensity needs to be greater. When you are saving energy by doing fewer long rides, you will be able to focus on interval training.

Training for short-distance events is less time-consuming than training for longer events – the focus is on intensity rather than endurance. But it's still important to have a balanced schedule, with long rides and interval training.

Events of around 1 or 2 hours are the staple diet of most amateur racers. Both road races and mountain bike cross-country events are around this length and the shorter distance and time spent on the bike means that the racing is more intense, so your training has to reflect this. There's little point in focusing your physical and mental energy on 5-hour training rides, if events that are important to you last for less than half that time. However, endurance training is of some use. Your training base should have incorporated plenty of long rides, since the endurance you build here will make your body more able to deal with the harder, more intense training that

Above: For an event like this one, in which you will need plenty of intensive effort to climb the hill, your training will stand you in good stead.

comes in the build-up to a race. Then, during a racing period, occasional rides of up to the same time as your target races will help maintain your endurance. The main difference between training for long events like enduros or sportives, and cross-country and road races, however, is in the intensity of the training sessions. Short races can involve intense efforts, and you must make such efforts in your training so that you can replicate them a race.

This eight-week training schedule focuses on doing two or three more

Left: You should train in all weathers, to be prepared for whatever conditions prevail on the day of your event.

intensive sessions a week. Everything in between should be at a more steady rate, and if fatigue builds, it is far better to go for a very easy recovery ride, or even take the day off the bike, so that you will be recovered for your next intensive session. These sessions should be as varied as possible, involving sprints, intervals on flat roads, and hard efforts on hilly terrain.

If you are aiming to compete in a flat road race, focus your training on sprints and intervals on flat roads. For a hilly road race or cross-country, train on the terrain you will encounter in the race. Your interval training should build gradually, so that you increase the length of your efforts.

Week one

MONDAY Rest

TUESDAY LSD ride 1:00, including
Classic intervals

WEDNESDAY LSD ride 1:30

THURSDAY LSD ride 1:00, including long
steady climbs

FRIDAY Recovery ride 0:30

SATURDAY LSD ride 1:30, including
Classic intervals

SUNDAY LSD ride 2:30

TOTAL HOURS: 8:00

From Tuesday, the days alternate between
intense training and steady training. If you are
feeling good, you can add sprints and jumps
or spinning drills.

Week two

MONDAY Rest

TUESDAY LSD ride 1:00, including
Classic intervals

WEDNESDAY LSD ride 1:30

THURSDAY LSD ride 1:30, including long
steady climbs

FRIDAY Recovery ride 0:30

SATURDAY LSD ride 1:30, including
Classic intervals

SUNDAY LSD ride 2:30

TOTAL HOURS: 8:30

The schedule is basically the same as week one,
with a slightly longer ride on Thursday, but you
can increase the length of your intervals from
week to week.

Week three

MONDAY Rest

TUESDAY LSD ride 1:00, including
Classic intervals

WEDNESDAY LSD ride 1:30

THURSDAY LSD ride 1:30, including
sprints and long steady climbs

FRIDAY Recovery ride 0:30

SATURDAY LSD ride 1:30, including
Classic intervals

SUNDAY LSD ride 2:30

TOTAL HOURS: 8:30

The schedule is virtually the same as week
two, but you can increase the length of your
intervals again. Sprints have been added
on Thursday.

Week four

MONDAY Rest

TUESDAY LSD ride 1:00, including
spinning drills

WEDNESDAY LSD ride 1:00

THURSDAY Recovery ride 0:30

FRIDAY LSD ride 1:00

SATURDAY Recovery ride 0:30

SUNDAY LSD ride 2:30

TOTAL HOURS: 6:30

After three intensive weeks of riding, you
now need to allow the body to have some
recovery time.

Do not be tempted to train hard through this
week or you will be vulnerable to overtraining.
Instead ride steadily or at a recovery pace
for the week.

Week five

MONDAY Rest

TUESDAY LSD ride 1:00, including
Classic intervals

WEDNESDAY LSD ride 1:30

THURSDAY LSD ride 1:30, including short
steep hill repetitions

FRIDAY Recovery ride 0:30

SATURDAY Long varied
endurance ride 3:00, including sprints

SUNDAY LSD ride 1:30

TOTAL HOURS: 9:30

The week builds up through steady rides and
a recovery ride on Friday. Then Saturday's ride
becomes the longest of the week, incorporating
high intensity sprints, followed by a steady
ride on Sunday.

Week six

MONDAY Rest

TUESDAY LSD ride 1:30, including
Classic intervals

WEDNESDAY LSD ride 1:30

THURSDAY LSD ride 1:30, including
short steep hill repetitions

FRIDAY Recovery ride 0:30

SATURDAY Long varied
endurance ride 3:00, including sprints

SUNDAY LSD ride 1:30

TOTAL HOURS: 9:30

The schedule has a similar pattern to week five,
but try to raise the intensity of your intervals
and climbing sessions. After this week, you
can reduce training volume in order to peak
for your event.

Week seven

MONDAY Rest

TUESDAY LSD ride 1:30, including
Classic intervals

WEDNESDAY LSD ride 1:00

THURSDAY LSD ride 1:30

FRIDAY Recovery ride 0:30

SATURDAY LSD ride 1:30, including Classic
intervals and short steep hill repetitions

SUNDAY LSD ride 2:00

TOTAL HOURS: 8:00

With two weeks to go, the week consists
of a rest, steady rides with some short hill
climbs. Reduce the volume of training this
week, but maintain a high intensity for the
intervals on Tuesday and Saturday and for
climbing sessions.

Week eight

MONDAY Rest

TUESDAY LSD ride 1:00, including
Classic intervals

WEDNESDAY LSD ride 1:00

THURSDAY Recovery ride 0:30

FRIDAY LSD ride 1:00, including some
spinning drills

SATURDAY Recovery ride 0:30

SUNDAY EVENT

TOTAL HOURS: 4:00

An easy week in which you should wind down
and get ready for your event on the Sunday.
Take a rest on Monday, ride intervals on
Tuesday, then spend the rest of the week
spinning the legs nice and easily to taper
for your event.

*Above: Intensity of effort, rather than
endurance, is needed for short races.*

Advanced Refuelling

Cycling is an energy-intensive activity. Racing, competing and riding seriously all burn up a lot of calories, and it is often necessary to eat on the bike. It's important to consume high-energy products such as energy gels and bars, and drink enough water.

It is impractical to eat a three-course meal in the middle of a bike race. On-the-bike nutrition needs to be more accessible and easier to eat. Directly after a race, the stomach is not ready to absorb food in its raw state – it is much easier and better to rely on easy-to-digest recovery drinks. Here are some ideas of what to eat and drink on the bike to avoid an energy crash.

Water

Staying hydrated is very important, and this can be difficult, especially on hot days. When exercising in the heat you lose a great deal of water, and it is essential to replace it. Dehydration can lead to a significant dip in performance, followed by a significant dip in health, such as headaches and cramps.

By planning effectively, you can help yourself avoid dehydration. Drink plenty of water the evening before, and an adequate amount on the morning of your long ride or event. Just before the start, drink 300ml (½ pint) of fluid.

For the ride, prepare by carrying bottles, and if possible, organizing replacement bottles during a feed zone. It is better to err on the side of caution

Below: During a race stay hydrated and maintain energy levels by drinking energy drinks on the go.

by drinking too much liquid and needing to urinate than to risk becoming dehydrated.

Energy drinks

As well as water, it is a good idea to consume energy drinks during exercise. These provide very quick energy compared with solid food, containing glucose for the muscles to use. This is important after an hour of exercise, when glycogen stores begin to drop.

Energy drinks come in powders that athletes can mix themselves with water. They consist of glucose, glucose polymers (polysaccharides), fructose, maltodextrin and any combination of

Above: Mix your own energy drinks from commercial powders and water. Try different brands to see which you prefer.

Above: Try different concentrations of energy drink – what works best for someone else may not suit you.

Above: Gels provide a direct hit of energy. If your gel is not isotonic, make sure you drink water with it.

the above, which are easily absorbed. It is best to use the concentrations recommended by the manufacturers, although some people can tolerate different concentrations. Experiment during training with different mixes, and see what works best for you – a race or event is never the time to try something new, as your stomach may react badly.

Energy bars
Just as your body needs fluids during exercise, so it needs solid food. Food for a race needs to be portable, digestible, nutritious and high in energy. There are two ideal solutions to this – bananas and energy bars.

Energy bars are very popular among cyclists, and they pack quite a punch with their energy content. You should aim for a product that is easy to chew, easy to digest, and is composed of about 80 per cent carbohydrate, 10 per cent protein and 10 per cent fat. Because they are so dense and concentrated, it is essential to drink plenty of water or low concentrate energy drink with an energy bar, or you may have trouble digesting and absorbing the energy.

Below left and below: Always carry a drink attached to your bike so you can reach it while riding along.

Energy gels
Because they are convenient small sachets, and contain energy-rich substances, energy gels are popular. Gels are easier to digest than an energy bar – they require no chewing and can be swallowed straight down. If the energy gel you use is isotonic, you will not need to drink water with it to ensure digestion. Some products need large quantities of fluid to be taken at the same time. Make sure you know about the product you are using and how many to take.

Below: Energy bars are ideal for long events, providing lots of fuel in a compact package.

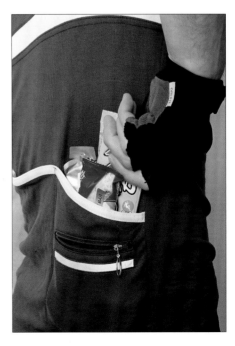

Injuries

Accidents are inevitable when you are cycling. At some point you will come off your bike or have a collision with another rider or an obstacle. There are also injuries caused by the general wear and tear that cycling inflicts on the body.

There are two major types of injuries for the typical cyclist. The first are caused by crashes. Injuries from crashes can range from a couple of scratches to, in the worst and rarest of circumstances, death. Most come somewhere in between. The second is the type of chronic injury suffered by riders through incorrect positioning or overtraining, and include bad backs and muscle strains – these tend to be less immediately painful than the first kind of injury, but they can keep you off the bike for extended periods of time.

Abrasions

For minor skin loss suffered in a crash, you can treat yourself. If you lose a lot of skin, it is a better idea to go to the hospital to get your wounds treated.

It is important, even with minor grazes and abrasions, to clean the wound thoroughly. Wounds are susceptible to infection, which can lead to illness and time off the bike. It is also important to make sure that you have had a tetanus booster in the last 10 years. If not, get one as soon as you can.

Soap and water is an adequate way of cleaning a wound, although some products are available from pharmacies to do the same job. Use a clean, sterile cloth and ensure that all the dirt is out of the wound. Once it is clean, cover it with a dressing that can be held in place with a bandage.

Broken bones

Collar bones, and to a lesser extent wrists, are susceptible to breakage in the event of a crash. When a cyclist goes down, his or her reflex is to break their fall with their hand, which can break the wrist or collarbone. If you do suffer a broken bone, you need medical attention – go to a hospital.

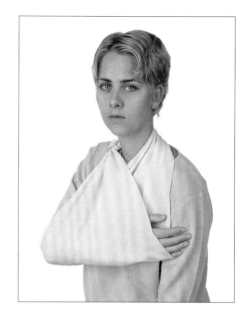

Above: Broken collarbones and arms mean extended periods off the bike. Below: Crashes are relatively common in road races – do everything you possibly can to avoid them.

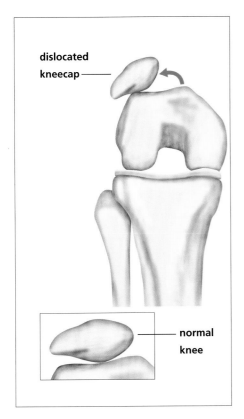

Above: The red arrow shows the direction in which the patella has dislocated. The knee joint is prone to overuse injuries – make sure your knees are aligned before pedalling.

Knee pain

All it takes is for your shoeplate to be slightly misaligned, or your saddle height to be a couple of millimetres out, or, as is more common than many people realize, your legs to be a slightly different length from each other. The repetitive nature of the cycling action will eventually exacerbate any of these problems and more, until you have chronic knee pain that prevents you from cycling.

The first thing to do when you have an injury like this is to stop cycling, which can be frustrating if you have been working hard for weeks or months. Rest, and an ice-pack on the knee, will address the immediate problem of pain and swelling. To cure the knee pain, you need to see a physiotherapist, who can assess what the root of the problem may be. Even though the pain is in your knee, the problem might be somewhere else in your body. A good physiotherapist will be able to work out why you are getting knee pain. Follow the exercise programme set for you by your physio, in order to strengthen whatever weakness is causing the knee pain, and you should be able to resume cycling within a matter of days or weeks.

Back pain

Cyclists suffer from back pain not because cycling is inherently bad for the back, but because their position or posture on the bike is putting pressure on their lower back. If your back aches during and after long rides, try to adjust your position so you are more upright, and hold the handlebars in different positions to prevent stiffness. Also, work on your core muscles to strengthen your lower back and abdomen.

Saddle sores

Cyclists spend a lot of time sitting on a narrow saddle, which puts pressure on and causes friction in their saddle area. Minute abrasions caused by the friction can become infected, leading to a saddle sore. Prevention is much better than cure. Before every ride, treat the padded insert of your shorts with antiseptic cream, and wash scrupulously after a ride. This will prevent a painful problem farther down the line.

Above: Cyclists are liable to have backache if they have bad or incorrect posture. This can lead to a curved spine.

Above: Being aware of your posture and standing up straight, can help strengthen the back and abdominal muscles.

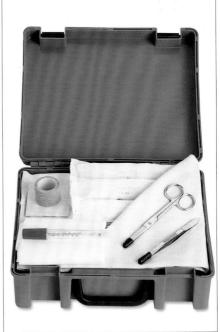

Above: Your first aid kit should contain dressings, antiseptic wipes, bandages, scissors and adhesive tape.

Resources

Further reading

SPORT

Dugard, Martin, *Chasing Lance* (Time Warner Books, London, 2005)

Fife, Graeme, *Inside the Peloton* (Mainstream, Edinburgh, 2002)

Fife, Graeme, *Tour de France: The History, the Legends, the Riders* (Mainstream, Edinburgh, 1999)

Fotheringham, William, *A Century of Cycling* (Mitchell Beazley, London, 2003)

Fotheringham, William, *Put Me Back On My Bike* (Yellow Jersey Press, London, 2002)

Fotheringham, William, *Roule Britannia* (Yellow Jersey Press, London, 2006)

Lazell, Marguerite, *Tour de France: A Hundred Years of the World's Greatest Cycle Race* (Carlton, London, 2003)

Rendell, Matt, *A Significant Other* (Weidenfeld and Nicolson, London, 2004)

Schweikher, Erich, *Cycling's Greatest Misadventures* (Casagrande, San Diego, 2007)

Watson, Graham, *Landscapes of Cycling* (Velopress, Boulder, 2004)

Wheatcroft, Geoffrey, *Le Tour* (Pocket Books, London, 2003)

Whittle, Jeremy, *Le Tour: A Century of the Tour de France* (Collins, London, 2003)

Wilcockson, John, *The World of Cycling* (Velopress, Boulder, 1998)

Woodland, Les, *The Crooked Path to Victory* (Cycle Publishing, San Francisco, 2003)

Woodland, Les, *The Yellow Jersey Companion to the Tour de France* (Yellow Jersey Press, London, 2003)

GENERAL

Andrews, Guy, *Road Bike Maintenance* (A&C Black, London, 2008)

Ballantine, Richard, *Richard's 21st Century Bicycle Book* (Pan, London, 2000)

Franklin, John, *Cyclecraft* (The Stationery Office, 1997)

Joyce, Dan, *The CTC Guide to Family Cycling* (James Pembroke Publishing, Bath, 2008)

Roberts, Tony, *Cycling: An Introduction to the Sport* (New Holland, London, 2005)

Seaton, Matt, *On Your Bike* (Black Dog Publishing, London, 2006)

Zinn, Lennard, *Zinn and the Art of Road Bike Maintenance* (Velopress, Boulder, 2000)

TOURING

Doughty, Simon, *The Long Distance Cyclists' Handbook* (A&C Black, London, 2001)

Hughes, Tim, *Great Cycle Tours of Britain* (Ward Lock, London, 1988)

Mustoe, Anne, *A Bike Ride: 12,000 Miles Around the World* (Virgin, London, 1991)

Penn, Rob, *A Place to Cycle* (Conran Octopus, London, 2005)

Woodland, Les, *The CTC Book of Cycle Touring* (Crowood, Marlborough, 1995)

TRAINING

Bean, Anita, *The Complete Guide to Strength Training* (A & C Black, London, 2001)

Bompa, Tudor, *Periodization Training for Sports* (Human Kinetics, Champaign, 2005)

Burke, Edmund, *Serious Cycling* (Human Kinetics, Champaign, 2002)

Eberle, Suzanne, *Endurance Sports Nutrition* (Human Kinetics, Champaign, 2007)

Fiennes, Ranulph, *Fit For Life* (Little, Hethersett, 1999)

Friel, Joe, *The Cyclist's Training Bible* (Velopress, Boulder, 1997)

Janssen, Peter, *Lactate Threshold Training* (Human Kinetics, Champaign, 2001)

Kauss, David, *Mastering Your Inner Game* (Human Kinetics, Champaign, 2001)

Sleamaker, Rob, and Browning, Ray, *Serious Training for Endurance Athletes* (Human Kinetics, Champaign, 1996)

Wenzel, Kendra, and Wenzel, René, *Bike Racing 101* (Human Kinetics, Champaign, 2003)

MOUNTAIN BIKING

Crowther, Nicky, *The Ultimate Mountain Bike Book* (Carlton, London, 1996)

Friel, Joe, *The Mountain Biker's Training Bible* (Velopress, Boulder, 2000)

Schmidt, Achim, *A Beginner's Guide: Mountain Biking* (Meyer and Meyer Sports Books, 2004)

Trombley, Ann, *Serious Mountain Biking* (Human Kinetics, Champaign, 2005)

Worland, Steve, *The Mountain Bike Book* (Haynes, Yeovil, 2003)

Websites

www.cyclingweekly.co.uk
www.cyclingnews.com
www.bikeradar.com
www.velonews.com

Magazines

GENERAL

Cycling Plus
Bicycling

ROAD RACING

Cycling Weekly
Cycle Sport
Procycling
Velonews
Rouleur

MOUNTAIN BIKING

MBR
Mountain Biking UK
Singletrack

Index

Figures in *italics* indicate illustrations.

Credits and Acknowledgements

The publisher would like to thank the following picture libraries for the use of their pictures in the book. Every effort has been made to acknowledge the pictures properly. We apologize if there are any unintentional omissions, which will be corrected in future editions.

l=left, r=right, t=top, b=bottom, c=centre

Alamy: 50.

Andy Jones: 4.3, 8b, 46t, 90t, 95tl, 97t, 98b, 102, 113c, 157c, 168tr, 170 (both), 174t, 182, 184br, 222, 223, 224 (both), 225 (both), 226t, 227c, 227br, 229tl, 229tr, 233 (both), 236, 237, 239 (both).

Corbis: 6t, 10, 12, 18b, 24, 25, 26l, 35t, 35bl, 36t, 40 (both), 41b, 41tl, 42r, 48b, 48tc, 54tr, 62 (both), 63 (both), 64, 66t, 67bl, 67br, 69 (both), 71tc, 72, 73, 93br, 95br, 98tr, 101tr, 111b, 112t, 114, 115tl, 143tl, 143bl, 143br, 149tr, 149b, 155tl, 162, 200br, 202, 203bl, 204br, 215tr, 215br, 227t.

Fotolibra: 13, 53tr, 55t, 60 (both), 61t, 65tr, 65bl, 65br, 140, 141 (all).

Geoff Waugh: 38, 39 (all), 52l, 74t, 77bl, 95tr, 116, 117, 118 (both), 119 (both), 120 (both), 121 (all), 122 (both), 123 (both), 124 (all), 125 (all), 126 (both), 127 (all), 128 (both), 129 (all), 130 (both), 131 (all), 132, 133 (all), 134 (both), 135 (all), 136 (both), 137 (all), 138 (both), 139 (all), 142, 143tr, 144 (both), 145 (all), 146 (both), 147 (all), 176, 206, 207, 208, 209 (all), 210 (both), 211 (all), 212 (both), 213 (all), 214 (all), 215bl, 252.

Getty: 15, 16, 19b, 54b, 65tl, 68t (Nathan Bilow/Allspor), 112bl
.

iStockphoto: 42l, 43l, 52r, 56bl, 56br, 58tr, 58tl, 61b, 66b, 70t, 152bl, 247tr.

Larry Hickmott: 222, 228t, 229tr.

Mike King: 35br.

Offside: 7t, 20 (both), 21 (both), 22, 23b, 108, 109, 110, 111t, 114 (both), 115tr, 115b, 178, 194br, 198 (both), 199 (all), 200 tl, 200tr, 200bl, 201 (all), 203tl, 203t, 204t, 204bl, 205 (both), 248b, 254.

Peter Drake: 57 (all).

Philip O'Connor: 1, 2, 3, 4.1, 4.2, 4.4, 4.5, 7b, 8t, 9, 17b, 18t, 19tl, 23tr, 26r, 27 (both), 28, 29 (all), 30 (all), 31 (all), 32 (both), 33tl, 33c, 33r, 34 (both), 36b, 37t, 37c, 37br, 44 (both), 45 (all), 46bl, 46bc, 48tr, 49 (both), 53t, 53c, 53b, 58b, 71tl, 74bl, 74br, 75 (all), 76 (all), 77tl, 77tc, 77tr, 77c, 78 (both), 79 (all), 80 (all), 81 (all), 82 (all), 83 (all), 84 (all), 85 (all), 86, 87, 88, 89, 90b, 91 (both), 92, 93tl, 93tc, 93tr, 93bl, 96t, 99t, 99c, 100t, 101tl, 102b, 103tl, 104b, 105 (all), 106 (both), 107, 113b, 150, 152t, 154 (both), 155b, 156 (both), 157tl, 157tr, 158 (both), 159 (all), 160 (all), 161 (all), 163 (all), 164 (all), 165 (all), 168bl, 169, 170tr, 171, 172 (both), 174bl, 179, 180 (both), 181tr, 181bl, 181br, 182bl, 183 (all), 184t, 185 (both), 186 (both), 187 (all), 188, 189 (all), 190, 191 (all), 192 (both), 193 (both), 194t, 194bl, 195 (all), 216, 217 (all), 218, 219 (all), 220 (all), 221 (all), 226bl, 226br, 228b, 229b, 230t,

231 (both), 232, 233 (both), 234 (both), 235 (both), 236, 238, 240, 241 (all), 242 (both), 243, 244 (both), 245, 246, 247tl, 247tc, 247bl, 247bc, 247br, 249bl, 250, 253, 255, 256 (both).

Photolibrary: 55b.

Photoshot: 59, 67c, 148, 149tl.

Schwinn Bicycles: 19tc..

Science and Society: 14 (both).

Science Photo Library: 155tr.

Superstock: 37bl, 43tr, 43b, 56t, 68b, 70b, 181tl, 249bc.

Triathlon magazine: 196 (both), 197 (all).

Wheelbase: 6b, 33b, 41tc, 41tr, 51, 100bl, 151, 251.

The author and publishers thank the following individuals for their valuable contributions to this book and the companies who kindly supplied equipment and clothing for photography:
Endura
Evans Cycles
Hawkes BMX Club: Margaret and Scott Dick
Triathlon magazine
Zyro

Models for photography:
Tyler Bowcombe
Dan Duguid
Jamie Newall
Edward Pickering
Elise Dick
Philip Mosley
George Pagliero